Life Interrupted,

Volume 2

A Collection of Memoirs

⚜

Living the unimaginable, Huntington's and Juvenile Huntington's disease patients and caregivers share their true stories of strength, courage, and perseverance as they travel the rocky road of what has been called the worst disease known to mankind.

Edited by Sharon McClellan Thomason
Published by Help 4 HD International Inc.

Dedicated to all our loved ones, caregivers and patients alike, who have already lost their battle to Huntington's and Juvenile Huntington's disease . . .

Fly, Angels, Fly

Help 4 HD International Inc.
5050 Laguna Blvd. 112 543
Elk Grove, CA 95758
916.698.0462

A Prayer

Dear God in heaven, up above,
I've come to talk to you about Huntington's
and what it does to those we love.

It takes these people, once so innocent,
steals their speech and abilities to function,
leaving them frustrated, feeling hopelessly spent.

Then it hurts those who have them in their care,
stretching their pockets, hearts, and good will.
Sometimes it is more than their faith can bear.

And then there are those who turn away,
breaking your teachings to help one another,
causing them to wander and stray.

There are some who say that you are only testing,
that you will never give more than we can handle.
Are you watching, God, and giving us your blessing?

The strength comes through our belief in your love
that helps us through the darkness of night
When our very souls cry out for help from you, above.

Oh, please, dear God, help those once so pure
to rediscover our faith unresolved,
and if it wouldn't be too much, send us a cure.

By Jean E. Miller, 9/5/96

Acknowledgments

Thanks to all of those in the Huntington's and Juvenile Huntington's disease community who selflessly share their stories each and every day so that those who are living with HD and JHD may learn from their experiences. Keep telling your stories!

Thank you to Randy Foster for formatting the cover so beautifully and to John Russo for the superb formatting of the authors' portraits.

Thank you to my partner, Sam, who supports me in all that I do and gives me the strength and the space to continue my advocacy.

Thank you to Help 4 HD International Incorporated, a small group of dedicated individuals, all affected by HD and JHD, who work tirelessly every single day to educate and support all those who are impacted by this horrific disease. You can learn more at *www.help4hd.org*

Table of Contents

Life Interrupted. Volume 2

About Sharon McClellan Thomason

Sharon McClellan Thomason was born in Georgia in October 1952. She has lived in south Florida and in Louisiana, and currently divides her time between Panama City and Tallahassee, Florida, where she lives with her son, a dog, and two cats. She earned her B.S. in English Education and M.A. in English from Florida State University. After teaching English, journalism, and hospital homebound classes in the public schools for 38 years, Sharon retired in June 2013. During her tenure as a teacher, she also worked for the *Tallahassee Democrat* as a copy editor and as a Newspaper in Education consultant. She has also done freelance writing, editing, and page design.

Sharon first learned about Huntington's disease over 30 years ago and has been hoping and praying for a cure ever since. In June of 2013, Sharon became the managing editor and a contributing writer for Help 4 HD International's online newspaper, *The Huntington's Post*. Sharon also serves on Help 4 HD's Executive Board as Executive Secretary and Director of Education.

Sharon loves animals, traveling, music, books, cooking, and gardening. She is passionate about raising awareness for Huntington's disease and believes that knowledge is power and education is key. Her greatest joy is her son.

Foreword

―――――❧❧❧―――――

Life Interrupted, Volume 2

Jimmy Pollard, a popular speaker for CHDI who lives in Lowell, Massachusetts, opened his morning presentation at Help 4 HD International's 2016 symposium in Sacramento with the theme of "Families Keep Telling Their Stories." His brief history of Huntington's disease (HD) told about Nora Ball and Charly Guthrie, who lived in Oklahoma and had four kids, one of whom was famed singer-songwriter Woody Guthrie. Nora Guthrie developed HD, and Woody moved to Brooklyn, where he married dancer Marjorie. As Woody developed symptoms of HD, Marjorie began to tell her story. Doctors told her to find other families, so she put an ad in the newspaper, found other families who were living with HD, and founded CCHD, the Committee to Combat Huntington's Disease, which is now known as HDSA, or Huntington's Disease Society of America.

Pollard said, "Families told stories, organized, partnered up with doctors and researchers, and now we have pharmaceutical and biotech companies interested in HD."

He noted that Marjorie always talked about the ripple effect of the pebble being tossed into the pond and said that's what happened and continues to happen in the HD community because, "Families keep telling their stories." Without those stories, he said, there would be no change.

We told twelve of those stories in the first volume of *Life Interrupted*, published in 2015. The response was overwhelming. The stories resonated with the Huntington's and Juvenile Huntington's disease community, and they opened the eyes of many who have never lived with HD or JHD. One pharmaceutical company purchased copies for all its reps who would be working with HD families so that they would understand what life with HD and JHD is like.

About a year ago, Katie Jackson and I decided it was time for a second volume. There are so many more stories to tell.

First, an update on some of the stories of the twelve original authors. Sadly, Frances Saldaña lost the last of her three children, Michael, this past year. Her story doesn't end, though, as she still has grandchildren at risk. Vicki Owen's husband continues to decline, especially cognitively, but he bravely forges on, attending education events and helping Vicki educate law enforcement officers across the southeast. Margaret D'Aiuto de Gallardo, a caregiver extraordinaire and founder of the first Huntington's foundation in Mexico, passed away this year at the age of 94. She cared for her husband and four of her seven children who had HD and brought hope to so many in her country who battled this disease. My own son, Randy, has been living at home with me for four years and is doing well, except for anxiety that barely allows him to leave the house. We've been blessed with the help of a wonderful community mental health program that supervises his care in between visits to the University of Florida Center of Excellence and pharmacogenetic testing through GeneSight that helped us pinpoint the medications most effective for his individual genetic makeup. Finally, Katie Jackson's husband, Mike, is in the final stages of HD, on hospice at the age of 39.

Since the publication of our first volume, there have been lots of advances in research, but there is still no cure, and despite exciting news on the gene editing front, a cure is not on the horizon; the reality of research and clinical trials means it could be at least another ten years before a therapy is available to HD patients. There is only one research study targeting JHD, and that is at UC Davis, under the direction of Dr. Kyle Fink and Dr. Jan Nolta. Clinical trials for the children who are suffering are nowhere in sight.

Sadly, many of the stories told here—from Australia to Canada to the United States—represent the hundreds of families who either didn't know about Huntington's or were given misinformation (or no information) about the disease before marrying or deciding to have children. As I said in the Foreword to *Life Interrupted*, "Huntington's is a monster. It is a thief. It steals the dreams and interrupts the lives of those who fall victim to this genetic anomaly. Once someone hears that devastating diagnosis, the whole family travels a rocky road, straight into the storm, and there is no turning back." For anyone in this day and age not to have that kind of information is truly a travesty.

Some of the names in this book have been changed. Even in the age of GINA (Genetic Information Nondiscrimination Act) and the ACA (Affordable Care Act), people with Huntington's and at risk for Huntington's rightfully fear being discriminated against in the workplace and when applying for healthcare insurance. Families still fight against the stigma of having HD and JHD, especially because of the psychiatric and behavioral symptoms that often come with the disease.

During the past couple of months, our community has been rocked by the suicides of both patients and caregivers. We desperately need hope and support, yet there is still a deplorable lack of knowledge about HD (and even more so about JHD), even within the healthcare community. The literature about HD still quotes the same statistics of 30,000 Americans with HD and another 250,000 at risk. These are the same statistics that have been quoted for as long as I remember; how is it that they never change? In fact, a study published in 2016, "The Prevalence of Huntington's Disease", would put the incidence of HD in North America at 42,441. That's an increase in prevalence of 15-20 percent per decade since 1950.
(*https://www.karger.com/Article/FullText/443738*)

There has been one more drug, Austedo, approved by the FDA for the treatment of chorea but nothing for the psychiatric and cognitive symptoms that plague patients and their families.

One of the young men who committed suicide recently did so not because he didn't want to live but because psychosis made him so fearful that he took his own life rather than be killed by imaginary enemies. His mother fought to get him appropriate, effective treatment, but the delusions of JHD were relentless. One caregiver committed suicide after struggling for years to get appropriate treatment, and education, for her son with JHD. She was overwhelmed and simply lost hope.

At a PDUFA (Prescription Drug User Fee Act) Hearing for Huntington's disease on September 22, 2015, patients and caregivers told the FDA about the challenges, concerns, and frustrations of living with this monstrous disease. In its March 2016 report on the meeting, the FDA concluded that four key themes emerged from the hearing:

HD is a devastating and debilitating disease that has a tremendous impact on patients and their families. Participants strongly emphasized that psychiatric and behavioral issues were the most significant symptoms of HD. A wide range of other symptoms were also described, including cognitive impairments, motor issues, depression, anxiety, and speech impairments. Many participants commented on the destructive impact of HD on multiple generations of their families.

Participants said that current treatments do not adequately manage their most disabling symptoms. Participants commented that while some medications were effective in managing some symptoms, most treatment regimens were altered to add more medication or increase dosing as HD symptoms progressed. Nearly all participants said that they value the benefits they see in non-drug therapies, such as exercise, dietary modifications, lifestyle changes (to minimize stress), meditation, and prayer.

HD impacts all aspects of patients' lives. Participants described severe limitations on physical activity, loss of independence and increased reliance on others for care, the devastating impact on relationships, and a constant fear of passing the disease onto their children. Participants shared that the cognitive impairments of HD often left them or their loved ones socially isolated, which worsened their depression and anxiety.

Participants stressed the need for medications that are effective in delaying the onset of symptoms or slowing the progression of symptoms. Other participants emphasized the need for improved research on a cure for HD (including gene silencing therapies and stem cell therapies), faster clinical trials and drug development, and expedited drug reviews. (*https://www.fda.gov/downloads/ForIndustry/UserFees/P rescriptionDrugUserFee/UCM491603.pdf*)

The report gives an excellent overview of the condition of HD and JHD in the United States, and I would encourage everyone to read it. *Note*: In the introduction, the FDA says that there were about 50 HD patients and patient representatives in attendance and about 60 web participants. I was there, and the room was filled to capacity, at least 150 people, I would guess. Gene Veritas, in his report on the meeting, estimated an "audience of some 200 HD family members and advocates" and "several dozen HD community members . . . via webcast." (*https://curehd.blogspot. com/2015/09/at-key-fda-meeting-huntingtons-disease.html*)

The HD/JHD community has a strong presence on social media, sharing stories, asking for advice, giving advice, praying for one another, and sometimes venting. I'm a member of many online HD/JHD groups. It's both a blessing and a curse—a blessing because, unlike when I began my journey over 30 years ago, I no longer feel alone, and a curse because the stories rip my heart out, over and over again.

And so we continue to tell our stories, hoping they will make a difference. The stories within this volume were written by people who demonstrate strength, perseverance, and courage .... but we are all getting tired. Some have now lived with three generations of the disease. We need understanding; we need effective therapies; we need hope; most of all, we need a cure!

Sharon McClellan Thomason

About Katrina Hamel

Katrina Hamel, Vice President and Chief Financial Officer of Help 4HD International, was born and raised in a small town on the central coast of California, USA, named Buellton. Growing up, Katrina's life was shadowed by HD. Her grandmother, who was experiencing movement issues, cognitive impairment, irritability and behavioral issues, felt lost and uncertain of what was happening to her body. Unfortunately, her grandmother committed suicide, and Katrina's mother was left with similar questions about the state of her own future, as she was experiencing similar issues. With symptoms that were growing progressively worse, she decided her only option was to leave the life she had made for herself and her family. Katrina lived there in Buellton until she had her three children and then moved 20 minutes away to Lompoc, California.

Katrina was a young mom who worked full-time, raised her children, went to school, and always volunteered. Katrina went to a trade school to study medical assisting in 2004, while also providing care to people in their homes. Eventually, Katrina moved on from medical assisting when she realized her love of caring for people on hospice.

In 2006, Katrina started working for Sarah House Santa Barbara, where she was a hospice caregiver to the dying poor. She was also volunteering in her children's school, at Help 4 HD, and with local nonprofits serving the homeless community. She eventually became the assistant manager and remained in that position for three years before leaving to provide in home support for her older brother, Kevin, who tested positive for HD. During this time, Katrina also opened Caring 4 HD, the first resource center and second-hand store for the HD/JHD community. This store remained open for two years.

Katrina continues to sit on the executive board of directors for Help 4 HD as the CFO/Vice President. She is a caregiver for her brother, who is experiencing the challenges that come along with being diagnosed with HD, and she volunteers with homeless organizations and her children's school. When she isn't working and volunteering, she enjoys spending time with her family, especially all her many nieces and nephews. She has always been interested in relieving people's suffering, if even a little bit. Suffering comes in many forms, not just physical; she just tries to help soften the struggle.

Katrina has made it her personal mission to educate everyone on HD and the need for treatments. She struggles daily with the fact that more people do not know what HD is and the integral part it can play in a family's life. She wants the world to know what HD is and to unite in the fight for a cure through more research efforts and studies into the complex workings of the disease and its symptoms. She believes strongly in the ripple effect, the belief that every person can spread the word of HD and ignite a movement across the globe.

1

Surviving Survival

I have two reasons for writing this memoir: first is for the people in this world who truly know Huntington's disease, like I do—living each day, staring it in the face; second is for the people in this world who have little or no relation to HD. This disease has plagued my family for generations, and I feel like I have a duty to spread awareness about how deeply this disease can affect one family.

A look inside my family's story:

1989

I hear her; she's yelling, again. I stop before I enter my childhood home on Second Street in Buellton, California. I imagine what is happening, and I freeze up, not wanting to go inside. Is she mad at my dad, Patches (our dog), or is it my brother? I had just gotten back from my friend's house (where I wasn't allowed to be), and I quickly thought of what I was going to say when I got inside, just in case she was mad at me.

You see, my friend Margot and I grew up together; we were stuck together like Siamese twins, yet I wasn't allowed at her house. My mom had Huntington's disease, and this altered her way of thinking. Among many other things, she thought that because my friend had a pool, I would drown at her house. Mind you, I knew how to swim; I grew up in the water, and both of Margot's parents were there supervising us. Years before this, I could go to Margot's house and swim all the time, but slowly my mom's reasoning changed as to why I wasn't allowed to go over there.

I open the door to my house, carefully and cautiously. I enter the house to see my mom standing above my dad as he sits on the couch. She is ANGRY. I notice the vein on her forehead protruding as she yells. My dad sits quietly with his head bowed as she speaks to him with utter disgust.

My house was upside down; it was off balance, and I could feel it.

April 1988

My family drove to the Santa Barbara Airport so my mom could fly back to Connecticut, where she was originally from, and where her family still resides. All I knew was my grandma had died. I didn't remember why or how she died; I didn't even remember her. I was almost 6 years old. I remember hearing of people's sadness and even my mom crying at one point.

Years went by, and slowly I started to learn how my grandmother had died. My grandma, Denise, had watched her mom, Agnus, become a different person over the years while she was growing up and knew that she had something described as Huntington's Chorea that caused her to have uncontrollable bodily movements and personality changes. As my grandma got older and had her own family, she started to notice changes about herself. These changes were physical, emotional, and psychological. She had troubles holding a cigarette, she stumbled when she walked, and her speech was impaired. My grandma reached out for help in Boston in hopes of being diagnosed and receiving care. The doctors she saw told her that she didn't have HD.

Despite her attempts to get help for what she knew she was feeling, no one would diagnose her or acknowledge her fears about herself and HD. My grandma Denise lost hope. She took her own life by jumping out of a seven-story building. THIS is what was wrong with the process of diagnosis and care, and some families still deal with this today, including my own family members. Without awareness and education, people often lose hope, understanding, and support.

As time went on, I started to experience my mom's lack of interest in mine and my brothers' lives.

1990

As I stand in our once very clean kitchen, I am feeling crumbs under my bare feet, slowly crackling with the shifting of my weight. I stand looking at the mess of a kitchen with piles of dirty dishes overflowing from the sink. My mom is standing at the far end of the kitchen with her back turned towards me; her hair is tangled, and most of it is in a ponytail. The rest of it is dangling on the side of her face. I stand still, watching, absorbing, confused. My mom hears me and turns around swiftly, her cigarette in one hand, and her other hand reaching for the pot of coffee that just finished brewing. I can smell the dark roasted coffee bean with a hint of burnt, old coffee – probably because she didn't wash the pot from earlier in the day.

This was something that I was used to, even at 3:00 p.m., when I got home from school.

She is still looking at me, wide-eyed, almost angry looking. She says, "What are you doing?!"

As I stand there looking at her, I notice her slightly spilling her newly poured cup of coffee. "Mom, your coffee ..." I start to tell her, but she interrupts.

"What about MY coffee?" and she is staring at me with eyes that look like they could pop out of her head and slap me.

I don't know what to say, so I just stand there. She isn't happy, and I can feel that in my chest.

I could often physically feel her reactions towards me as a child.

In runs my little brother through the front door, yelling, "MOM! MOM! Where are you?"

He comes racing into the house, and Mom and I make our way towards the front door, and he is holding a piece of paper. My mom, who I thought was leaving the kitchen in response to my brother coming home, walks past him and continues to her room.

Korey, who is six at the time, runs after her, not noticing her demeanor at all. My mother, Allyson, slams the door to her bedroom as Korey's heart is crushed into a million pieces. He stands in the hall, in shock as the paper he's holding slowly falls to the ground like a feather in a breeze. He stands there, still, with his hands down to his side, slowly turns and goes into his room and closes the door, defeated, broken, and sad. I stand there alone and can't understand what just took place, but I know something is wrong. I can feel my mom's anger and sadness.

At that time, in that moment, I didn't know she had Huntington's disease. In fact, I hadn't even heard of it, yet. As time went on, things continued to change and shift. Some days were pretty good and full of warm memories.

My mom was always first in line to see our school events, the first to be at our softball and football games, cooler and chair in hand. She was the first to sign up to make donations for a bake sale or to make sure we made a cool gift to give to my friends for their birthdays. My mother would laugh, a lot. Good people and friends always surrounded her. My house was never just my house, which was a beautiful way of growing up. We always had friends to play with and plenty of family to make up a few baseball teams. There was also the flip side of things, too, though. Strange outbursts, lies, anger, and disappointment ... and it always seemed to get worse.

I remember one summer evening, we were playing catch in front of our house, and the neighbors came over and started playing catch with us. My dad's best friend and his family showed up (which was a common happening), as well as my cousin Keith's two friends, all unplanned and spur of the moment, and next thing you know, we were across the street at the school, playing a full-on game of baseball. My dad was the coach of any sport his kids wanted to play. He coached baseball, basketball, football, softball, and even a little cheer from time to time. That night, after playing a few innings of baseball, it started getting dark, and we walked home to find my mom in the backyard, chain smoking, and her whole body was moving.

It is a vision I will never forget. She was fuming. I could almost see the heat radiating from her body. I looked at my dad and was wondering if he knew anything. Did he realize? Was he going to do anything about it? Our friends all met us at the door and said their brief goodbyes and even said bye to my mom, who didn't respond. My mom walked in from the backyard and slammed the sliding glass door as though she were trying to break it. The house sure quieted down; my brothers and my cousin went to their shared room, and I went to my room (which was also their room, but my parents put up a partition, so it was my own space, seeing as I was the only girl). There were four of us in one room. We all sat there knowing this was going to be a long night. I could hear my mom yelling and my dad apologizing. Not so much in the words they were saying, but in the tones of their voices.

My dad was so good at calming the storm. There was always a flip in my mom, like a switch and a light. She would be calm and happy, and quickly that would turn into a memory that I would like to soon forget. My dad, Kevin Hamel, Sr., was the love of my mom's life. My mom and dad met when they were teens in Lompoc, California. My mom was born in Connecticut and moved out to California with her dad and her brothers after my grandparents split up. My dad, born in Hawaii, moved to California from Hawaii when my grandpa was stationed here. My parents met when my mom was 15, and my dad was 19. My mom became pregnant at 16 and had my older brother, Kevin, Jr., at the age of 17. They went through many challenges as a young couple. They dealt with many things that young parents are faced with, and in the 70s, there wasn't a ton of support. My parents grew up together and created a beautiful family together. They share three kids, my older brother, Kevin, then myself and my younger brother, Korey. My cousin Keith also lived with us for a period of time while growing up.

1994-1995

Over the next few years, we, as a family, experienced more frequent events that included anger and reactions that were not understandable. I would see my mom bring home shopping bags ... maybe not from expensive stores, but LOTS of shopping bags. We were very low-income, and her bringing home multiple bags wasn't strange to me growing up; now, though, I see that this was poor financial judgement on her part and something she wasn't able to control. My dad started talking about something called Huntington's disease, to us, not to my mom. I was confused. I couldn't believe that as a teenager, I was just hearing about a disease that my mom could have and that her mom may have had as well. At this point, there wasn't much information and education available. The internet was not in most people's homes, and our encyclopedias weren't much help.

My mom and dad started arguing almost daily. My mom would blame my dad for things he didn't do or things he may have said or done, but she would blow it out of proportion. As kids, we were constantly talking about how mean Mom was. We didn't like to ask her questions, request anything, or cross her path on a hard day. We kids would go out of our way to stay on her good side. My mom was fun, and as young children, we enjoyed her a lot, but as teens, it became harder. We spent a lot of time in our rooms, as many teenagers do, but we did it out of necessity. My mom eventually made my dad move out. I remember the day we sat down as a family and listened to my dad explain why he was leaving. We sat at our round, oak table centered in the middle of the dining room. My mom was drinking coffee, legs crossed and bouncing, chain smoking with a furrowed brow. Her coffee was spilling, and ashes were falling onto our burnt orange colored shag carpet. My dad looked like a sad puppy, abandoned and broken. He was still wearing his chef's uniform from his morning shift. He looked so tired.

"You guys know that your mom and I love you, right?" he started. My dad has always been the light of a situation, and this day was no different. He tried.

We nodded, with confusion—Kevin, Korey, and myself.

"Sometimes, parents stop being able to get along." He paused, looked at my mom, who was staring out of the window in the dining room. He was holding back tears, which made no difference because his mouth was literally turned so far upside down that you could tell he wanted to sob.

I was 17. Kevin was 19, almost 20. Korey was 12. I also had a one-year-old daughter who was playing on the floor next to us.

My dad continued talking: "No matter what, your mom and I will always be a part of you guys' lives. We love you. None of this is your fault; none of this has to do with anything any of you did."

My brothers and I looked around the table at each other, and I'm sure we were all thinking the same thing ... *What the hell is going on?* My dad wasn't close enough at the table to comfort Korey, who was visibly upset, so I remember putting my hand on top of his as if to say, "I'm here."

My mom didn't say one word, except the occasional snort or loud exhalation as if to say, "Yeah, right," or, "Are you done yet?"

This made me so deeply sad. My dad took all the blame. He gathered some clothes, told us that he loved us and said he would work his hardest at trying to fix this. My mother didn't hear him say that, or she would have flipped out. For the next six months, my dad lived at his job. He worked 12-hour days and slept in a private dorm. During the time he stayed in this small bedroom, we would go visit. It was so depressing to see my huge-hearted Hawaiian daddy in so much pain and misery. He wept, moped, and was so quiet, something that, for those who know my dad, is almost impossible. He was losing weight rapidly and was so lonely. He had a small twin bed, a smaller mini fridge, and a couple of piles of folded clothes.

After a few months of this, my dad moved about 20 miles away to Lompoc, California. He still had hope that my mom would take him back—even though she wouldn't say one word to him, except, "I need money." He got a studio apartment and was still paying all my mom's bills. He worked several jobs to afford this type of living. He knew my mom couldn't work, and besides, he wanted to support her.

2001

My mom was manic. She was on the phone with 'a guy from Connecticut' every minute of every day. Talking fast and excited like. I hadn't been living at home, but my brothers told me what was happening daily. She wasn't engaging with them, was sleeping all day, and was on the phone all night. She would go in and out of wild amounts of energy, then crash.

One day I got a call from my brother Kevin. "Mom moved Dick in," he said, monotoned. Later, I find out that my mom had asked both of my brothers if it would be ok for him to move in; they both said no, and she did so anyway.

"Who's Dick?" I asked and could hear the immediate angry tone in my voice.

"The guy she always talks to on the phone, apparently."

Silence.

What the hell? I was so lost in this conversation. I had no idea my mom planned on moving someone into our childhood home. I had no idea because she'd told no one.

"I'm on my way."

I hopped in my car and drove to my parents' house. There he was, standing in MY DAD's front yard that he'd just mowed days prior. He was smoking a cigarette, chest out, glaring in my direction. My mom, with the biggest smile on her face, was draped on him. I took a deep breath and approached them. He had a very thick east coast accent. He put his arms out to hug me and said, "You are so beautiful, just like your mom!"

I wanted to barf. I was looking at him, up and down, and most definitely judging him. I deflected his hug and gross comment and looked at my mom. "Ma, are you serious? Who is this guy?"

Her happy smile turned to anger within a second. "This is Dick, and he's living here now!" she shouted back at me, turned on her heels, and stumbled into the house. I walked in behind her, and there were multiple empty liquor bottles and piles of ashes.

Great. They both drink and smoke.

I started to walk down the hallway, and Dick yelled out, "This isn't your home! Where are you going?"

I kept walking and said nothing. He followed me, saying, "Young lady, I'm talking to you." His voice was creepy, and he sounded like he was trying not to explode.

Both of my brothers came out, and we went to the front yard to talk a little more privately.

My brothers were both visibly upset, and they told me that right away Mom and Dick went into the house and started throwing things away and moving furniture, etc. I immediately went to the trash and found my dad's clothing, some shoes, and even some of his belongings from around the house that he has had for years. I was fuming. I retrieved all that I could, went back into the house and took things that I knew belonged to my dad. The entire time, Dick was yelling at my mom to stop me and that she needed to have control.

Dick came up to me and literally tried to act like he was the nicest man in the world. "Hi, sweetie, I was hoping we could talk. I love your mother. I want to marry her, and when we do, I will get to be your dad."

What the hell did he just say?

"I know you have a dad, but I can be your other dad."

I looked at him and simply said, "I have the best dad in the world. You need to get out of my way and leave me and my brothers alone!"

He backed up, which was wise, and went to yell at my mom some more.

At this stage in life, I had very little empathy for my mom. I witnessed a lot of bad decisions, screwed up priorities, and her hurting my family. I told my brothers that we would figure this out, and I left for the evening.

Dick continued to live in my dad's home while my dad paid the bills there. He didn't lift a finger or get a job, nor was he kind. I had to break the news to my dad. This broke my heart. He really had no words in response, only tears.

Over the next couple of months, things in our family shifted. Dick was acting like the king of all humans, and my mom was erratic and wanted nothing else but to please Dick. I moved into my dad's studio with him and was trying to figure out what to do about my brothers and my mom.

2002

Late one night, I got a call that sent my world spinning around. It was Korey, and he was hyperventilating and sobbing. I tried to help him calm down as I got my keys ready to go to wherever he was. He was at home, Dick screaming in the background, and I finally got Korey to be audible.

He said, "Dick is screaming at me because of Mom. Mom is mad at me for having an attitude, and I have an attitude because of Dick." He paused, and I heard him crying. "He spit in my face and pushed me. Mom was watching, and she didn't even stop him."

He was now bawling, and so was I. We did not grow up in a home of violence. Before my parents broke up, there were a couple of times when my mom smacked us, but it hurt more emotionally than it did physically, for sure. I asked Korey if it was over, and he said it seemed to be, so I told him I'd be there ASAP, and if anything else happened, to immediately call 911. I was beyond pissed off. I drove like a maniac and got there ten minutes sooner than it usually took me. I busted that front door in and yelled as loud as I could, "WHERE IS HE!?" I started walking towards my mom's room yelling, "DICK!" He started coming out of my mom's room, sweaty and fixing his pants.

"Are you serious? What do you think you're doing coming into MY family's home, being an ass to my mom, and messing with my brother?" I yelled. He was definitely intoxicated; I could smell it on his breath. Out came my mom as well, and she wasn't saying a word. "Answer me!" I demanded.

"Listen, YOUR brother is being a little jerk to YOUR mother! He is not listening to her, or me!" There was a quick break as he was waving his finger in the air and shaking his head. "What are you doing in our house, anyway?"

I looked at him and wanted nothing less than to strangle him. I looked at my mom in such disgust. This was the woman who always went to bat for us; she was THE mama bear. My brother was standing behind them and was still visibly upset.

"Korey, get some of your stuff and get in my car," I instructed him.

He moved so quickly because he knew that this was an opportunity to get away from the madness that he had been living with for the past few months. After Korey went outside, I looked Dick straight in the eyes and said, "Don't you EVER spit on my family or put your hands on my family again, or you will regret it, and that's a promise." I shoved his shoulder, and I turned around. My mom still had nothing to say. I turned around and said, "Ma, you've chosen him, and you've lost us in return."

She flipped me off and said, "I'll get my son back!" and they both laughed.

I responded with, "I promise you won't." Which I literally only said, because legally, I knew had no control. I walked out and got in my car. They were both standing at the front door with disgusting smirks on their faces.

Korey whispered, "He's wearing my jersey."

I turned to look as we drove off, and sure enough, he was walking into my house with his back turned; the jersey read HAMEL with the number 11.

Korey came home with me. I had moved two doors down from my dad, into an apartment with my boyfriend, Fred. I didn't have a plan, and I wasn't sure what to do. Over the next couple of months, we figured things out and got Korey enrolled into Cabrillo High School. He stayed with me and sometimes my dad. My dad was working seven days a week and from 6 a.m.-11 p.m. most days. When Korey had a baseball or football game, my dad would do his best to leave work and watch him for at least part of every game. Korey started getting in little bits of trouble here and there, and it was most likely a call out for attention because my mom didn't fight for him. She didn't reach out, didn't ask for him back, didn't want anything to do with him, but she didn't want anything to do with any of us. When my mom wasn't home, and neither was Dick, I went to the house and collected all of Korey's things. They never mentioned it. I did, however, get a call unrelated to this where my mother disowned me, threatened me with calling the police, and called me every name in the book. I remember saying some awful things to her, too, that I now regret.

One day, while my dad was at work, he noticed my mom's van pull up (which he was making payments on). It was Mom, and Dick was driving. My mom got out, and my dad met her at the back door. "I'm moving, and I need money," she stated. My dad already knew she was leaving, and originally, my little brother, Korey, was going to go with them. Korey was both relieved and hurt.

My dad told me he was shocked, not so much that she was moving, but because of her reasoning for asking him for money. "When we first broke up, I had Korey, and you never paid me child support," she said with an annoyed tone.

"Well, Allyson, I paid all of the bills and bought all of the food for the house. I paid everything; isn't that considered support?"

My mom wanted money, and she was willing to pull any card necessary to get it.

"I'm moving to Connecticut. If you give me some money, I won't ask for another dime, and I won't ask for support in the divorce," which they still hadn't finalized.

My dad eventually gave in and went to get her some money.

That same week, my mom and Dick left. No goodbyes, no calls, nothing. This affected us all, but my little brother never did recover from this pain. He wanted nothing but love from her at that point. I was relieved. I'm sure there was some sadness, but it was masked by rage and disappointment.

A year went by, and I became pregnant with my second child. During this pregnancy, I was considered high risk and needed to be on bedrest. I was unable to work, and my dad had offered to have us move into the house in Buellton where my older brother, Kevin, still lived. Fred, my daughter Alyiah, and I moved from Lompoc, and my dad helped us pay our bills while I was unable to work. When I was approximately six months pregnant, my family members were telling me they thought my mom was back in California. After talking to more family members, I found out that my mom was indeed back. She was also homeless and pregnant.

When I was told that my mom was pregnant and homeless, I was scared, confused, and I felt really bad for her, and after little thought decided to reach out to her and see if I could help. I went to pick up my mom from a filthy, run down shelter in Santa Barbara, California. She came waddling down the flight of stairs, trying to balance her gait, trying to carry a giant duffle bag. I noticed something was different, that she walked funny, and that she carried herself differently. At this point, I had read a little more about Huntington's disease, but wasn't sure if what I was seeing had anything to do with the disease that she may or may not have. My mom got in the car and was so different than I remembered. She was so filthy and unkempt. My mom used to be known for her long, thick, beautiful, bright pink nails that she would take care of by herself, and this day they were broken, some completely torn off, all of them full of dirt. I wasn't shocked, simply because I had cared for many people in the homeless community, but I was deeply saddened by what I saw.

On the hour drive home, it was very quiet. Occasionally, I would ask her a question or tell her a little something about her granddaughter. When she responded to me, it was with extreme excitement, but very few words. I wasn't sure how to really talk to her, and I felt nervous, as if I were meeting someone for the first time. In a way, I kind of was, the new version of my mom.

Early January 2003

Being pregnant at the same time as your mom and being the same number of months along is an experience that I cannot describe correctly. We were both showing. I was exhausted, my mom was exhausted, and I know things were still awkward for me. She didn't seem to feel the same way, that's for sure. She told me so many stories about Dick and how he was always yelling at her and being physically abusive. Even while pregnant, Dick hit my mother—in fact, that is why she left Connecticut to come back to Santa Barbara; he hit her, and he ended up going to prison, again. I have said that sentence, in different variations, many times to family members, and it never comes out easily. Allyson was strong, never putting up with anyone's crap. She despised men who hit women, so of course this came as a shock to me.

A month went by. and we were starting to get into a comfortable groove. We were gathering things for both of our babies and even starting to get sleeping areas arranged.

February 6, 2003

I woke up to my water breaking. I needed to wake up my brother, Kevin, to drive me, then wake my four-year-old daughter to get her dressed, and finally my nine months pregnant mom. We all drove to the hospital, and my contractions were intense and close together; I must have caesareans, so this situation became emergent. The stress, plus her own pregnancy, caused my mom to start acting out. When we arrived at the hospital. she grabbed my daughter's wrist and was pulling her through the hallway, stumbling more than I had ever seen. The nurse stopped her from going into the pre-surgical room. She wasn't happy. They wheeled me right past her; it happened so quickly. Shortly after, I could hear her yelling, "That's my daughter; I am her mother!"

Soon, I was in surgery, and Joseph was born. I got home after a couple of days in the hospital, and the first couple of days were good. I was healing; Mom was resting and getting ready to have my brother. My mom started using the phone on a regular basis, and soon I found out that she was talking to Dick. I was so angry and really concerned about this disruption to MY world. Looking back, I see that she couldn't know any better, that her mind literally couldn't process what was good for her. Looking back, those reactions make me feel so selfish.

February 20, 2003

Dick showed up in California. My mom's 41st birthday. I was infuriated and wanted nothing more than to protect my mom. My mom asked me if it was okay that he come over, and before she could even finish her sentence, I said "NO!" I instantly regretted my reaction and told her how I felt and why I was worried about them getting together. He got a hotel room down the street from my house. She decided to leave and spend the day with him. Two days later, my baby brother, Joshua Elijah Church, was born. I was absent because my brother's father was present during the birth. At that point in my life, I don't think I could have faked the kindness needed to be in the same room as him. My mom came back to my house shortly after Josh was born. Her chorea was getting worse, and I could see it when she tried to change Josh's diapers and clothing. She was also a bit frustrated with his crying and sometimes would just let him cry.

I wish I could go back in time to so many different events in my life, but the one event that sticks out the most is when Josh and Joseph were three months old. My mom came to me and let me know that she and Josh would be moving back to Connecticut ... again. Just as my mom had started making amends with my younger brother and the rest of our small family, she was leaving. My dad came over to the house with Korey and told my brothers to say their goodbyes. He told them how important it was, because he never had the chance to say goodbye to his mom before she passed away. Kevin came out to the garage where I was standing, talking to my mom, and he said, "Mom, I love you, but I hate the situation that you are in."

He gave her a hug and went inside. Korey stood in the open doorway that led to the garage, and he was just staring at my mom. When he finally spoke, he said, "So you're gonna run out on me again, huh?" and went back inside.

My mom started bawling, and my dad went and got him and made him come back to the garage, and he did end up giving her a hug and saying goodbye. Then my dad took him back to Lompoc. I drove down the street with a few of my mom's and brother's belongings and pulled up at the extended stay hotel where Dick was staying. I had no control, and I knew that. I was hurt. I was unsure of what the future would hold, and I was angry. Full of tears, I pulled away, knowing it would be a while until I got to see them again; never did I imagine that it would be almost six years.

I continued life, raising my children, planning family get-togethers, working and going to school, all with my mom and baby brother in the back of my mind. I never thought that my mom was lying when she told me that she would call me as soon as she reached Connecticut. I believed her. I waited years for her to call. I continued to pay for my childhood phone number because I knew my mom had that number memorized.

When Joseph started sitting up, walking, talking, eating, running, biting, smiling, laughing, and giving kisses, I always wondered if Josh was doing the same thing. When Alyiah was about six and Joseph was around one, I found clear and accurate information about Huntington's disease that specifically stated that it is a neurodegenerative, GENETIC disease. I don't even remember thinking that I could have this; I instantly thought about how awful it would be for my kids to get this, or for them to have to deal with a mom that was sick.

Panic started to set in, and all I could think about was getting tested. I was experiencing a lot of emotional issues that included depression, heavy, uncontrollable tears, unannounced, and I was also starting to 'see symptoms' in myself. I would look at my kids and feel so guilty. I knew that I didn't have the ability to know if they had HD, but I needed to know if they would ever be able to get HD. Over the next year, I was terrified, I was depressed, I was scared, I felt alone—no matter who was around. I wasn't able to afford testing, and I wasn't sure what I would do if I tested positive. All I could think about was my kids. I saved money, and I made an appointment at the UCLA movement disorder clinic and spoke to a genetic counselor. This was a very informative appointment because I was new to education about Huntington's disease. I knew just what I had grown up with and the little bits of what I'd read. Basically, they wanted to be sure that I would be safe, no matter how my test came back. I gave a blood sample and went home for two weeks. During those two weeks, I had the biggest mind trip I have ever experienced. I felt every symptom, every sign that pointed to a positive test result. I was having trouble finding my words, I dropped things, I stubbed my toe, and I was irritable. Each and every time something like this happened, I would break out in the loudest, most painful crying. I'm sure people could hear me. I sounded like a siren and sometimes like an uncontrollable baby. I was a mess. That was a very long year, and those were, without a doubt, the longest two weeks of my life.

I got to UCLA, just Fred and me. We sat down at a round table with three serious looking people in lab coats. The room looked cold and sterile. My head was saying, "You have it, you definitely have it … how are you going to tell your kids?"

The woman sitting across from me said, "You have nothing to worry about; your test came back negative." My CAG repeats came back as 17 and 19, which meant I was definitely in the clear.

I was sobbing like a newborn taking its first breath of air. I just couldn't stop. I had been so sure I had it. I was so happy to be wrong.

The drive home was interesting, crying, laughing, daydreaming, planning, and finding simple joys in life. I imagine that experience to be a slow version of someone who has had 'their life flash before their eyes'—unimaginable.

2007

The more I read, researched, and studied HD, the more empathy I had for my mom, and the more I wanted to find her. I started slowly looking for my mom and brother. The very first thought I had was, "Is she alive?" I called around, looking for death records, something that is so wrong for a child to have to experience. I then started reaching out to relatives in Connecticut, which was hard to do because I barely had any names to go off of, let alone cities, addresses, and phone numbers. I really got no help from my mom's family because she had very little left, and the ones who were still alive had no idea where my mom was. I started looking into the Church family to see if I could find out where Dick was and see if that may get me somewhere. My Auntie Sallie, who was also my mom's best friend growing up, had an ancestry account that helped her track people down in her family, and she offered to help me. After many attempts and many numbers, I found Dick's mom. I called, even though it was literally 3:30 a.m. in Connecticut and 12:30 a.m. in California.

A very tired voice answered the phone, "Hello?"

"Hi ... my name is Katrina Hamel, and I am looking for my mother, Allyson Hamel." I choked the words out.

Silence.

"Hello?" I said through my tears.

"Hi, honey ... how did you get this number?" the woman on the other end of the phone said.

"My aunt found a few numbers, and I am looking for Dick's family, so I can find my mom and my brother," I said, hoping she could give me a lead on who to call.

"Hold on a second, okay?" she said, sounding half asleep and shocked.

I could hear her talking to someone, but the phone was covered, so the voices were muffled. Then, clear as day—"Just talk to her! Tell her what you know, damn it!"

As the phone was being shuffled around, I heard a man's voice come on. He cleared his throat and said, "Sweetie?" I froze.

Seriously?? I wasn't sure if my anger for him outweighed my shock or vice versa.

"Hi, Dick, I am looking for my mom and for Josh. Are they ok?" I skipped over all of the small talk and got right to the point.

"Honey." I HATED that he always called me honey and sweetie. "I must tell you, I don't know."

Fear was setting in, and my mind was racing. "Well, do you know where they are?"

He said he'd heard my mom was staying in a homeless shelter in Willimantic. I started getting more info from him as far as she was concerned, and then the bomb dropped.

"I ended up in prison because of your mother..." which was what he always said; there was always blame... "I never put my hands on her, but she called the police and told them I did."

"You hit my mom, again?! What kind of man are you? You disgust me!"

Of course, he denied it, and I had to accept that because I was interested in getting all the information I could from him.

Over the next couple of days, I continued to talk to him, and he told me many stories of the types of things my mom would do, like spending her entire check within five days, getting mad at people she was staying with and walking out, never to come back. I kept asking about Josh, and I would get beat-around answers. He would never answer me.

May 2008

I found her. She was staying in a shelter for the most part, sometimes in a hotel when she had a few extra bucks, sometimes sleeping on a bench outside. My first contact to The No Freeze Project, homeless shelter, was emotional to say the least. They told me my mom had a medical bed there, and that they could not provide shower care or incontinence care for her, but that she was in desperate need of both. I instantly felt ashamed and embarrassed. After talking to them a few times over a couple of days, they said they would get her to call me on one of their phones. I needed to know what was going on with her before I talked to her. I knew that before she'd left California, she was slurring her words, walking with an unbalanced gait, using poor decision-making skills, and exhibiting many psychiatric issues. After speaking to staff members at the homeless shelter, I could see that things had gotten worse, as expected.

The beginning of the last trip to Cali:

My phone rings as I am kissing the kids and waking them up for school. It must have been about 7:15 in the morning. I know the area code, but not the number.

"...Hello?" I say, nervously.

"...Hi" A quick, gargled female voice says.

"Ma?" I can't tell if it's her, but I feel it in my stomach like little butterflies racing around.

"Yeah, yeah, hi," she responds.

"I love you!! I'm so happy I found you!!" I blurt out.

"Me, too, Rae. How you been?" she asks, but I didn't want to do that; I wanted to talk to her about her and Josh and how I could make things better for them.

"I'm good, Ma. Really good. The kids are growing, and we all miss you."

We talk like this for a good thirty minutes, and then it is time for her to get off the phone because she was on an employee's cell phone.

Over the next couple of days or so, I learned a lot about her daily living and her struggles. I learned about her battles and her triumphs. I couldn't bring up Josh, because she wasn't talking about him. I was scared, and I didn't know what to do. I eventually was able to talk to a social worker from the homeless shelter, and she said my mom didn't come in with a young boy. The worst thoughts flooded my mind, and I specifically remember not sleeping that night. I called the shelter in the morning in hopes of getting hold of my mom before she had to leave the building for the day.

"Ma?" I say softly.

"Yeah, yeah, hi, Rae." She, my dad and my brother called me Rae; it's my middle name and makes me feel good when I hear it, this morning especially.

She often said words twice as she became sicker.

"I love you. I need to ask you a question." I pause, and she says nothing, so I continue, "Where is Josh?"

"They took him from me. They are liars and won't let me have him." She has anger in her voice, and I can tell I've hit a nerve. She closes up and won't talk to me, not one word. A few days go by with her not wanting to talk, and I feel like I'm going to lose her again.

Over the next couple of months, I sent her packages with food, warm clothes, hygiene items, pictures, and nail polish to lift her spirits. She was talking to me on a pretty regular basis, and I was saving money to fly out there, get her, and fly her back because employees at the shelter didn't think she could fly alone. My mom had no glasses and no identification, so I tried setting up appointments for her to get to a doctor and to the DMV, but she couldn't navigate times, locations, and situations necessary to get her there.

Beginning of January 2009

I got a call that literally dropped me to my knees.

Basically, there was a couple who volunteered at the shelter. The husband was a retired employee of an airline, and he talked to the airline management about my mom. They came to an agreement for this gentleman and his wife to fly with my mom from Connecticut to California, drop her off to me, and fly back to Connecticut. She would be excused from needing an identification because this man was willing to go in front of management and vet her. I didn't even need to pay for the ticket because the shelter had a grant to help pay for families reuniting. I have never been so grateful and appreciative as I was in that moment.

My mom was coming home!

Arrival:

I'm nervous, putting bunkbeds together so my daughter and my mom can share a room. We've moved our son to the living room and created a bedroom for him, using a large piece of furniture as a wall. We have a very small two-bedroom duplex, but we are excited to have her back. I've gotten her a few new outfits and things like a brush, toothbrush, towels, and a new warm blanket. I start getting things situated for her, then leave on the three-and-a-half-hour drive to the airport. Joseph and Fred come along. Joseph sits in the back seat with a huge smile on his face, holding a bag of my mom's favorite chocolates. He's spent six years hearing good stories of my childhood and about how fun my mom was. I also explain in an age-appropriate way about my mom's brain and how we have to get to know her. We've always had pictures up in our house of her and the kids together. Gram is finally coming home!

The three of us enter LAX, and we stand there, waiting for her plane to land. Soon after, the screen tells us they have arrived, and people soon start to shuttle in to the baggage claim area. The line of travelers stops, and I look around, confused, because I don't yet see my mom. Then I see her. It has to be her. A man pushing a wheelchair to my left is looking around. I see his wife pointing at people and asking a question. They're looking for me. I'm stuck in the quicksand that is my shoes, and I whisper, "That's her."

I slowly gain the strength to walk towards them.

"Ma?" *I say as I approach.*

The man accompanying her sticks out his hand and says, "Hi, I'm Dale, and this is Leslie," pointing towards his wife.

I bypass his hand and throw my arms around him, praising his kindness. He wants to be sure I know what I'm getting myself into, which, in retrospect, did he think I was going to say, "Nope! Take her back!"? I'm not sure, but my mom is sicker than I anticipated.

I think it was honestly hopeful or wishful thinking. Our next stop was for a cigarette and a meal.

I'm helping my mom walk back to my car, the smell of urine engulfing a ten-foot radius. Her clothing is dry, and the urine is old, so old that it smells of ammonia. Her hair is matted into what looks like a helmet. She has one, two, three, four – at least five cigarette burns in her jacket alone. She is filthy. She looks at me, though I know she is blind as a bat because she can't see a thing without her glasses, and she smiles. I'm so warmed by her smile, but that is overshadowed by her broken, grey teeth that look so painful. She is smoking a cigarette and dropping it on the ground several times, picking it up after many attempts, and once she gets it into her stiff fingers, she flings her entire stiff body up and backwards, almost falling in the process. She notices nothing; I notice it all. We stop at a diner, and she is having trouble getting food into her mouth. I look around, and people are looking at her with expressions of disgust, and when they notice I am watching them, I get a sympathetic look as if to say, "You're so good for taking someone like that to dinner."

Of course, nothing was said, but it was felt.

That was the ONLY time that I didn't take an opportunity to educate.

At home, I was thankfully on the beginning of my scheduled three-day weekend, and this gave me a few days to get things in order.

The first day of my life-changing situation:

I wake up at seven in the morning and start getting the kids ready for school. My mom is asleep with her blanket over her head. Once the kids are off to school, I'm ready to get started on helping my mom get comfortable and cleaned up, but I also want to let her sleep in. So, I wait, till 4 p.m., and the kids are already home from school. I start by giving my mom a pack of cigarettes, a huge cup of coffee, and I bring her outside.

I detangled her hair for three days. Three exhausting, long days. I cut pieces I couldn't get untangled, and she cried through the whole thing. She took a warm shower and let me brush her teeth. I cut a half inch off of each toenail. I soaked her feet. I popped about 25 blackheads and put lotion all over her body for several days. THIS is not what a woman of any age should go through. My mom was 46 and dependent on her daughter but didn't realize it. I was a caregiver at home; I was a caregiver and manager at work.

My world became very small and overlapping. I noticed that I needed help, but I didn't know where to start. I started doing my research for California low-income assistance programs and kept coming up short. Eventually I stumbled on IHSS (In-Home Supportive Services), which is a program for helping disabled adults and the elderly population remain in their homes as long as possible. I reached out to someone in my county and was able to get someone to come by my house and assess my mom's needs. For the first couple of weeks, my mom seemed rational to a point, calm and even-tempered. That sure changed quickly, and it was fierce. When the social worker came to the house, my mom showed signs of paranoia and delusions. She told the worker that she thought there were people coming to find her from Connecticut.

She kept her composure for the most part. When it came time for my mom to sign papers for receiving assistance, though, my mom refused. She said that she didn't want me to take her money. Mind you, she made approximately $800 a month. I didn't need nor want her money; plus, this program did not touch her personal income; it was there to help. Eventually, I was able to convince her to sign the papers to allow me to be paid for caring for her. It wasn't easy; I told her if she didn't sign them that she would need to find a way to get the things she needed. Though this sounds harsh, it was the only way to make things work. I had to call into work several times, and though I was a manager, I was not salaried, so every day missed was pay I didn't receive. I was trying to make ends meet, missing work, growing out of the size of our rental, and really needed the small amount of money from this program to replace what I had been missing. Long story short, she signed the papers, and I went down to four days a week.

Eventually, I left that position and started a caregiving group and managed private care duties within my community. This kept me home more often, and I also was able to get a caregiving client that lived across the street from me. Things started to fall into place, and I was slowly feeling some relief, but in a Huntington's disease family, that is usually short lived. The issue now was space.

My mom started taking over my daughter's room to the point that my daughter couldn't spend any time in there. She would wake up and get her clothes in the morning, and the noise of her drawers or her walking around the room would disturb my mom's sleep. My mom would wake up and yell and sometimes throw a fit where she would wail like she was crying, but no tears would come out. We made adjustments for Alyiah's morning routine, and we moved some of her toys out of the room, so that Alyiah wouldn't disrupt Mom's naps while playing and getting ready for school. My daughter and my son made sacrifices at young ages that I don't think they realized, but it most definitely impacted *their* character.

October 2009

I found out that I was pregnant with my third baby, which was great for many reasons! We decided we needed to move and couldn't afford a bigger place in Buellton, California.

Before we moved, I needed to get my mom a pair of glasses. That appointment was eye-opening. Basically, the optometrist and my mom were having troubles communicating. She kept saying, "I can't see it," and he would adjust the machine and would get frustrated with her. At one point, my mom actually started crying.

I bent down and noticed that she literally could see nothing; there was no view. I told him, and he finally started to talk with respect because HE messed up. She couldn't verbalize what was going on.

Moving on:

We found a three-bedroom in Lompoc, California. It also had a sunroom that worked as another room and was perfect for my mom because she could access the backyard to smoke. I had recently found another job at Sarah House, which is a nonprofit care home that serves low-income dying adults. I worked three days a week and was able to take care of things at home as well as maintain clients in the Buellton area.

I had a lot of complications with my pregnancy, and I am sure now that some of it was due to stress. My mom was angry all the time; she would yell and cuss, daily. I would watch her in the middle of the night, pacing, screaming, talking to people that I didn't see, and blaring the T.V. Her sleep was irregular; so then was mine. I worried about our future as a family, about finances, and about how long my mom would need to suffer. Every day, my mom was miserable. Her quality of life was nonexistent, and she was falling more frequently, which added to the misery.

Some days were manageable; most were unbearable.

January 2010

I got home from a shift that was longer than usual because someone I was caring for at work had passed away.

I walk in, everything is pitch black, and I can see the dim blue light permeating through the house, which is a sign that my mom hasn't yet restarted her VCR movie. This means she is likely sleeping. I quietly go to peek on her through the sliding glass door, and she is lying on the floor. There is blood smeared on the cream-colored linoleum floor, and it leads to her side. I was taught years prior through work that I need to remain calm in high-stress situations. I'm looking at the pool of blood, and it feels like I was there for 15 minutes staring, frozen, but it must have only been seconds. I slow my breaths, slide open her door, and I kneel next to her. "Ma, I'm here. Are you ok?" My hand is on her rib cage and is slowly rising and falling with her shallow breaths. I feel a sense of relief wash over my body; I feel heat rushing out of my body as soon as I know she is alive.

I am now sitting next to her on the floor, and she is responding to me. She tells me a story about her going outside to yell at the neighbor's dog, which was a daily event, and she fell. After I help her off the ground, slowly, and clean her all up, I notice that she has blood coming from her elbow and her forearm. When I get her into bed, she tells me she was trying to change her movie in the VCR, and she tripped and fell.

At this point, I was worried that she had a concussion. I asked her repeatedly if she would go to a doctor, and she refused over and over. I knew if I called 911, she would refuse all care, and in turn, they wouldn't be legally allowed to tend to her. I was stuck in a very hard place and had no idea how to go forward. I sat in her room. All night. I gently woke her in the middle of the night to make sure she was even wake able, and she was. I hadn't slept in 24 hours, and it was time for work, yet again. I remember that day well. My mom was awake, bruised up and causing a ruckus, the kids were ready and off to school, and I was heading to work needing unmeasurable amounts of caffeine. I had to stop halfway to work to take a nap on the side of the freeway, and I only had 15 minutes. I got to work, and unfortunately, someone had called in to work and was unable to come. I tried calling others to fill in and was unable to find anyone available in such a short time. I worked alone and ended up sleeping at work that night, after my shift, for a couple of hours because I was afraid to drive home. These types of days became more common as my mom became sicker.

More frequently I was finding myself in need of support, but not knowing how to get any. I was drowning myself in work to make ends meet, and I was trying to take care of all of my mom's needs, but also finding myself grieving, separating myself from her. I can't fully describe it, but what I can say is, I didn't like who she was turning into. I didn't like my style of care with her, either. I was impatient and at times mean. I was frustrated that I didn't have a mom, yet she was there.

One day, on my first day off in ten days, I sat on my couch, sipping a warm cup of tea. The kids were at school. I was about four months pregnant, and I was starting to watch a movie on Lifetime, and all I could remember was the overwhelming stench of bowels starting to make me feel sick. It was like an ugly cloud in the sky that is warning of something to come.

I stand up, walk to the most obvious place, my mother's room, and I find her awake (which was rare for the morning). Not only is my mom awake, but she has stool in her hair, on her face, on her shirt, pants, and toes. It. Is. Everywhere. I am instantly hot. I am boiling at the thought of me having to give up my peace and quiet for the day and not only clean up but disinfect EVERYTHING!

I feel guilty admitting that now, but this day only continued to get worse.

I open the door and sharply say, "STOP!" She's trying to take her clothes off, and that is making matters worse. She continues, of course, and it takes her a few moments to process my demand. She is sitting on her chair in front of her TV, and I know this will be a process that takes some organization. I ask her to stay where she is and tell her that I will help. I start by taking all of her soiled bedding and soaking it in hot water outside, because I can't throw excrement into the washing machine. At this point, I am crying with overwhelming amounts of anger, not at my mom, but at this disease. I then disinfect the bed, which takes a long time, and my mom sits outside, unbothered by her uncleanliness and smoking a cigarette. I complete her bed, with fresh linens, so that when she is done in the shower, she can go directly to bed, like she likes. I wash the wall next to her bed, and then I start to scrub the floor on my hands and knees. Everything is clean, but mom.

"Ma, let me help you into the shower now. The room is clean, and when we're all done, you can get into bed," I say, exhausted.

"No, no, mmmm, no," she mumbles. I'm beside myself.

"What do you mean, no?" I question with such frustration

and anger. She has declined taking showers in the past, even refused. Never has she refused when she was this filthy.

I continue to try and help her into the shower with different strategies and techniques, and nothing works. I sit on the freshly cleaned floor and stare at the wall. All I can think is, "What am I supposed to do?" "How am I going to get her into the shower?" I try bribing, borderline threatening, being friendly and downright pissed. I even try to physically overpower her while she hits me. Nothing is working. I have to work in the morning, and it's very apparent I need help with her.

I called APS, which stands for Adult Protective Services. I told them of the situation, and I was sure to go into depth about Huntington's disease and what might happen when they arrived. The woman on the phone listened; she asked questions and was thankful for the learning experience. When the two caseworkers arrived, they seemed to have been told of the circumstances and did a decent job at not making it worse. They came inside, and I remember feeling ashamed and embarrassed for the way my house smelled and the way my mom looked. They approached my mom and asked her if there were any issues that she had and wanted to talk about. They proceeded to tell her that she had choices. I was concerned, at first, but quickly understood. Choice one, let your daughter help you into the shower. Choice two, let the woman helper give you a shower. Choice three, leave with them and be taken to a hospital to take a shower.

She instantly chose option one and answered as if it had never even been a problem. It was now 8 p.m., and my mom was lying in bed, exhausted. Twelve hours of this, and I didn't know what to do. I lay in bed, thinking about my future and that of my family. The next day, I called the agency that was paying me a small amount of money each month to take care of her. I told them that I needed help. They only offered to help by slightly increasing her hours. I needed someone to help me get her to a doctor or help me with local resources. I had heard of an organization called Help 4 HD International that was local to my area and had talked to the president previously, but at that point in my struggle, I didn't have energy or time to attend a support group. I did, however, listen to the radio show and did find a lot of it to be informative. I connected with people via Facebook, which helped a lot because I felt like my stories were validated when others believed the absolute craziness that had become my life.

After that day of explosion of BM, my mom never really went back to *normal* toileting.

I had to implement routine in order for my household to work and in order for my mom to have days with the least amount of negativity and problematic situations. I was working four days a week and sometimes five or six, depending on clients that I had outside of my hospice care job. Planning was a necessity.

I worked in the morning and would leave for work at 6:00 a.m. I would return by 4:00 p.m. At 5:30 a.m., I would make three peanut butter sandwiches, cut up or peel some fruit, and brew a pot of coffee. I would put this on the table where she sat to watch TV. The sandwiches would be in Ziplocs, and she had three large drink cups, with lids and straws, full of coffee. She would drink cold coffee all day long. She also typically wouldn't wake up until noon, so by the time she drank all the coffee and ate her sandwiches and smoked a few cigarettes, I was home.

At 5:50 a.m., I would change her brief, if needed, and pants. When I was away at work, I would constantly worry about her ability to eat, her ability to use the commode I'd put in her room, and her ability to smoke without lighting herself and our house on fire. From 6:00 a.m. to 4:00 p.m., I was gone.

When I got home at 4:00 p.m., I would start by cleaning out the commode, making her something to eat to tide her over until dinner, and cleaning up her room that looked like people were having a food fight, daily. Her chorea was debilitating at this point. Some days, she walked like a robot; other days, she moved frequently but with fluidity.

After cleaning up, it was time for a shower or laundry or taking her to the store or a fast food drive-through and then, time for dinner. Her care was more than my own children combined. I continued this type of routine for a while, and then I started having to limit my physical activity because my third baby, Elias, was not gaining weight or size. I had full-time work, a complicated pregnancy requiring appointments every five to seven days, my own family, and, of course, my mom. I had no time or even thought of self-care. I didn't spend time after work with friends, and I didn't sleep well. I started becoming bitter, especially as my mom started needing more of my attention and time. I was starting to spend less and less time caring for her, partly because of my resentment and then because of having a new baby.

One Saturday morning before leaving for my morning shift

I walk into my mom's room and start to do my usual routine. She needs her brief changed and needs clean pants. My mom throws off her blanket, rolls over, and tries to stand, all in one movement. She has a hard time pausing between movements or tasks.

She has crusted coffee mixed with tobacco grounds surrounding her dry, chapped lips. This is when I start realizing she is eating more of her cigarettes than smoking them.

I started with a warm washcloth and washed her face. I put Vaseline on her lips and worked my way down. After calling my work and letting them know I'd be an hour late, I gave my mom a bed bath. She was all clean, food was on her table, and she decided to go have a smoke before lying back down.

Standing right in front of me, she looked as though she had a jolt of electricity going through her body; her chorea was so intense. Her arms flew up in the air, she took a giant step back and over corrected and fell forward and to the side. Her head grazed the side of her table, which we had rigged up with soft towels, and she fell to the ground. It shocked me because it happened so quickly. I helped my mom up, and the side of her head was wet. I pulled my hand away, and my hand was full of bright red blood. After fully checking her out, I found that her ear lobe was detached from the side of her head. She was unable to acknowledge the pain, but as you can imagine, it hurt. I tried to give her some over-the-counter pain medicine, and she refused.

This was always her response, as she thought I was giving her medication for HD, which she *didn't have*. I asked her to please allow me to call the ambulance, and, of course, she said no. I held onto her ear lobe for about 15 minutes, and as soon as the bleeding slowed, I used medical superglue to reattach her ear lobe. At that moment, I felt such deep gratitude for my background as a caregiver. I had dealt with many wounds and injuries over time. After several layers of superglue, I helped her back to bed. On my way to work, I called the woman in charge of her IHSS and reported what had happened. I also documented it and called APS. I wanted to always cover myself in the event of a misunderstanding.

Several months went by, and my mom seemed to get sicker, quicker. She was choking on soft foods and beverages. I started leaving her blended smoothies and shakes, and the weight of her care was starting to fall on my family more and more. If my mom soiled her pants while I was gone, my daughter would typically need to bring her in fresh pants. Fred would help with food/drinks and cleaning up. I know it was stressful for everyone, and I know we were all holding on by threads.

Around this time, my mom was having difficulties smoking. One evening, I was cooking dinner, and I could smell something burning.

I check all the food, I check the house, and I walk to the sink in my kitchen and open the curtains to the window that overlooks my mom's smoking area. Her hair is on fire, literally smoking from her head.

She always got burn marks on her clothing, but never had I imagined she would light her hair on fire. I flipped out!

"MA! What the hell!" I yell as I run to the backyard. I take her cigarette, and I throw it on the cement. I start patting her head to get the burning to stop. Her eyebrows are singed, and half of her hair is, too. She has no idea. At this point, I am cry-laughing because I know this is sad, and scary, but all I can think is, "Are you kidding me? What's next?"

I washed and cut her hair, which was matted anyway because she hated showering and especially getting her hair brushed. I needed to implement rules pertaining to her smoking at that point. I told her that I, or someone else, if I'm not home, would need to light all her smokes from then on. She immediately said okay and agreed to this, but as you can imagine, that didn't last very long. About five days into this arrangement, she flipped out while I was at work. She started screaming, yelling, and throwing her belongings all over her room. This ended by having to call 911 and asking for them to come and help with the situation. We had had to call the police in the past, and I was sure to give them a little bit of background and education prior to their arrival. The police came and went, and, of course, when they arrived, she would contain her emotions, or at least be calm. I wanted, more than anything, a paper trail of her outbursts in case I ended up needing it, which I did.

One evening I was taking my mom to cash her monthly check, and all seemed like a typical third day of the month.

I am exhausted. I take Eli and my mom and head to the store. We get inside, cash her check, and purchase snacks and cigarettes. The next stop, like every other month, is Jack in the Box. As I pull out of the liquor store parking lot, my mom opens the door and jumps out ... mid-street. Eli is in the car, so I have to back up, park the car, and lock him inside. He is one-and-one-half. I run to the middle of the street and try to help her stand. She wasn't walking well at this point in her life. She is unable to walk, and cars are stopped in both directions. I finally drag her to the side of the road, and she is hitting me off her. She manages to hobble to the liquor store and is thrashing all over the place. She starts pulling large chip shelves down, magazine stands are thrown across the room, and she is SCREAMING. She is acting like a bull in a china shop. I stand there in shock, thinking of a strategy to stop what's happening.

My mom wasn't very verbal at this point and was yelling noises more than words. Then, clarity hit, and she said, "Call 911!"

I said, "Ma, I will call, if that is what you want, but you have to understand that they will likely take you away because of the way you are destroying this store."

She insisted I call, so I did. I again told them about Huntington's, but I also requested a psychiatric team to come so they could evaluate her. I called my Auntie Sallie and asked that she come and get Eli from me because I knew this would amount to a very long night.

Two police officers arrived first. Mid thrash, they tried to *contain* my mom – bad idea. My mom threw both officers to the ground. She must have weighed 120 pounds, max. Rage in Huntington's creates such enormous amounts of strength.

The people who came to assess my mom were so gracious and kind. They helped my mom into the back of the police car and assured her that she was safe and told her they needed to talk to me. She gladly got in the back, and she and the police officers and the CARES (Crisis and Recovery Emergency Services) team asked their questions. (CARES provides psychiatric evaluations for involuntary hospitalization in conjunction with American Medical Response. Adult and children evaluations are done under the direction of the Behavior Wellness Department's on-call psychiatrist and are provided countywide 24 hours a day.) The woman from the CARES team told me that I was correct, that my mom needed medication for her safety and for others' safety. I was told she would be put on a 72-hour hold and that I would be able to see and talk to her after that.

The next three days were very intense. I would cry out of nowhere. I didn't want to look at her room, I didn't want to talk to people who asked me what was going on, I was in mid-grief, and I wasn't sure how to manage my emotions. When that police car pulled away, my mom looked back at me through the rear window with eyes of defeat. I felt guilty, and strangely enough, I still do. I wish I had known about HD sooner, so I could help her get care before it had gotten to where it was.

The social worker from CARES decided it wasn't safe for my mom to come home, mainly because I had young children. I understood it as my kids were in jeopardy of being taken out of the situation if need be. After her assessment, the hospital was then in charge of helping her find placement. I was calling all over California, trying to find a home closest to me, so I could recommend it to her team. I really wanted my mom close, so when she was under control, we could take her out or go visit frequently. I got a call on day six; the social worker basically told me they were releasing my mom. I was instantly confused, and that confusion turned to anger. How could I be told that it wasn't safe for my mom to come home, then be told that they were releasing her?

I told the social worker at the hospital all that the CARES team had told me, and they didn't seem to care. My anger elevated and turned into problem solving, luckily. The social worker continued to ask me to come and get her, and I refused. She then told me that if my mom wasn't picked up, they would discharge her, and "How would I like it if my mom was walking the streets of Lompoc?"

This still upsets me. The lack of compassion was unimaginable and hard to put into words. I told this social worker that she had a responsibility to my mom and her safety and that she should reconsider what she was threatening because the hospital would be liable. I don't think she expected that. Conversations went back and forth over the next few days, and then they found a care home willing to take someone with behavioral problems. This home was in Los Angeles, four-and-a-half hours from me. My choices were limited, so I accepted her fate. I followed my mom down and what I was forced to do was so heartbreaking. I had to leave her in a home that smelt of urine, with people who were yelling at themselves and walking into walls. I was crushed, but she didn't seem to mind.

I purchased her all new clothing, labeled everything, and did the same with her toiletries. I bought her linens and labeled them with washable, permanent labels. The paramedics unloaded my mom. She had been given medication to safely transport her, so she was groggy. They helped her into bed, and she didn't wake up. I sat next to her bed, thinking about all the times we'd gone to the beach and how we'd never had any money, but she and my dad always produced happiness. Sitting beside her for two hours while she slept brought me a lot of resolve emotionally. I felt selfishly relieved that I wouldn't have to care for her every need for the time being. I felt relieved that she was sleeping. I felt relieved that she was finally getting rest, mentally and physically. I was looking forward to her getting stable enough to come home.

A few months went by, and I started to get discouraged. Some days would be quiet. I would call her, tell her I loved her, and let her know when we would be down to visit. Some days I would get a call, and the nurses would let me know that she wasn't willing to take her meds, and she was acting out to where it was dangerous for staff and other residents. I, my mother's daughter, had to authorize for them to hold her down and inject her with a sedative. I had to do this a few different times, and it never got easier. I saw huge changes in her between visits. She was losing weight and becoming more and more withdrawn.

On my last visit to the care home, I noticed such dramatic changes that I confronted the nurse on duty. I was upset that no one had contacted me to tell me she hadn't eaten food in a week and that she was only accepting high caloric shakes. Now, I am all for her making that choice; I was simply upset that after day two, I wasn't notified. I requested to speak with the doctor on call as it was a Saturday. When I spoke to the doctor, he informed me that he thought my mom could benefit from yet another medication change. We had been going through a list of medications that he felt would most benefit my mom. I was getting the feeling that because she was 50 years young, he was having a hard time with her becoming so ill.

The medication he had suggested did not change her heath, her symptoms, or her comfort.

Because of my background in Hospice care, I knew where we were. I knew that my mom's body was no longer able to fight. I noticed her change in skin, her change in breathing, her sleepiness, and her inability to keep fluids in her mouth. It was time. Before this moment, I had held hands with hundreds of people during their last days, many of whom had no one in the world who cared for them. I was honored to be sitting beside a large number of people during their last breaths on this planet. But this was my mom. My one and only mom. Over the next few hours, I had to figure out how to get my mom from Los Angeles to

Santa Barbara. I was, and had been, working at Sarah House Santa Barbara. This is a unique home that cares for the dying poor. My mom fit the criteria, and there was one room open. The medical transport was hundreds of dollars, and I had saved for this moment. I spent all we had in savings to get her to the right place to take her last breaths.

When she arrived, she was awake and smiling, which was a breath of fresh air. She was unable to say much, but she did say yes, no, and an occasional curse word. The next ten days consisted of family time, sitting in silence, bed baths with warm water, rose petals, and lavender oil. It was refreshing to have my mom 'home' and being able to work while taking care of her. I repositioned her, changed her briefs, and gave her medication to be sure she was comfortable. I slept on a recliner next to her bed and woke up every two hours to continue her care. The mix of emotions poured over me. Was it okay to be happy that my mom was finally comfortable and relaxed? – but also dying? She sure did fight with people till her last moments. She would holler out, "NO!" when people would try and bathe her; she would give the eyes that meant no, even if she couldn't produce the words. On day nine, she said, "Love you," and I knew what that meant.

I said, "I love you, too, Ma. Thank you for being your best self and teaching me to be so strong."

On the eleventh day of my mom being at Sarah House, Kevin, Korey, Fred, Alyiah, Joseph, Elias, and I were all in my mom's room. My mom had shifted, and her lungs were filling with fluids. We were writing notes to put on her walls where our family's pictures hung. I noticed a change in my mom's breathing. It became shallow and paused. I told my brothers that if they wanted to say anything to her, now was the time. We all took our turns whispering into her ear. I made sure to tell her that I forgave her and that I hoped she forgave me. Moments later, my mom, our mom, died.

The next couple of days were a blur. I wanted to dive into work and volunteerism. I wanted to move forward and swallow my emotions, which is exactly what I did. I started working even more, and I began volunteering with Help 4 HD International.

Two years later, my uncle died from the complications of Huntington's disease. A year after that, my cousin, his son, was diagnosed with Huntington's disease. That same year, my other uncle became severely combative, causing injury to my aunt, and was placed in a home. That same year, another huge blow came and hit me upside my head.

Kevin was worried about his future pertaining to HD. He was adamant about being tested quickly. He had little movements in his body, but they were different than my mom's; they were more like tics. He would move his hand from down by his side to his glasses and back down again. We went to his primary doctor to talk about the process of testing. This is, by far, not a typical situation; however, it is what worked for Kevin. His doctor was amazing about sitting with Kevin, hearing his concerns, and asking questions. She said she would be happy to order the test for us because we came prepared. Again, not typical. Kevin took the test that day.

About a week and a half later, I went on a camping trip for Father's Day; on the last day there, I received a call from Kevin's doctor. She very sweetly said that she didn't have the news that we all hoped for. I could tell before she finished her sentence that the result was positive for Huntington's; her tone of voice when saying "Katrina" gave it away.

I sat down right where I was and cried. I wondered what my brother was thinking because he'd just gotten the same call I did, seconds before me. We ended the call because Kevin called me. I was his first call, and I didn't know what to say.

"Hey, Rae," he said with a broken voice.

"Hey, Bubba," I said hesitantly. Bubba is his nickname.

There was a silence like no other. I slowly said, "I love you," and I silently cried.

He said, "I love you too," and I proceeded to tell him I was sorry and that I will be here for him no matter what and forever.

"We'll figure this out together, Bro."

I knew I had to be strong. I knew I had to suck up my sadness for that call.

"I guess I'm just in shock," he said before we got off the phone.

I had to call my dad, which I was dreading. I had been warning my dad about the possibility of Kevin having HD, but it was so definite. My fears were placed in front of me without choice.

I broke down when I heard my dad's voice on the other end of the phone. Through tears, I said, "Dad?" – he instantly met my tears with his own fears and was already crying when he said, "What's wrong, sweetie?"

I told him that his son, his firstborn, has Huntington's disease. Parts of me wished I wasn't the one who had to tell him, but other parts of me knew my dad needed to hear it from me. It was a short phone call as there wasn't a lot to say at that moment. We were shocked and already grieving.

After that call, I called my HD family at Help 4 HD and bawled like a pissed off toddler. I complained, I got angry, I was scared, yet they understood, accepted what I was going through, and helped me justify my emotions. I will forever be grateful.

I found myself very spaced out, not really thinking of anything specific, but more a blank sadness, if that makes sense. I eventually started thinking about specifics, things like, will he ever get married? Will he allow me to take care of him? What do I say when I see him? Is he going to be upset with me because I tested negative? How can I be sensitive to his feelings about our different fates? I felt a heavy weight on my shoulders, and I felt myself falling into a depressive state. I didn't have insurance, so a doctor was out of reach for me. I had to live through what I was feeling and do the best I could. The last thing I wanted to do was impact Kevin in a negative way.

I wrote this shortly after he was diagnosed:

What are you feeling and what do you see?
Sometimes I watch you and don't know what to say. I
imagine your thoughts, and I begin to fray.
Do you see me and become unhappy? Do you feel angry that
it's you and not me?
I know your fate seems limited and predicted, just as mine,
yet completely different.
Do you imagine your life without this? Do you believe in my
dedication and selflessness?
I dream of you walking gracefully, with ease, and doing so
without your need for me.
Do you think you're a burden to me and the rest? Do you
enjoy your time with all of us?
I need you, I want you, and I hope that you know – forever
and always that will be so.
Do you trust me? Do you know that I'm here?
I will always do my best for you, to try and keep you near, if
you are safe and happy –
That's my fear ... that things will change so drastically, and I
will somehow fail.
Huntington's is all around, but so are we; there is nothing
that can stop us from being family.
I will walk, stand, sit, and lie beside you till I am alone. Then
I will continue this fight for people like you and Mom.
I hope you see that we love you and will always remain;
nothing, not even HD, can change that, any day.

I don't know what is in store for my brother, I don't know how his body and his mind are going to change and when. Would I want to know? I'm not sure that I would. Someday I know that I will be the little sister, helping the big, protective brother get to and from the bathroom to take a shower. I will have the job of making him the appropriate foods and changing his adult briefs. I also get to be his voice and help him remember the power of his own, while he still has it. I have made no promises other than to do my absolute best. I just don't ever want him to feel like a burden.

As time moves on, we work on getting Kevin medical coverage and Social Security—he hadn't been able to keep up with the work load and quick responses needed to do his job, and he was let go prior to testing. We had to apply, and I was lucky, in a way, that I had helped very ill people obtain deserved Social Security in the past and knew how to navigate the system. We did not get denied the first time, which is more common than some people realize. We did, however, have to see a psychiatrist that the Social Security Administration assigned. I came prepared. I had been taking notes about when he was let go at work, dates and reason. I wrote down stories with dates that might be pertinent. One entry read *On July 4th, 2013, Bubba tripped and skinned his knee and both palms. He needed a hand up.* Short stories with important info. Eventually, he was awarded disability, and I would have to be his payee, due to him being incapable of processing bills and managing money.

My brother is my hero. He watched my mom die. He watched her get sick. He has taken this diagnosis with such grace. I admire him, and though I obviously hate Huntington's, it sure has made us very close as a family.

Kevin, since diagnosis, has become an advocate. He has volunteered with Help 4 HD, providing videos for teaching tools and has come along for law enforcement trainings. He wants the world to talk about Huntington's, to acknowledge what it is that he must withstand. He knows I will stand beside him; he knows he is fully loved by all his family.

Recently, I have had to talk to Kevin about specifics of his care. I want to be sure I honor his wishes as much as I can.

"Hey, Kev. I wanted to talk to you about yeaaaarrrs down the road. I want to ask you some questions, so I know what it is you want me to do when we get to a point that I would need to make those decisions. Is that ok with you?" I say while we sit at my table eating mac 'n' cheese.

"Yeah, sure," he says, which is a response he uses often.

"First of all, I want you to know that I will do all that I can to do exactly what you would like, as long as we are all safe. Do you

think you would rather live in a care home, or would you rather live with me? – Or even at home with caregivers if we can pull that off?" He is quiet, and you can tell he is processing.

"I don't want to go to a home, ya know?" He is quiet.

"Yeah, Bub, I hear ya. I will do my best to keep you home as long as I can, as long as you continue seeing a doctor, taking needed medications, and if we are all safe."

I don't recommend people promising anything they can't commit to. That is why I said I would do my best.

Our conversation continues, and I ask him how he feels about me caring for his bathroom needs, and as soon as I say it, I have to stand up and turn around to 'clean the kitchen counter' because I instantly start to cry. I know this is hard for him. He is my older brother, and hello, I am a girl. I see the need to ask these questions now, because I want to be sure I know what he wants even when he can't tell me later. But that sure doesn't make it any easier. He comes to the conclusion that he would like to have a caregiver come into our home to help him with those needs if we're able to figure that out financially. He does say that he knows that may not work out but that ultimately, he'd like to stay home.

During these times of deep sadness, there was more weighing on my mind. My mom's older brother passed away in Connecticut, leaving behind a son who also tested positive—he is my age. My mom's younger brother severely hurt my aunt who was helping to take care of him, and he ended up in a care home in Connecticut. I also have my two younger brothers who have not yet tested. I have nephews and a niece at risk, and I can't tell you how frequently I think of their futures. I have been in my nephews' and niece's lives since the day they were all born, helping raise them and take care of them. I may not have my own children at risk for this disease, but I do consider my nephews and niece to be darn close, if not the same, for me. I worry. I fight. I wonder. I cry.

My mind won't shut up. There are other things that come up as well that make me watch, stare, observe. I watch the way they talk, I watch how they perform in school, I watch how they do medically and socially. The possibilities of them having HD are scary; the thought of JHD is terrifying.

My dad taught me to laugh often. To find the good in people and situations, to love and love unconditionally. My mother taught me strength; she taught me the separation between disease and person, even if it wasn't intentional. My brother taught me that we are all different, yet so alike; he taught me selflessness. I am my family, and I am thankful.

About Ginnievive Patch

Ginnievive Patch (pseudonym), RN, grew up in southern California, born in Anaheim and raised in the mountains and high desert, where she and her husband had their first son in 1987, until age 24, when she and her husband moved to Sacramento, California. Their middle son was born in Sacramento in 1990. At age 28, they moved to Missouri, where they currently live. She and her husband went to the same high school in the high desert and re-met during college break and got married. She is the mother of three sons and grandmother to a beautiful little girl. Two of these sons have tested positive, including the one who is now a father.

Ginnievive started out young in medicine, becoming a candy-striper at age 12, then working as a pharmacy tech at age 18, becoming a pre-med student at age 19, but then deciding to go on to get her associates as an RMA and then becoming an RN in 2006. She has a background in family medicine, lab, psychology, pediatrics, oncology, and for the last 12 years, medical aesthetics and rejuvenative medicine, including stem cells therapy.

She ran a local support group for Huntington's disease until her mother-in-law, Nana, who was in the end stages of HD, moved in with them. She now takes care of her ex-husband, who has HD. She is also the author of *I Fight for Understanding: 31 Days of Coping with Huntington's Disease.*

She and her ex and their children have all participated in HD research, especially the youngest son, who went yearly to University of Iowa to do the Kids HD study. Her passion is to educate caregivers and help them survive the turmoil HD/JHD can cause in the early stages, primarily if the psychiatric symptoms outweigh the physical chorea.

HD/JHD is a wild roller coaster ride, and her goal is to make the ride smoother for others; her motto remains, "IF I can help one family avoid being shredded as my own was, then I have accomplished my goal."

2
A Little White Lie

I have been sitting at my computer, staring at the screen. I cannot think of the best way to tell our story. You see, it is not MY story; it is OUR story as a family, a family with a dark secret, a skeleton in the closet, that has emerged and wound its boney fingers around all family members, refusing to let go. Huntington's disease is an illness that does not just choose one victim. It may be devouring several victims at once, in the same family, generation after generation. The count today in our family is 34 who will or possibly will die from Huntington's, some already testing positive and symptomatic, some born to these folks, some passed away, and some yet to be born.

You may have heard of this illness; you are probably reading this because it somehow has come across your path, either slamming you in the chest because it is in YOUR family, too, or because a friend or co-worker or maybe a patient of yours has it. This illness is terminal. It is a genetic illness, a family thing. It is autosomal dominant, meaning it is not linked to an x or y chromosome, and therefore, every child of someone who has Huntington's has a 50 percent chance of also having it, regardless of being male or female. It does not skip generations; there is still no cure or even a super effective treatment or medication. This monster can mutate and even be passed along in a juvenile form, which is even more severe and claims its victim even earlier, in a crueler way, taking the life and quality of life away from an innocent child. I had never heard of Huntington's until it was in my life, our family's life, to stay.

I have changed my family's names to protect them because even in this day of so-called political correctness and tolerance, folks at risk can still have their lives affected by their risk or gene status being known to insurance companies and employers (although an employer does risk a huge lawsuit if found to be guilty of genetic discrimination).

A Brief Description of the Disease

Huntington's disease and Juvenile Huntington's disease have a plethora of symptoms, but no two people, even siblings with identical CAG counts, will display the same symptoms or display them in the same order. As an advocate and ex-support group leader, I have often used this analogy. Picture a whole pie. It is cut into pieces and given to different guests. Some guests will eat the crust first, then the part with the filling. Some will eat from the tip back, leaving the crust for last; others may kind of mash it all together and eat it; some may even scoop out the filling, eating the crust last. The pie gets eaten and the plate cleaned, yet each guest ate it his/her own way. Huntington's is like this. Huntington's victims may have the area of the brain that is in charge of executive function start to die off first, while others may have the area directing motor function die off first, and others may have the brain dying off in both areas at once. The area of the brain affected is the basal ganglia, especially the caudate and putamen of that region. This, in turn, can affect neuronal transmission to the frontal lobe. The area that begins to die first will, in fact, dictate how symptoms will occur in that individual.

The USCF Memory and Aging Center of California puts it like this: "Huntington disease (HD) results from degeneration of neurons of structures deep within the brain, the basal ganglia, which are responsible for movement and coordination. Structures and circuitry responsible for thought, perception, emotions, and memory are also affected, likely due to connections from the basal ganglia to the frontal lobes. Subsequently, there is great variability in the expression of HD, even within the same family."

They also call the gene dynamic, meaning it can change and mutate within the same family and with each generation. It had been thought that it would expand to a longer CAG mutation with the passing to the next generation, but like all things HD

(Huntington's disease), in our family it has been the opposite. Nana and one son and her sister have the exact same count, 43, but Skip's is 38, and two of our sons both have 37. Very unusual, especially among males. We still do not know our oldest son, Brett's, CAG or even if he has HD. He chooses not to know or let us know just yet.

Something I feel is extremely important to understand is that in some families or some people with HD, they can have behavioral and psychiatric issues for years, even decades before they have chorea, and some may have decades of movement issues with all the strange jerking, twitching, gyrating, flapping, head bobbing, grimacing before any psych issues begin, and some may be a very consistent form of both. There are folks whose chorea is never really noticeable, but they are very demented. It goes back to how they eat their particular piece of pie, if you will. In Skip's family, the psych issues have predominantly preceded the motor issues. This was true for Nana, Jerry, Justine, and Skip. Aunt Jeannie, however, had more chorea, subtle psych issues like obsession and impulsive buying, but never anger or hostility. Nana herself had more depression, lack of initiation, trouble organizing time, visual tracking issues, and swallowing issues decades before her chorea became big and noticeable. Our story is one in which the psych issues, left untreated, dominated and shredded our family to bits. I hope this gives you a clearer picture of the importance of acknowledging and treating these symptoms.

Falling in Love

I attended a private Christian high school. In this school were two extremely handsome brothers, Skip and Jerry Griff. They had a beautiful blonde mother, who I thought was the most classy, gorgeous mom I had ever seen. They drove nice cars and lived in Spring Valley Lake, the most elite neighborhood that the high desert in California had. They played sports, and they dated all the popular girls. These two brothers had beautiful, perfect hair. They were tall with long, black eyelashes and brown eyes and tan skin. Skip was blonde, and Jerry had brunette hair. Skip was in the class behind me, and Jerry was in the class above me, but we did have some classes together, like PE and Spanish. I was a cheerleader back then, so I was often cheering them on at ball games. However, you never could have told me that I would be related to them one day. Two of my friends dated Skip, and a couple of them dated Jerry, but one girl in my class married Jerry and became my sister-in-law, because I married Skip later on.

During high school, I was not really interested in the Griff boys. I did not swoon every time they walked by or flirted. In fact, ironically, my most distinct memory of Skip was standing at the lockers with my hands on my hips, chastising him for hurting one of my friends. It was not until I came home from college, for summer break, that I got reacquainted with Skip. I was dating a mutual friend by the name of Dennis. The relationship was not really going anywhere, and my friend Eve asked me who I was interested in if it did not work out. Skip was leaning against his car in the driveway of Dennis's house, talking to a girl named Julie, and I looked over at him and said to her, "Skip Griff . . . I am going to marry him."

She told her boyfriend and sent the guys on a beer run. While they were gone, her boyfriend told Skip that I liked him. When they returned, Skip took Julie home and came back to where the rest of us were. The rest is history. We were together after that, every day.

Once Skip and I told Dennis, our courtship began. Every time we were apart, I could not sleep, and every time we were together, my stomach did little happy flips. Unfortunately, I became pregnant too soon into the relationship. Skip had wanted me to get an abortion, but due to my beliefs, I refused. Sadly, at four months, I had a bad miscarriage and ended up in the OR. Two weeks after that, Skip roundaboutly asked me to marry him. He said since we could not keep our hands off each other, we needed to make it right before God and get married. He had already picked out matching wedding sets and watches from a catalogue.

Our wedding day came on January 25, 1986, like a fairy tale. It was perfect. Skip looked like a Greek god with his muscular, lean, tan body, long blonde hair, and his white tuxedo. Our wedding party consisted of Jerry as best man, my sister Amy as the maid of honor, Jerry's wife, Lee, as another bridesmaid, ironically, Dennis as a groomsman, and a couple other close friends. We marched down the aisle. Still, I had never heard of Huntington's disease, that family skeleton waiting to jump out of the closet. Little did we know that four people on that stage would be dramatically impacted by that disease. Little did we know that two other family members in that audience also would be impacted.

After Skip and I got married, I decided that I would return to college. I was not sure I still wanted to be a doctor, so I decided to get an associate's degree in Medical Assisting, then maybe later become an RN, which is what I did.

My Introduction to Huntington's

During the school year of 1986, in my studies at college, my clinical instructor was going to be discussing genetic illnesses and how they are passed as either autosomal dominant or recessive. She assigned us a documentary called "The Venezuela Project," by the Wexlers. I now know how important that documentary was.

Skip's grandparents had stopped by to give us a picture. Once they left, Skip flipped on the TV to MTV. I told him that I had to watch a documentary that we were going to have a quiz on in our genetics course the next day. I told him it was on an illness called Huntington's disease.

"Oh," he said. "My grandma died of Huntington's when she was 48 years old."

I looked at him and said, "What? Your grandma just left here. You mean on your dad's side?"

Skip replied, "No, my mom's mother. Grandma is really my step-grandma."

Well, that was the first I had heard any of this. I cuddled up beside him and turned to the documentary.

As we sat there together, Nancy Wexler walked through villages and clinics filled with horribly disabled and disfigured patients with Huntington's disease. They were emaciated, jerking and writhing, unable to feed themselves, wearing diapers. This area of the world has an exceptionally high count of folks with this illness. As she described this incurable monster of an illness that wreaked havoc on families, generation after generation, the blood began to drain from my face, and I could hardly breathe, and the world was spinning. I looked at Skip, his face pale, too, and I said, "Oh, my God! "We can never have children. You are at risk for this!"

We sat there in quiet devastation. Then I became indignant. WHY had NO one told me about this while we were dating? WHY was I just now hearing about this? WHY did his mom not talk to him more about it? WHY? WHY? WHY? I had a million questions. I got out my medical dictionary and looked it up, but there was just a small paragraph about it. It was not very descriptive. I was on the hunt. I needed more info.

I went to the local library and found next to nothing on Huntington's disease, once again finding one-paragraph writings in medical books describing chorea and brain death and possible dementia. Wow. Not much to go on.

Skip and I decided that we at least knew his grandma had died early and had been in and out of psych wards. We knew she was only 48 when she died, and we knew all of her siblings had also died in their late 40s. We did not know how many of them there were; we do know at least five or six had HD. We do not know who they inherited it from, their mother or their father. From the little I had dug up, I suspected his Aunt Jeannie was showing signs of it. She flicked her fingers, bobbed her head, and did very eccentric things, like buying $600 worth of groceries for just her and her son. She was a diehard liberal and was obsessed over the news. Since we did not know his mom's status, we decided we would adopt children to prevent passing it along. Aunt Jeannie had three kids, and two of them had decided to never have kids.

Life went along, and Skip and I decided to announce at his family Christmas party that we would be adopting, due to Huntington's disease. As the family gathered around in the gaming area of Aunt Jeannie's home, Skip held my hand, and we told the family about our choice. By this time, his sister had already had a daughter, and Jerry and Lee also had one baby girl that Lee was breastfeeding. The announcement went over like a lead balloon. Jerry and his sister Justine and his grandfather jumped all over me. They said I was a know-it-all and, "Who did I think I was?" and that just because I was in school to be a medical assistant did not mean I knew everything. They were hostile and unsupportive. Later that evening, Lee was sitting on the staircase landing, nursing her baby daughter. Lee whispered to me she was not going to have more kids after hearing this. I told her I was going to stick to adopting. Nana, Skip and Jerry's mom, overheard us and came to sit on the landing with us. If I had known what I know now, I would have noticed that she already had symptoms. I did not notice. She told Lee and me to relax and not worry and to go ahead and have as many kids as we wanted because she had flown to New York and had a "special" test and did NOT have Huntington's, and we could feel safe. We believed her, and we each subsequently had three children. This was 1986. The test for HD would not be available until 1993.

Deciding to Have Children

Skip and I were so relieved that we went home and began trying to get pregnant. I had lost our first baby because, according to my OB/GYN, I had polycystic ovarian disease. My body fat ratio was too low (it was 10 percent at the time) and my weight was too low (98 pounds), and I did not have enough progesterone. I researched and researched. I let myself gain weight up to 112 pounds and let my body fat get up to 22 percent. I took herbs and used positioning, and when I went in to start fertility drugs, my pregnancy test came back positive! "Congrats!" was what my doc said. We never once even thought about Huntington's disease. It had drifted away like a feather in the wind.

About 18 months after our firstborn son, Brett, was born, we moved to Sacramento to be near Skip's biological father and his oldest brother, Matt. Little did I know, but I was expecting, again. The timing of this pregnancy was horrible. We had just moved to a new city, we had a toddler still in diapers, and Skip was not making stable money. We could barely pay rent, daycare, and buy groceries. Skip kept working out of town, leaving me alone with our toddler in the big city of Sacramento. Being pregnant, in a new job, in a big city was devastating. I did not know anyone. We were struggling so bad financially that I felt overwhelming guilt for bringing another child into this situation. How would we feed another mouth? How would we pay daycare for two? Could I love another child as much as I loved Brett? What if I could not afford to clothe this new child? My head swirled. I finally decided, I had to abort this baby. I had already made an OB appointment, and the doctor did an ultrasound to determine how far along I was. I had insisted that Skip attend. The nurse doing the ultrasound kept moving the handpiece over my belly.

"Look! He is playing hide and seek; he hates the ultrasound," she said.

Skip and I looked at the screen, and sure enough, every time she tried to catch him, he moved to the other side of the womb. Then she caught his face, and he stuck his thumb in his mouth. Skip and I left with a totally different view on abortion. This was a thinking, feeling human!!!! No way on earth were we going to abort the child we'd just seen.

My belly grew, and Skip and I had decided we would put this child up for adoption. Our marriage was rocky and financially unstable. I felt we were unstable and could not provide for another child. We began searching for the perfect couple. Time went by, and I began to feel my baby move and kick. I began to feel very protective of this child and very connected. Finally, I confessed to Skip, I could not do it. This was our child, conceived in love, and God would provide. I was keeping him, or I was going home to my mother. End of story. So we had our lovely little boy. He was a strapping 9 pounds, 8 ounces! He was born with long, flaming red hair, and he nursed like a champ. He had this strong, independent spirit. He became our biggest blessing, and he never went hungry or without proper clothing.

About 15 months later, we moved back down to Southern California. Being near my family and his mom seemed much better than trying to build a relationship with his biological dad, who did not take much interest. Skip was so hurt by his dad's disinterest that moving back to Southern California was fine with him. Our two boys were chubby and cute and content. We bought our first home in Silver Lakes and lived mostly on mac-n-cheese, potatoes, eggs, apples, and peanut butter. Sometimes, I had only $20 for food, but Food for Less and the day-old bakery saved the day, and no one went hungry.

Huntington's Creeps In

Things were going along, rather rocky, but going along. Nana, Skip's mom, did a few really odd things. She left her husband and moved into a condo with another man. Several months later, we were moving her back home with her husband. She bought piles and piles of material and started all kinds of projects and clothing for the grandkids, but never finished a single one. Lee and Justine had both had more children. Nana would get depressed and sleep for days. She was always extremely late for any family date or appointments. It took her hours to run simple errands. She started not keeping herself as immaculate as she always had. Then her husband passed away. He had been an alcoholic. He was a retired fighter pilot with the U.S. Air Force, and he left Nana with a hefty pension. Nana, however, unknown to us, was in the early stages of Huntington's disease. After her husband died, she did nothing. I mean nothing. She had been a dynamic real estate agent, but she did not work. She sat in her house, with it dark, without showering, until the bank foreclosed on her home.

I cannot recall everything that happened, but Jerry and Lee's life became very chaotic, and at one point, Nana, Jerry, and Lee, along with their three kids, were homeless, living first in a tent in a camp ground, then in a hotel, and then finally in a house in Sacramento. Fortunately, God intervened. The church that Skip and Jerry's biological dad attended had a house for rent. Jerry landed a good job with an International Lighting Company. Then their life stabilized for a very long while, and Nana lived with them. Their life seemed to run along smoothly for a good stretch of time. Skip's sister had also begun a long string of behavioral and lifestyle turmoil. She was admitted to a psych ward one time. Her life was a general mess, consisting of lots of relationship issues, drugs, outbursts, and illogical choices. Skip started having a little trouble here and there with clients and a few little, unreasonable outbursts. I chalked it up to stress and money being tight. We were around 28 years old when Skip and I had some real arguments about him being overreactive or inappropriately angry at one of the boys. I just thought he was stressed from work. Still, Huntington's disease was not really even a thought. I just thought Nana was flighty, and her many marriages and moving around had caused issues that Jerry and Skip were now dealing with as adults.

We moved around a lot. To Sacramento, to Carmichael, back to the High Desert in California, eventually to Missouri. During this time, my parents decided to retire and return to the Midwest. They sold their home and moved to Missouri. They kept telling us to sell our home and raise our kids in Missouri. Things were scary back then; the Los Angeles riots had occurred, kids were getting shot at bus stops for their name brand shoes, and kids were getting kidnapped right out of shopping carts. My parents tempted us with real estate ads and had Skip come see the area. He loved it. It was lush and green, and the pace of life was slow and easy. He moved the boys and me into my parents' guesthouse and stayed in California to sell our house.

Eventually, Skip joined us, but we had not made even a dime off our house and were unable to purchase our own home as planned. The guesthouse was unfinished and small, but we managed for a bit. Skip went through several jobs, from Lowes to self-employment to a cabinet shop to self-employment again. He was never happy. He jumped from job to job and even returned to do jobs in California, leaving the boys and me alone. One time, I arranged for him to stay with friends in L.A. who had two beautiful girls. When he got home, he was determined to have a baby girl. I got pregnant.

During my pregnancy, a series of crazy things happened. Scott had been complaining for a few years of not being able to concentrate. He also had these moments when his left arm and wrist would writhe uncontrollably. He could not get along with clients, and people called and complained about him lying and not showing up. I defended him vehemently. This was not my Skip. Things were strained between my parents and me, and finally we found a little place of our own to rent and moved out. I did not get it. Skip was hardworking, and everyone loved him. The day I delivered our youngest son, Kegan, Skip was fired off the job he had been doing. It was a snowy, winter day, temperatures in the below-zeros.

Deciding to Test

Things improved after a while, and Skip got a job in a cabinet shop. I continued to work at a pediatrician's office, and we moved into a bigger house. Later, my parents decided to move closer to town and mom's church and sell their house. They offered it to us. After coaxing and several turndowns, we finally accepted. Kegan was three and a half. We bought my mom and dad's house. Skip was working two jobs, delivering newspapers and working in a cabinet shop. I was working in a doctor's office, and life was rolling along a bit better. However, things were very strained between Skip and me. He was never happy and complained about everyone and everything. He found fault in me all the time. I could not please him. He said I was frigid. Said I was not a good housekeeper. He would yell at me over nothing.

Then one day, his cousin called. Aunt Jeannie had tested positive for Huntington's disease, and we should check into it. The internet was up and rolling. I got online to look up things because things were niggling at the back of my mind. I came across an article on the Huntington's Lighthouse website. As I scrolled down the very descriptive explanation, my blood ran cold. Every word described Nana . . . and Skip! I could not breathe. I got dizzy, and my heart was pounding uncontrollably. I ran into the other room and made Skip come read what I read. I said to him, "Your MOM has this! Read this. She has it! I know it! You have to be tested! Oh, my God, we have kids, we have kids! You have to be tested for our boys!"

I did not tell him that the article also very much described him. We were so young and so uninformed. We went to our general practitioner and asked for the test. We waited four grueling weeks. The waiting just about killed Skip. One afternoon, I was mowing the back yard. He came running to me and asked me to turn off the mower right now. I turned it off, and he encircled me with his big arms. Tears were in his eyes, and his voice broke. "I cannot have this disease. I just can't," he cried.

We just stood there, holding each other. When the results came, they were not interpreted correctly, and they were given over the phone by a medical assistant. We were told he only had one positive allele. Duh. That is all it takes. Our GP was not familiar with the test or how to read it. I asked for a copy of it. When I sat down to read it, I knew it was positive.

One summer, Nana had been to Kentucky to visit her sister Jeannie, who had moved from California back to Kentucky to be closer to her own kids. Jeannie had broken her ankle from a fall, and Nana stayed with her. Nana bought a bunch of furniture while she was there but had no way of getting it back to her home in California. We had not seen Aunt Jeannie since her HD diagnosis. Nana found out Skip was going to do a job out in California and asked us if we would drive to Kentucky from Missouri and get her furniture for her. We thought it would be a fun trip. Skip and I loaded up Kegan, who was around four, the big boys staying with friends, and went to see Aunt Jeannie. When we arrived, we were absolutely stunned by what we witnessed. She was emaciated. Her face was badly bruised and swollen. Her head bobbed and twisted severely, and she shook and stumbled, trying to walk. Her hands were curled inward, and she moved clumsily, knocking things over as a movement would interfere with her trying to reach and grasp things. Aunt Jeannie was still the sweet, loving hostess, though. Once we left, I found money she had smuggled into my coat pocket. The drive home was silent. Skip and I were in total shock. At one point, he looked at me and said, "THAT scares the shit out of me."

His face was pale the whole ride home. He called his brother to tell him what he had seen.

Seeking Help

Time went on. I had become obsessed with learning about HD. I searched and read and looked on the internet. I stumbled across two things, a Center of Excellence in St. Louis and a chat room called "Huntington's Disease, the monster." I wrote down the number to the COE and joined the chat room. I called the number I had found and spoke to a social worker named Melinda Kavanah. She was an angel. She listened and explained everything. She scheduled us an appointment. Our first experience was confusing. The doctor told Skip he had it and had symptoms, even giving him a prescription, but that he would not put a diagnosis in the chart because he did not have life insurance or health insurance yet. He told him to get his things in order, to get insurance, especially life and long-term disability.

I thought the visit had gone well. For the first time, I had opened up about the verbal abuse, aggressive behavior, anger, and strange things Skip did. I told them I was afraid of him. I was relieved to have people who understood. On the way home, Skip thanked me for going with him. Three days later, however, Skip let me have it. He accused me of exaggerating, lying, and making things up. I was completely floored. He said he would NOT fill his prescriptions, that I just wanted to control him. He said I was masculine and wanted to be the man. I was totally blindsided by his unreasonable response. I could not wrap my head around his behavior. Little did I know what all would come next.

Once we had Skip's diagnosis confirmed, I was furious with Nana. I wanted to tell her, and I wanted to hurt her. I called her and told her that Skip had HD. She was quiet at the other end. Then she said, "How did he get that?"

I was so angry, I blurted out, "FROM YOU!"

I clenched my teeth and told her that it did not skip generations, that she had symptoms, and that she had lied to us! She was never tested. The predictive genetic test was not out until 1993, and our boys had been born in 1987, 1990, and 1995! I hung up, shaking. Later, she went on to be tested and has a CAG of 43, the same as her sister, Aunt Jeannie. HOW could she tell us this lie??? This was not a white lie. This was a life changing, earth shattering, devastating lie. This lie could impact the entire family! We all had kids! What the hell had she been thinking?? Now that I am an RN and know a ton about HD, my blood still boils a bit, but I also understand her denial and fear. Even though I hate that she lied, I have come to realize that on some level, she thought it would make things easier. I guess. She regrets that now. Sadly.

Things Come Undone

Skip was the first to be tested. Then Jerry tested positive with a CAG of 43 as well. It was all beginning to make sense, but it was all beginning to come undone.

Our marriage began to crumble under the strain. Clients complained about Skip. He lost jobs, he pissed people off, and then he began to get obsessed with the internet and other women, romance chat rooms and porn. No matter what I did, it was wrong. He began to find fault with our boys. Things were stressful and rocky and confusing. My gentle giant had begun to be hateful and short tempered, even throwing things. At one point, I found out he was having an affair with a woman in Texas. Unfortunately, our middle son, Shelby, had found out before I did. Earlier that year, I'd found a $600 phone bill in the drawer. It was full of phone numbers I did not recognize. I called AT&T. The rep told me it was for adult entertainment. Since we have boys, I automatically assumed they had been curious. I ran into their room to dole out punishment. Skip overheard me telling the boys they were grounded. He knocked on the door and asked me to come into the hall. He closed the door and told me it was him, not the boys. I could not believe my ears.

Other things happened that put a strain on the family. Skip did things like tearing the siding off the house, gutting the kitchen, removing the old roofing off the garage roof, but then he took years, like ten years, to finish the remodeling. Our new carpet sat in a roll for more than five years, and the siding stayed off for nearly a decade. We argued over it all the time. He would start one project and not finish it before he moved onto the next. At one point, I was so tired of it I finished the drywall patches around the new windows, finished the half-painted walls myself, and hired men to install the carpet and put the finish on the hardwood floors.

For the next few years, Skip continued to carry on with his other woman. We tried counseling. I tried being more romantic. Nothing helped. Skip even tried to convince me we needed to have a threesome to spice things up. Thank God, I did not give in. One day, he blamed the boys for his affair. He had not been working, and we were behind on our bills. He spent all his extra time having cybersex and camera sex with his other woman. His brother had managed to get him a job with the lighting company he worked for. Skip left to go train in Washington. I came home from work, found the electricity off and a foreclosure notice. That day, I moved our three boys and me into a tiny two-bedroom apartment and applied for a divorce, Medicaid, and food stamps. I found Skip's truck in the airport parking lot and left a note and money for parking. He came home to an empty house with no electricity.

Skip did not seem to put two and two together. He was devastated. He could not believe I had done all this. He came to our door. He cried. Said he was sorry, said he would go to counseling. He asked me to stop the divorce. He spent the night often, and we managed to stop the foreclosure. Then one day, I came home to find he had contacted his girlfriend from my computer. He lied to her and said his goodbye letter was from me. I kicked him out and finalized the divorce. All this time, I kept in contact with my new-found HD family in the online chat room and via email. I was slowly learning that losing inhibitions, promiscuity, and exacerbation of flaws could be aggravated by Huntington's disease.

After a while, a girlfriend of mine had a house for sale that had not sold, so she rented it to me. The boys and I were happy, and Skip continued to try to win me back. Our house was now rescued, and he promised to finish remodeling it. During this time, our middle son, Shelby, had begun to have trouble at school. He had nightmares, and his grades declined, and he was very depressed. I took the boys to a child psychiatrist at Burral Institute in Springfield, Missouri. The doctor had experience with Juvenile Huntington's disease. She ordered an MRI. It was abnormal. She ordered the genetic test because my son met the criteria. His pediatrician called me with the results. Positive, but not for the juvenile form; his count was 37. Now I was determined to put my family back together. If I'd known then what I know now, I would not have had Shelby tested.

One day, my friend told me she had a buyer for the house we were renting, and the boys and I had no choice, so we moved back home with Skip, into the unfinished house. For a while, things seemed okay. He worked on the road and was gone all the time. I was frustrated with how little he came home, and when he did come home, it was like walking on eggshells. I never knew what would set him off. The boys began making plans with friends whenever he was home to get away from all the fighting. Skip was cold and angry. I felt like I had to have the house perfectly clean and cook all his favorite meals and make love furiously to keep him happy, but nothing made him happy. He found fault in our boys, fault in me, fault in my parents, my siblings, his siblings, his co-workers, everything. He acted like he just hated life.

Fighting to Save My Family

I had done a lot of research on Huntington's disease after I joined the online chat room. The more I read, the more I spoke with others, the more I knew Skip's behavior was HD. I also knew that I needed to go back to school and get my RN because Skip was not going to be able to work later on, and I had to make enough to support us. Going back to school was more than stressful. We had three boys, a pool, five acres to mow, three pets, and a husband who was on the road all the time. I took care of all of it. I did nothing but study and work at keeping the house up. I had no outside help and had to take care of all of it myself. The boys did some of the mowing, too, but teenagers are messy people. Skip harassed me the whole time I was going to nursing school. He would try to prevent me from studying. He called me a parasite because I had stopped working while in school because of all the responsibilities I had. I had figured out that my student loans would bring in as much as a part time job would, and that way I could get it done quickly. Skip demeaned my education and always brought it up during fights, saying things like, "Oh, I guess I am just not college educated like you." It was horrible, and he constantly berated my faith in God. Tension was so high at home.

Time went on, and our boys became teenagers that tested the rules. Our middle son, in particular, tended to bend the rules a lot. Skip and Shelby butted heads, and at one point, Skip kicked him out. It took me three weeks to convince him that Daddy was just mad and get him to come back home. Our oldest boy, Brett, turned 18 and moved into his own apartment. Shelby was 16 and acting out big time. Things were so bad at home that when my oldest needed a roommate, the boys convinced me this was the best choice, that he should take his GED and move in with Brett. Shelby felt responsible for the fights between Skip and me. I felt like Skip was cruel to Shelby and that it was unfair to him. I let him move out after he passed the GED, at age 16. My heart broke.

I finally managed to graduate, I do have to brag, even graduating Cum Laude. I went to work in the hospital, then switched to a pediatric clinic. The house was quiet with only Kegan and me home alone most of the time. Skip stayed out on the road longer and longer. The boys had gone to work for him. They called home upset all the time. They said Skip did not give them enough food money. They said he was selfish. They said he had lost his people skills. When he was home, he was hateful and verbally abusive to Kegan and me. The house remained unfinished. During this time, Skip would just show up at home with large major purchases. A boat. Jet skis. ATVs. A big, expensive truck. He even went as far as to rent a storage unit in another state and hide his toys in them.

At some point during all this, Skip and I volunteered to be in some Huntington's research. It was a very positive experience. We met Dr. Kevin Black at the St. Louis Center of Excellence in Missouri, and they treated us like royalty. I thought we were making progress. I felt strongly that the more we educated ourselves on HD, saw the HD specialist, could get Skip on meds, were honest and open with our boys, joined support groups, and read up on it, that we would survive this monster of an illness. I thought I could keep our family together. I was wrong.

I found out Skip was at it again with another woman. This time, though, it was with a girl he had gotten pregnant in high school. Her father had forced her to have an abortion, and she had never gotten over Skip. She was married, with grandchildren, even. I happened to run across an email with a hotel itinerary. I called the number and asked for Skip. The woman asked who this was, and I told her, "His wife."

She hung up. Her husband found out, and both our families were torn apart. I made Skip move out this time.

Skip kept trying to get back together, and by this time, I had learned that promiscuity and obsession were a big part of HD for some folks. After about a year apart, Skip's lease was up, and while I was at work, he moved himself back home with Kegan and me. I did not know what to do. I thought God wanted us to try again. God had provided me with a great job opportunity, and I had gone to work in a Preventative Medicine Medspa. Life seemed to improve for a bit. Skip finished the kitchen, which was gorgeous. He still did not have the outside done, but he was working on it. He still refused to take any medicine. He said he was fine, and I was a control freak. His anger flared on and off. He became so petty.

Nana Moves In

Meanwhile, out in California, his brother Jerry's HD was out of control, he and Lee had divorced, and Lee had put Nana in a nursing home to keep her safe. Jerry had become super violent, physically assaulting Lee and even their son at one point. He had turned to street drugs to self-medicate. Skip and I were still rocky, but we learned that Jerry had taken Nana out of the nursing home and was trying to keep her with him. Two people with HD. This did not work out. Jerry got arrested, and Nana accidentally locked herself out of the house. The landlord saw her out alone in the 102-degree desert heat and took compassion on her and brought her to his home, and he and his wife kept her until they could find family. They called us. Nana came to live with us in 2009. She was heading into the end stage of Huntington's.

The time Nana lived with us was bittersweet. She was very thankful and easy to care for in terms of attitude. Since I was an RN, I knew how to arrange our home to suit her disability. Kegan hated how it seemed like a nursing home with medical equipment in the bathroom, adult diapers in the pail, medication and doctor visits scheduled. Nana's speech had declined to hardly intelligible. She had to be on pureed food and had lots of issues with choking. I had to bathe her, dress her, and help change her diapers. She could walk some in the house with a walker, but she had to have a wheelchair if we went out in public. The walker eventually became too dangerous, and she mostly lay around and watched tv while I was at work. We hired my mom to care for her during the day while we worked. Kegan became more and more depressed. Scott became more and more hostile.

Survivor's Guilt and Depression

I want to take a moment and explain some things that happened to me personally. I became extremely depressed. Not only did I have survivor's guilt, but I also felt sadness so profound for what we may have done to our own flesh and blood. I loved my boys so, so, so much. They were my life, my joy, my purpose. Everything I did, every choice I made was to help them grow up confident, self-assured, and well taken care of, both emotionally and physically. I made sure their immunizations were always on time. I breastfed them and made their baby food. I sat in the sandbox with them. I read to them every night. I made sure that we told them we loved them several times a day. HOW could we have done this to our own flesh and blood? We had played Russian roulette with our own children. Anticipatory grief and depression over our chaotic life began to weigh on me like a boulder. Mornings, it was hard to get up. My head spun, and I was distracted. My mind was foggy, and I spent long walks screaming and crying to God. WHY my family?? How could He do this to us???

I cannot fully explain what it is like to line your own kids up on the edge of a cliff with no safety net and a storm blowing and have no way to pull them back to safety. I began to hate my normal friends who complained about toilet seats being left up. I wanted to scream at everyone who complained about their life. Arguments broke out between Skip and me and between my oldest son and me because they could not even understand why I would be sad. I felt guilty then for that because I am not the one sick or facing this sickness. HD became my mission. I went and got on an antidepressant, a supplement by prescription called Cerefolin. I went to therapy. I joined online groups and became a nurse advocate for HD.

After my mom started watching Nana for me, Mom began to get a clearer picture of what Huntington's disease was all about. She had great compassion for Nana, but also for me as a caregiver for two of them! She helped lighten the load as much as she could, cleaning house, folding laundry, and being so sweet to Nana. Some nights, I was up all night, cleaning up diarrhea and vomit for Nana. I was so tired. Skip was also having job issues. Sometimes he had a job; sometimes he didn't. When he was out of work, he would stay home with his mom. He became resentful of her and started directing his anger at not only Kegan and me, but also at her. One morning, while I was cooking breakfast and waiting to go for a walk with Skip, Skip came into the kitchen. I was putting away the clean dishes. He picked up his breakfast plate, took a few steps, and turned around and shouted, "Did you just put that plate away fucking wet?"

I was stunned. The plate literally had one drop of water on it. I started to say no, and Skip let out a string of how I was a fucking disrespectful bitch, that he worked his ass off, and I did not respect him. The plate of fresh breakfast was hurled across the room and landed on the counter with a crash, spraying food all over the kitchen. The noise woke up Nana and Kegan, who came running to see what was the matter. Skip slammed out the front door. Things like this happened frequently. It was intimidating and draining.

One time, when Skip was out of town, working, Kegan climbed in bed with me. He was crying and saying how much he hated his life. He was suicidal and desperately wanted a normal dad, a normal life. He was envious of his friends' fathers who were loving and family oriented. He was only 11 or 12 years old. I held him, and we sobbed together. I felt so helpless as a mother. I felt like a failure. I had been feeling suicidal, too, but I managed my depression well. When Kegan told me how he felt, I finally realized I had to do something to protect everyone in the family. I began searching for a nursing home for Nana and a place for Kegan and me to move into. Skip still worked, and I had to give Kegan a normal life.

I had everything in place. Nana was thriving in the nursing home. I went every week and picked up her laundry, did her mani-pedi, and took her out for a walk in her wheelchair. Skip and I brought her pudding cups, Reese's peanut butter cups, and pies. I was searching for a place to live with Kegan that I could afford and was stashing money away. I had opened a separate savings account. I had cashed in my retirement.

One of the days during this time, I had come home and heard screaming and cursing coming from the house. I could hear Skip yelling at Kegan, "What are you fucking doing? Are you fucking insane? Do you need put in a mental institution?"

Kegan and his friend had been playing with water guns in the house and gotten the floor wet. I rushed in and asked, "What is going on in here?"

Skip was flustered. We argued. For days, Kegan went into a deep depression that I could not pull him out of. I tried to tell Skip that even though discipline was in order, he should not have spoken to Kegan that way. He denied any wrongdoing.

Fighting for Our Lives

Finally, I found a perfect house for Kegan and me. I had

planned on moving out and then speaking to Skip, but something went wrong. I got a call at work from Skip. He said, "What the hell is going on, Ginnievive? Are you moving out?"

My heart sank. I told him I would talk to him when I got home. When I got home, he was drunk and siting on the porch with a wine glass in his hand. I no sooner got out of the car than he was screaming at me for being a fucking bitch, fucking cunt, whore, at one point breaking the wine glass and saying he was going to "fucking kill" me. I backed up, called 911, and waited by my car until law enforcement came. I explained to the officers I was moving out, that Skip had Huntington's disease with dementia, and they stayed until my boss came with her horse trailer and helped Kegan and me move out the bare essentials we would need. It was the worst night of this family's life.

Kegan and I had gotten out with our clothes, Kegan's bedroom set, and the guest room furniture. I left everything else for Skip. I felt he should stay in the house and finish it until we could sell it, and I did not want to be one of those wives who took everything. Kegan and I needed a fresh start. I slowly bought new furniture and made our house a home. Skip went into a black hole. He stalked me. He sent venom-filled text messages not only to me, but to Kegan as well. Skip sold off all the furniture and even got rid of our dog. He stopped making the house payment and let the house get filthy. Eventually, he moved out of it. He was going to sell the appliances, but I had bought those, so I went in and got the fridge and sold the oven and dishwasher. He was not living there anyway. I cleaned the house up and got it ready to sell. The neighbor helped me fill the holes in the walls and get it ready. Skip refused to sign auction papers or real estate papers, and the house went into foreclosure again. This time, I did not care. I did not have the heart to move back in and try to salvage it. When the bank locked it up, Skip went in and tore out the mantle. It sold on the courtroom stairs. We made $900. This house had appraised for $163,000, unfinished, and we were told it would bring $200,000 if we finished it. It sold for $65,000, just what we owed.

Kegan and I adjusted. I got him a therapist, and our doctor put him on antidepressants. Dr. Dawson and Dr. Abraham did more for him than I can say, and I am so thankful they brought him back from the brink of suicide. Once Kegan turned 18, he was adamant about knowing his gene status. I was very supportive because I know he is like me and must know things. I felt he should wait until he finished college, but he wanted it asap. I scheduled him to see the genetic counselor, and we received the all-clear to test. His results were positive, and he received the results with gene-positive brother Shelby and myself for support. He is so brave and strong. He took it so well, and it drew Shelby and Kegan closer together.

Time went on. I tried dating, Skip tried dating, but we kept in touch, and we also dated each other some. I still loved him, and I knew that most of our trouble was that he was unmedicated, and HD was running his life instead of the other way around. I knew he loved me, but I could not live with this out-of-control, angry, promiscuous man.

Things were on and off with Skip and me. He refused to pay what the court ordered, but he did pay hit and miss. He did not go to Kegan's high school graduation and blamed Kegan for me leaving him. I kept visiting Nana, doing her laundry and nails and trying to be friendly with Skip. Our oldest son and his wife moved to Seattle for a job opportunity, our middle son Shelby is working for a big company and has also moved to Seattle and awaits the birth of his new baby, and Kegan went out into the workforce and attended college off and on. I finally got a really good job offer in the St. Louis area and moved. Kegan currently rents the house we were in.

My oldest son, Brett, and his wife, Kathleen, have decided to get in great shape to begin IVF. They do not want to take the risk of passing the gene on. Brett has not undergone testing as far as we know, but he and his wife do live as if he could have it. They own a beautiful spa and seek a therapist and use natural remedies. I cannot explain how brave I think my sons are. I cannot explain how brave I think my daughters-in-law are. Facing each day with the dark cloud at the edge is tough; imagine if that cloud only grew darker and closer with each passing year.

Since I moved, Skip has come up to visit for weekends, on and off, and we spend holidays together. He finally did go back to the HD clinic and sometimes is good and takes his medication, and sometimes he does not. We continue to love each other and hate each other. My goal is to make happy memories the best we can. Skip is a big man, and we have moments when we sit cuddled up, and he cries. He cries for our children. He cries for us. He cries for the progression he feels. I see him slowly deteriorating. His balance is bad. His movements are getting more discernable. He does not think correctly. He used to be neat and clean and well organized; now he is not. It is getting hard to be in public with him because he will become unreasonable with help sometimes. His driving can be scary at times. He chokes often on food and even coffee. He has vertigo. He is so forgetful. He drinks a lot. Once in a while, I get something he needs, like a microwave or groceries. I spend time with him.

As of this date, Skip and I do not live together. He would like us to. I sometimes do, sometimes don't. Skip talks about his plan for suicide. I argue with him. We have a grandchild due soon to our middle son, Shelby. Shelby and Kegan have the gene. Waiting on the test results for your own child is something I cannot even explain.

Kegan wanted to be tested as soon as he was 18. I took him to the genetic counselor and his psychologist, and they gave us the all clear that he could handle the news. His count came back the same as Shelby's, and it has brought them into a type of bonding that is truly deep and binding.

Today, as I write this, there are 34 people in the family at risk for or with Huntington's, including our grandchild. Our oldest son has not been tested, as far as we know, and remains at risk. All of the above is because of one white lie. One lie, "I don't have Huntington's disease." The actual fact is, Nana has a CAG of 43. This legacy continues. Nana is currently nothing more than a tiny bag of bones. She sleeps most of the time. She can no longer make her speech intelligible. If she is awake, her movements are severe, and she cannot walk. She cannot eat or swallow well. She struggles to eat baby food. She is in diapers and has to be dressed and bathed. Her eyes light up when we come in, and she can give the tightest hugs ever. This was once a gorgeous, dynamic realtor who looked like a fashion model. She had so much talent. I miss the grandma she was to our kids . . . now I miss her more.

Update

A few things I would like to share since I originally wrote this chapter. We recently lost Nana, who passed on December 17, 2017, losing her battle with HD shortly after I wrote the above. We had a celebration of her life on her birthday this August and buried her ashes with her late husband at the Riverside, California Veterans Cemetery. Looking at our family picture of that day, the attendance held seven at risk for HD and two currently ill, and only part of the family was present.

Scott became homeless, while still working, and has moved in with me. It has been a journey getting his meds straight and helping him continue to work. Nana passed away. Our middle son, gene positive, had a baby in November of 2017, which caused a huge amount of turmoil for the entire family. Her birth has been bittersweet because she is the most beautiful, smart, loving little child . . . and she is now at risk. My at-risk niece is pregnant with another child. The legacy continues.

Currently, we still do not have a cure or even a good treatment. WE have been waiting for a cure for more than 18 years. I encourage you to participate in research. Educate your children. Educate yourself. Never lie about Huntington's disease. It is not a white lie.

I thank you for purchasing this book and reading our chapter. Huntington's disease is not an illness that claims only one victim. It seeps into families and takes over. It picks and chooses whom to destroy next. Young and old, male and female, it is not picky. It shreds families, dismantles the beautiful and the talented. It causes chaos and turmoil. This illness has made me a better person, though. It makes me appreciate the little things. It makes me love my family ferociously. It makes me strong and compassionate. It has helped me learn to love unconditionally, under wretched circumstances. I hate Huntington's. My goal is to kill this monster. You have helped by buying this book.

About Nancy Sweet

Nancy Sweet was born in Cheverly, Maryland. After she graduated from high school, her family moved to California where she met her first husband. They had only one child from that marriage, a beautiful baby boy. Unfortunately, the marriage lasted less than three years due to her husband's erratic and violent behavior. It was not known at that time that her husband had Huntington's disease.

Nancy proudly raised her son as a single parent for 16 years and truly enjoyed the adventures of raising a boy, i.e. little league games, track meets, cross-country races, baseball games, Boy Scout events, surfing, hiking, etc. She also started taking college courses in general education and engineering, while working full time in real estate and then construction. She married the man of her dreams, Rudy, when her son started college and shortly after the death of her son's father. Nancy recently retired from a major utility company in California as Designer II, where she designed residential and commercial electrical distribution projects for new construction.

Tragically, Nancy's son was diagnosed with Huntington's disease five years ago. He is now 41 years old and requires 24-hour care in a nursing home. Her son has two precious, beautiful, and gifted children who are also at risk. Nancy has fought and won battles for her son's health care and benefits. She will continue to fight for the sake of her grandchildren by raising awareness about Huntington's disease in hopes that this horrific disease will soon be eradicated.

3

"I Love You, Mom – Be Strong"

When I was young, I dreamed of a future where I would fall in love with a wonderful man, get married, and have healthy, perfect, and beautiful children. I imagined growing old with my husband and celebrating the births of our children, grandchildren, and hopefully great-grandchildren. I imagined years of happiness in our perfect home with a white picket fence and a garden of flowers. I believed in happily ever after.

Love and Marriage

Shortly after my 18th birthday, I met my future husband, "Ben," at a church function for single adults. All of the ladies were smitten by his good looks and kind nature, but I was the one who caught his attention. He was my knight in shining armor . . . or so I thought. Early in our relationship, I noticed that Ben's moods would change without warning. I made excuses for his moodiness, as well as some other instances of unusual behavior, chalking it up to stress from his job. Ben was a medic in the Air Force when we met, and he struggled with his supervisors as well as his schedule. I thought that his superiors were being unfair to him and could not understand why they were so hard on him. Hearing only one side of the story, it sounded as if everyone was ganging up on Ben. Eventually, I learned the truth. Ben's insubordination and poor job performance had become a real problem, and he was indeed fortunate to leave the Air Force with an honorable discharge.

Ben and I dated less than a year before deciding to get married in 1976. Once the date was set, we called his parents to tell them the happy news. I had never met my future in-laws because they lived approximately 3,000 miles away. Literally moments before making our phone call to his parents, Ben briefly mentioned that his mother had Huntington's Chorea disease, and then he quickly changed the subject. I had no time to ask questions. During the phone call, Ben's mother's voice was very shaky. She was a little hard to understand and didn't talk for very long. Although it was a short conversation, my future mother-in-law was very sweet to me and seemed happy to hear the news about our upcoming wedding. After the phone call, I pressed Ben for more information about his mother's illness, but he refused to talk about it. I was so young and extremely naïve. I had no idea what Huntington's disease was, and nobody that I knew had any knowledge of the disease. The internet didn't even exist at that time, and Ben adamantly refused to discuss the subject. I had absolutely no idea what was in store for me.

Our wedding was very small, and Ben's parents could not attend due to his mother's illness. Very soon after our wedding, my silly and childish dreams of a fairytale life were shattered. There would be no "happily ever after" for us. Instead, my marriage marked the beginning of a long and scary nightmare.

The Long Nightmare Begins

The day after our wedding, my new husband was very angry and refused to talk to me for the entire day. He was obviously very unhappy and made no secret about it. I had no idea what I had done wrong. Ben was a little nicer a couple of days after our wedding but remained very distant and quiet. As days and months passed, I never knew what kind of mood he would be in. I soon found out that his good moods never lasted long and would change to very dark, ominous moods at the blink of an eye.

The verbal abuse started immediately after we got married. One of Ben's favorite things to do was to call me a whore because I had dated others before him. He constantly told me that I was stupid and couldn't even carry on a conversation worth listening to. I was criticized about my looks, my housekeeping, and my cooking. His mean and angry words absolutely crushed me. My self-image was soon shattered.

My new husband controlled how I dressed, how often I visited with my family and friends, the amount of television as well as the types of shows I watched, the food I ate, the music I listened to, the books I read ... the list goes on. But, through it all, I kept thinking that he would change. All that I needed to do was pray, believe my prayers would be answered, and strive to be a better wife.

Within the first year of our marriage, I gave birth to a beautiful baby boy. The subject of Huntington's disease (HD) was never discussed after our wedding, and I still had no idea what it was. Instead, another serious problem plagued my mind during my entire pregnancy. Hemophilia, an inherited and serious blood disorder, ran strong in my family. Both of my brothers had severe Hemophilia A, and both my sister and I were carriers of the disease. If I were pregnant with a boy, my baby's chances of having hemophilia were 50/50. My older brother had died within days of birth, due to severe hemorrhaging. My younger brother spent most of his life in and out of the hospital, requiring endless treatments to stop the constant internal and external bleeding. We lost him a few years ago at the age of 37, due to complications of hemophilia, and I will never stop missing him.

My baby boy, "Luke," was born in May of 1977, at an Air Force base in Fairfield, California. After many blood tests, I was so very thankful when the doctors finally determined that my baby did not have hemophilia. Again, Huntington's disease was a complete mystery to me and was the last thing on my mind.

During my pregnancy, my husband made it very clear that he did not want our baby. He refused to let me buy maternity clothes, and I had no other option than to borrow from some of my young mom friends at church. For the entire nine months, I suffered from anemia and was very fortunate that the Air Force provided me with prenatal vitamins. At one of my OB visits, my doctor was concerned about my health and questioned me about my diet. After learning that my husband did not feel it was necessary for me to have milk or to eat healthy foods during my pregnancy, my doctor set him straight (for a while anyway) and gave Ben a lecture on how important a good diet was for me. Afterwards, I ate a little better and actually got to have real milk. Ben was afraid of job repercussions should my doctor find out that my health and well-being continued to be neglected.

When I was approximately five months pregnant, my husband decided to get a vasectomy to ensure that we would have no more children. He did not discuss his decision with me, and I was completely unaware until the day of his surgery. I remember being shocked and very sad about his decision. It broke my heart that he hated the thought of having children. Looking back now, I realize what a true blessing his surgery was.

Ben started having unexplained and unexpected fits of rage before our child was born. Knowing how much he did not want our baby, and having already suffered several instances of abuse myself, I made every effort to keep my husband from being alone with my sweet baby boy. Ben told me on more than one occasion that he would hurt our baby if they were left alone together. I cannot even put into words the horror, fear, and heartbreak I was feeling. There was nowhere that I could run without Ben tracking me down. Things were so different back then. There were no battered women's shelters where I could go and hide with our baby. Calling the police did no good, as I found out on several occasions. Whenever my husband found out that I called the police for help, I suffered even more abuse.

Early in our marriage, Ben started refusing to let me use our car. Visiting my family, going shopping, or just taking a drive was strictly out of the question. One day, a friend called and offered to take me shopping, and I happily accepted her invitation. Being in my last trimester of pregnancy, I was in need of larger clothes. I had grown out of all the maternity clothes that had been loaned to me, so I summoned up the courage and asked Ben if I could have some money to buy some clothes. Our budget was solely controlled by my husband, and he did not allow money to be used for maternity clothes or for any of my needs, for that matter. As expected, his answer to my request for money was an emphatic no. I made a bold and unwise decision to use ten silver dollars that I had received as a high school graduation gift a few years earlier, in hopes of finding some very cheap clothes that would get me through the last few weeks of my pregnancy.

Abuse Turns Physical

When Ben found out, he punched me in the arm so hard that I lost my balance. The blast of pain was incredibly intense! I was shocked and frightened, and certainly didn't see it coming. As a result, I was badly bruised (physically and emotionally), and was unable to lift my arm for days. I really could not believe that Ben would ever actually hit me. At first, I was too ashamed and embarrassed to talk to anybody about what had happened; however, I eventually confided in my friend, and I will never forget her response. She stated in a very matter-of-fact way, "Once the physical abuse starts, it will never stop." She was right. That day marked the beginning of constant physical abuse.

During the first summer after my baby was born, the weather was very hot, with temperatures of over 100 degrees on many days. Shortly after Luke was born, I received an offer in the mail from Sears Portrait Studio for a free picture. Since my husband had refused to let me purchase newborn pictures of our baby, I was eager to get at least one portrait of Luke while he was still very young. The photo session was extremely tense, and Luke cried non-stop. It took a while, but the photographer was finally able to get a decent picture. After what seemed like forever to finish the photo session, I had to go over some paperwork and details.

By that time, my baby was crying uncontrollably, and my husband was getting very angry. He took Luke from my arms and started walking out to the car, telling me that I had better hurry. I quickly finished the paperwork and ran to the car. What I found was my baby locked in the car alone with all windows rolled up. It was over 100 degrees outside, and I had no keys to unlock the car. Luke was screaming, and my husband was nowhere to be found. People started gathering and staring, but no one helped. I finally managed to pry a window open and unlock the car. My baby was okay, thank God. Ben eventually showed up about ten minutes later and yelled at me for taking so long in the store. He felt no remorse whatsoever for putting our baby's life in danger.

Not long after our Luke was born, my husband left me on

several occasions, stating that he would not come back until I put our baby up for adoption. I was horrified! How could he even think that I would give up my beautiful baby boy?! Each time my husband left, I prayed that he would stay gone. But he always came back, and things were always worse afterwards.

My husband eventually left the Air Force and decided he wanted to go to college. So, off we went to a small Christian college in Tennessee with very little money. We were fortunate to live in some apartments close to the college, and I was able to make some good friends. Classes did not go well for Ben, and he constantly took his frustrations out on me. Our neighbors heard the "domestic disturbances" and eventually reported Ben to the school. As a result, an official from the college came to our apartment and told Ben that he would be kicked out of school if any more abuse occurred. Of course, the abuse continued, but officials from the college did not follow up, as there were no more reports from our neighbors. Out of desperation, I decided to leave Ben late one night. I had secretly packed enough for me and my baby, waited until Ben was asleep, found the car keys, and snuck out to the car with my baby. No matter how hard I tried, the car wouldn't start. Little did I know that he had removed the spark plugs and disabled the car. That became a regular practice for Ben in the years to follow, as he wanted to make sure that I would never leave. He would often hold the car wires up for me to see, then laugh at me.

Seeing Huntington's for the First Time

When Luke was approximately six months old, we made a trip to Maryland to visit family for Christmas. It was the first time that I would meet Ben's mother and father. My mother-in-law had recently been placed in a residential care facility, due to her condition. She had her own room in a nice large home, and it appeared that the care she was receiving was very good. When I walked into her room, I was totally unprepared for what I would see. To say that I was shocked is an understatement. She looked nothing like the old photos that I had seen of a beautiful, healthy lady. She was unrecognizable. Her hair and clothing were in disarray, she was hallucinating about a chair that was "wet and was unsafe to sit in," and her constant uncontrolled movements (chorea) were shocking. I was thankful that my husband was being unusually nice that day. He and I sat with his mom on her bed, he on one side and me on the other. We wrapped our arms around her and cradled our baby in her arms, enabling her to hold her grandson for the first time. My dear mother-in-law was still a beautiful woman on the inside, but her life was being destroyed by a devastating and horrific disease called Huntington's. I wish that I had had more of an opportunity to visit with her and let her know that I cared.

Immediately after our visit with his mother, my husband's fury returned, and he left me again for a short time. Fortunately, I had friends and family in Maryland that my baby and I could stay with. Ben soon returned, and we made the trip back to Tennessee so that he could return to school. It finally started dawning on me that my baby and I were in serious trouble, and that all the prayers in the world were not going to change my husband. I started gathering as much information as possible about Huntington's disease through an organization I had found. I contacted the "Committee to Combat Huntington's Disease" as soon as I had some privacy to talk. The lady I spoke to was very kind, and she told me that Huntington's disease ran in her family. She also shared some very disturbing information, giving me an example of how Huntington's disease affects large families. In a family with twelve children, it was possible that most of those children would inherit the disease and become sick by the time they were adults. I assumed her information was based on personal experience, though I am not sure. Shortly after our conversation, I received the information packet in the mail as promised. The report on Huntington's disease was quite lengthy, and I had almost finished reading it when my husband found it. He immediately ripped the report into small pieces and threw it in the trash, forbidding me to keep any information about HD in our home.

As time passed, and the abuse continued, I became fairly certain that my husband's irrational behavior and violent tendencies were due to Huntington's disease. But there was absolutely nothing that I could do about it. Although I had tried to leave him on several occasions, I'd never actually considered divorcing my husband because of my wedding vows "in sickness and in health." However, I often dreamed of taking our baby and just going into hiding somewhere. There were just no options available. In less than three years of marriage, we moved several times, which made it very difficult for me to plan my exit. We lived in California, Tennessee, Indiana, Maryland, Arkansas, and Texas.

My husband's rage was not always directed at me. On one occasion, he stopped to pick up a hitchhiker in California. My baby and I were both in the car, and I pleaded with Ben not to stop, but he refused to listen to me. After picking up the hitchhiker, Ben decided that this poor guy needed to accept the Lord. When the guy said that he wasn't interested and asked my husband to pull the car over and let him out, Ben went into a rage and started driving erratically. I begged him to stop and told him that he was scaring me. That made no difference. After yelling and cussing at the hitchhiker for what seemed like an eternity, Ben finally skidded to a stop on the side of the road and screamed at the hitchhiker that he was going to hell. That poor guy could not get out of the car fast enough. I'm sure he still remembers the event to this day.

On another occasion while living in Maryland, Ben had had a bad day at work. Upon leaving his job, he went to the parking lot, smashed out the windows of our car, and then drove home. To this day, I don't know if he did damage to any other cars. Ben told me that someone had committed an act of vandalism, but he refused to file a police report. Of course, the truth finally came out. And he was soon fired from that job for stealing money.

On one particular occasion that I had left my husband, he used an axe to demolish my favorite wooden rocking chair. We were living in Indiana at the time, and I had gone back to Maryland to escape the abuse. In his rage, Ben destroyed irreplaceable baby pictures of Luke and threw them in the trash. We had only one family portrait that had been taken by an amateur photographer for a church directory. My husband decided to modify that portrait. He cut out the section that showed our baby sitting in my lap and then put the picture back in the frame and hung it on the wall. The altered portrait showed only my husband, me, and a huge gap. Our baby's picture had been removed.

During the first summer break of school, Ben decided to take a part-time temporary job in Indiana. We lived in a farming area, and our closest neighbor was about a quarter of a mile away. Much of the physical abuse I suffered was during that time. No one could hear what was going on, and I had no way to escape, as my use of the car was forbidden. I was constantly on alert, trying to protect my little boy from the physical abuse that I was suffering.

Once, during a shopping trip there, my husband had graciously given me a certain amount of money for groceries. Since there was a little money left over, I decided to use it to buy chocolate chips for baking. Ben had stayed in the car, and I took our baby with me in the store. I could never trust my husband to be alone with Luke. When I returned to the car, I excitedly told Ben that I was going to make chocolate chip cookies when we got home. He totally flipped out and started yelling at me about how stupid I was for spending money unwisely. He demanded that I go back in the store, tell them how stupid I was, return the bag of chocolate chips, and ask for our money back. I was crying so hard that I couldn't go back in the store. Ben finally gave up and started driving home, yelling vicious insults at me the whole way. Luke was in a car seat in the back, hearing and witnessing everything. He was only one year old at the time. I kept thinking to myself that if I would just stay quiet, Ben would finally calm down. I was so wrong. Ben figured that since I wasn't talking or trying to explain myself, I was ignoring him. With his fist, Ben hit me so hard in the chin that I blacked out temporarily. He never, ever apologized because everything was always my fault. Buying chocolate chips earned a hard blow to the chin. Forgetting to make a salad for dinner earned a stinging slap across the face. Not looking at him when he spoke earned being jerked by my hair.

I have managed to forget some of the reasons for the constant physical abuse, but I will never forget the abuse itself, the busted lips, the black eyes, the fingerprint marks on my neck from being choked, the handprints on my face, and the constant bruises. But though it may sound odd, the *verbal* abuse hurt the most. Constantly being told that I was worthless, that I had "a backbone of jelly" (his favorite saying), that I was a terrible wife and mother, that I was stupid, that I was ugly, and all the other constant insults were incredibly hard to endure. I was so sad and broken. It seemed that just about everything I did or said would set Ben off.

Eventually, it became impossible for my husband to finish school. Our lives were in such chaos, and I had no idea where we were going to go or how we were going to survive. During a winter break from school, Ben agreed that we could go and visit my sister and brother-in-law for Christmas. They were working at a children's home in Texas. While visiting, my husband and I were offered a job as house parents. Since Ben was very close to being kicked out of school, we agreed to take the job. Luke was two years old at the time. Our cottage consisted of seven children, ranging in age from six years old to 17 years old. All of these children had come from broken homes, and all suffered from one form of abuse or another. I quickly formed a strong bond with my new family, and they adored my little boy. However, none of them trusted or liked my husband. They instinctively knew that he was a mean and dangerous person. Living at the children's home did not change Ben. The physical and verbal abuse continued behind closed doors.

The Final Time I See My Husband

In 1980, a couple of months before Luke's third birthday, on a day when the kids were at school, I endured the worst beating of my life. Fortunately, it was the LAST time I would ever be beaten. It was also the last day I would ever see my husband. On that fateful day, I wanted to use the car to go have coffee with my sister. Of course, the answer to my request was no. I made the very stupid mistake of arguing with Ben, trying to convince him to let me use the car. My sister also tried reasoning with him, but to no avail. I didn't realize that he was having a bad day, a sure sign that bad things could and would happen. As a result, Ben snapped and went into an uncontrollable fit of rage. He started threatening my sister, and he would have followed through with his threats if I hadn't stepped in between them. Fortunately, my sister was able to run and get help from next door. And thank God that my little boy was with his uncle at the time. As soon as my neighbor arrived, and Ben realized that he was being watched, he stopped beating me.

By that time, I had been choked, punched in my mouth, eyes, and ears, thrown to the floor, and kicked in the ribs, arms, and legs, over and over. The beating wouldn't have stopped if my neighbor hadn't shown up. I was rushed to the doctor and was strongly encouraged to have Ben arrested. Instead, I chose not to press charges, under the condition that Ben would leave and not come back. My husband left that day and was not allowed to return. I don't know how I would have survived that day and the many that followed without the love and support from my sister. My brother-in-law was also very caring and supportive. I am so thankful that they were there for me when Ben finally left for good.

The months that followed were far from easy, but Ben was gone. My little boy and I were finally safe. Unfortunately, the phone calls from Ben went on for months. He would scream at me, plead with me to take him back, beg my forgiveness, and then threaten my life in the same breath. He frightened and intimidated me constantly. Although I knew that I could never allow Ben back into our lives, I did not really want a divorce. I became convinced that my husband's behavior was due to Huntington's disease and that he really couldn't control his erratic and violent behavior. He didn't drink, and he didn't use drugs. There just didn't seem to be any other reason why he would treat me and his son so badly. I pleaded with Ben to go to the doctor and be tested. He eventually agreed, and a friend of ours went with him to his appointment. At that time in 1980, only a clinical diagnosis could be offered if one could find a doctor that actually knew about Huntington's disease. DNA testing was still many years away. Our friend called me shortly after Ben's appointment and told me that the doctor had ruled out Huntington's disease. Evidently, Ben was not exhibiting any physical symptoms. In the doctor's opinion, my husband was just a very cruel and dangerous person. Upon hearing that news, I immediately filed for a divorce. I also moved my little boy and me to a place where my ex-husband could not find us, I got an unlisted phone number, and I basically hid from him for a long time.

Starting a New Life

As the years passed, my son and I lived happy and peaceful lives. I eventually managed to buy a little home in Temecula, California, a perfect place to raise a child. Being a single parent was challenging at times, but I had been blessed with a child who loved me, respected me, and never got into real trouble. When he was very young, my son would ask questions about his father. I will never forget the time when he asked me why he didn't have a dad, and why I didn't just "go to the store and get one" for him. He was such a sweet and innocent child. Though I had been physically and emotionally scarred from my marriage to Luke's father, I made it a point to never speak unkindly about Ben when my son asked questions about his father. Sometimes, I would even lie. I felt that my son did not need to hear negative and harsh comments about the father he hardly knew. When asked, I always told Luke that his father loved him very much, even though I knew it wasn't entirely true. The limited memories of his father that Luke still held on to were not good, so why add to his pain? He had already suffered enough and continued to have nightmares for many years. Counseling that had started in first grade and continued for several years was helpful, but it was still very difficult for my boy.

Sometime after the age of five, and unbeknownst to me, my son decided that he did not have a father at all. This fact came to light during a first-grade class project where the students were learning about families and the roles of mommies, daddies, sisters, and/or brothers. Shortly after the project began, I got a call from my son's teacher, stating that Luke had gotten very upset during class. His teacher had made a statement that all children had fathers. My son adamantly insisted that he did not have a father, and the more his teacher tried to explain that all children had fathers, the more agitated Luke got. As a result, I was asked if the school psychiatrist could give my boy some exercises that would help shed some light on his true feelings and thoughts. In one of the exercises, Luke was asked to draw a picture of his father. At the tender age of six years old, Luke's vision of his father was both shocking and heartbreaking. He had drawn a picture of our home with a giant man stepping on it and crushing it. The giant (his father) was holding flowers and crying. Professional counseling for my boy began immediately.

Halfway through the second grade, Luke's teacher urged me to take him to the doctor, as she felt that he was showing signs of Attention Deficit Disorder. Though Luke never really misbehaved, he couldn't sit still, couldn't concentrate, and was causing disruption in his class. So off to the doctor we went. During the visit with his pediatrician, Luke was SO amped up. It was everything I could do not to burst out laughing while the doctor was trying to talk to me. Luke had turned onto his stomach on the patient table, put his forehead into one of the stirrups, spread his arms out as if he were flying, and started pretending that he was a pilot on a fighter plane. His head and arms were going from right to left, and his "war" sounds were so funny! All that he needed was a pair of goggles, a helmet, and a pilot scarf. His doctor never even cracked a smile. After only five minutes, Luke's doctor diagnosed my boy as "extremely hyperactive and in need of Ritalin."

When his doctor finally convinced me that Ritalin would be safe for Luke (this was in the early 80s before the internet and extensive research), I agreed that we would give it a try. Honestly, Ritalin did help. Luke's grades started to rise, and he did much better in school and at home. In fact, we could finally go to restaurants without drinks and ketchup and mustard and place settings accidently being knocked over or chairs being toppled. Luke did not take Ritalin for long. He had decided that he could channel his energy in positive directions without the help of drugs, and I was in full agreement. He and I got very creative in coming up with ways to release some of his limitless energy, i.e., jumping jacks, running in place, jumping on a miniature trampoline, and doing sit-ups; however, what helped the most was getting Luke involved in every activity and sport available. He started surfing at the age of eight, mowed lawns for friends (and loved it), joined the Boy Scouts, played Little League baseball, rode his bike or skateboard everywhere, and went on endless hikes with me.

While in high school, my son continued to do well with his grades and was even placed in some college prep classes. He was on the high school cross-country, track, and wrestling teams. But in his spare time, he did what he loved the most . . . surfing! I loved taking him to the beach and could sit for hours, watching him do what he loved so much.

From the age of 14, my son worked part-time jobs at Kentucky Fried Chicken and a local grocery store. He had dreams of buying his own car, and he had one particular make and model in mind. Our neighbor rebuilt BMWs as a hobby and got my son hooked. Luke bought his dream car at the age of 15, an old blue BMW 2002 that had been built in the late 60s. The body was in great condition, but the engine needed rebuilding. By the time Luke got his driver's license, that little car was ready.

From grade school through high school, my son was a good student, earning above average grades. He chose to attend college after high school and, when the time came, Luke picked a community college close to the beach so that he could surf before and after classes. Life was good.

Although my son had not seen his father since the age of two, he never forgot about him and continued to love him. I kept Luke updated on his father's condition and hospitalizations throughout the years, trying to make the situation as easy as possible for Luke to handle. As he grew older, my son began asking me more questions about Huntington's disease. The day finally came when he asked me if he might "get the disease" later in life. I did not hide the truth from Luke, and it broke my heart to tell him that there was a possibility he could inherit Huntington's. But I also told him NOT TO WORRY BECAUSE THERE WOULD BE A CURE SOON. Sadly, I actually believed there would be a cure long before my precious son would ever be faced with this horrific and terrifying disease.

When my son was 19 years old, his father passed away. I thought that he would be upset when hearing the news. Instead, it was me who was upset, and Luke was the one consoling me. He told me his father had gone to heaven and was no longer suffering.

New Marriages

Shortly after my ex-husband passed away, I got married to my true knight in shining armor. My son was still attending college and was given the opportunity to move to Florida in order to finish school on a full scholarship. Off to Florida he went, with his surf boards in tow. Not too long after his move to Florida, he graduated with an Associate's Degree in Fine Arts. Instead of coming home to California, my son chose to stay in Florida after he graduated. He had met a girl and had fallen head over heels in love with her. Marriage soon followed as well as the birth of their first child, a beautiful baby girl.

Luke worked a full-time job, with a part-time job on the side to help put his wife through school and to pay the bills. He eventually saved enough money to buy a home for his new little family, and within a few years, their second baby came along, a beautiful baby boy. There was no question that my son was one proud daddy. He adored his wife and children, and he worked hard to provide a good home for them. The difference between Luke and his own father was night and day when it came to loving his children. His complete love for his family was endless and knew no bounds.

After working all day, Luke would take on all parenting responsibilities for his two children at night while his wife studied, attended school, and eventually started working graveyard shifts. He cooked dinner for them, made sure they were bathed and ready for school the next day, helped with homework, and spent quality time playing games and having fun with his children before tucking them into bed. When not spending time with family and working full time, my son was also very involved in church work. He became a deacon at his church, helping others in need and participating in church services. Anyone who knows my son knows that he has a heart of gold.

Though my son and his wife had their share of ups and downs, all seemed well for a few years. And then Huntington's disease started to take over, hurting everyone and destroying everything in its evil path. Luke started having problems in his marriage, trouble with his employers, and constant disagreements with his family and friends. He could no longer remember his responsibilities at work, and he started losing job after job. He became extremely irritable and moody, started having minor car accidents and getting traffic tickets frequently. Road rage became very common.

Looking back now, I can clearly see what I tried so hard to block from my mind for many years . . . the cold, hard truth that my beautiful son had been showing signs of Huntington's disease as far back as his early 20s. Perhaps the most obvious symptom early on was his forgetfulness. He had a terrible time remembering appointments, dates, times, schedules, etc. His once perfect handwriting skills deteriorated to the point that he could no longer write legibly by the time he finished high school. Luke had problems answering questions and carrying on conversations, which he told me was really embarrassing. He also experienced clumsiness and some involuntary movements in his legs from time to time.

My Son is Diagnosed with HD

By the time my son was in his mid-30s, his life started going downhill at a rapid speed. He was clinically diagnosed with Huntington's disease, his wife left him, he lost custody of his children, he lost his home to foreclosure, he went bankrupt, he lost his job, and he lost his truck, all within a one-year period. Thoughts of suicide started playing heavily on his mind, and as a result, he spent numerous short stays in psychiatric facilities.

At that time in his life, my son refused to move to California to live with his stepdad and me. He could not stand the thought of leaving his children in Florida, even though he rarely saw them anymore. And his pride just wouldn't let him be dependent on anyone, let alone his stepdad and me. Fortunately, my parents lived close to Luke, and they did everything in their power to help him. The love they have for their grandson knows no bounds, and I am certain that things would have been much worse for Luke without their help. I am so thankful for all that they did to help my son.

After Luke lost his house, I arranged for him to live in an apartment and had food delivered to him on a regular basis. I made sure that all utilities were paid and that he lacked for nothing. But Luke's life continued to spiral out of control, and he started wandering the streets, suffering from hallucinations and extreme paranoia. Many dear friends from church also tried to help Luke, often spending time with him and delivering food to him. They even gave him two bicycles to get around with. Unfortunately, due to coordination problems, he had a couple of accidents where he got banged up pretty badly. People nearby witnessed one of his more serious bike accidents, but they did nothing to help him as he struggled to get up and limp home. His glasses broken, he was bleeding, his clothes were torn, and the bike was too messed up to ride home. Yet no one helped him! Instead, they just stared and made comments about him. Eventually, both of his bikes were stolen, and he resorted to walking everywhere.

During one of his days out wandering, some drug addicts followed my son home and would not leave his apartment until the manager threatened to call the police. After a couple of days, they finally left his apartment, stealing the food from my son's refrigerator, his clothes, his shoes, his radio, and many other personal items.

It was no longer possible for my son to live alone, so I started the legal process of obtaining guardianship in order to move him to California. The attorney I hired had no problem taking the money she was paid, but she never quite finished the job. I managed to get one thing out of the whole ordeal, a letter signed by the court, stating that I would be granted guardianship. What a sad world this is when our laws won't allow a mother to help her adult son who is completely losing his mind and his body to Huntington's disease.

In my quest to move my son to California, I finally got a break when Luke's psychiatrist gave him two options. He told Luke that he could either go to California to live with his mom, or he could stay in a psychiatric hospital indefinitely. Finally, my son made the decision on his own to leave Florida and move to California so that my husband and I could take care of him.

Nearly three years passed wherein my husband and I took care of my son. Luke started seeing a neurologist at UCLA shortly after arriving in California. He was placed on a full regimen of medications and given the genetic blood test in 2015. As expected, Huntington's disease was confirmed. Luke's CAG repeat came back at 47. As the disease progressed, it eventually became obvious that my husband and I could no longer meet all of my son's needs. His hallucinations and paranoia had returned, he was falling constantly, he was often unable to eat without choking, and he did not want to live with us anymore.

Struggling to Find Care for My Son

In the summer of 2017, shortly after he celebrated his 40th birthday, my son had to be hospitalized in San Diego for kidney problems, dementia, and psychiatric problems. The emergency room in San Diego was the only hospital that would not turn him away. Our local emergency room refused to take him because he had Huntington's disease. Even the hospital in Los Angeles where his doctors and neurologist practiced refused to admit him. I was informed that his doctors only dealt with Huntington's patients one day a week, and taking him to that hospital was not an option. Oh, how I wish that my son had Huntington's disease ONLY one day a week instead of seven days a week!

Within a week of Luke being admitted in San Diego, the hospital started harassing me about taking my son home. They made it very clear that they did not deal with Huntington's disease. At one point, they even threatened to send my son to a homeless shelter. Their final threat was to send him to a 24-bed psychiatric lock down facility, a place that clearly did not deal with Huntington's disease. I frantically searched for a skilled nursing facility that would accept my son before the hospital in San Diego released him to God knows where.

Now comes the real shocker! Our great state of California had absolutely nothing to offer when it came time for my son to be placed in a long-term skilled nursing facility. We came very close to having him placed in a facility near San Diego, or so we thought. But in the end, he was turned down. I'm not sure what the true reason was for denying my son because we were fed so many different stories and lies by hospital staff and board members. All I do know is that for several months, we did everything that was required to have my son placed in that facility. We transferred his medical records to San Diego and had him set up with a neurologist, we obtained permanent residency in San Diego, we completed tons of paperwork, we attended meetings, and we called weekly and sometimes daily to follow up. We were told that my son was a "perfect candidate" and that they were just waiting for a bed to be available. We were strung along for months, lied to, and given false hope, only to suffer from the worst let down ever. My son never stood a chance of getting into that facility, yet no one had the courage or decency to tell us.

In my relentless search for a skilled nursing facility that would accept my son, the only places I could find were approximately 3,000 miles away, in New Jersey and in New York. I had only days to decide before the hospital in San Diego followed through with their threat of sending my son to a psychiatric lock down facility. After being turned down at the facility in San Diego, I thought all was lost. However, one very sweet and caring person who was the case manager at a facility in New Jersey gave me some hope. She helped with all the arrangements to have my son transferred, showing compassion and understanding throughout the entire heart wrenching ordeal. I was devastated at the thought of moving my son so far away, I was worried sick about how he would handle a non-stop three-day drive via medical transport from California to New Jersey, and I couldn't stop crying as I packed his clothes and belongings. I arrived at the New Jersey facility just hours before Luke, and I was an absolute mess. But there waiting for me with a big hug, true kindness, and encouraging words was this wonderful lady, the case manager who had been helping me for several months regarding placement for Luke. Although my son's stay at the facility in New Jersey was short, I will be forever in debt to that amazing lady and to the incredible nursing staff that took such good care of my son during his stay.

My son now resides in a wonderful facility in upstate New York that specializes in Huntington's disease. The staff is awesome beyond words, the facility is immaculate, and the building is surrounded by beautiful countryside. My son has a room of his own and is spoiled rotten by the nurses and attendants. His beautiful smile has returned.

I miss my son so much, and I cry every night over the thought of losing him. The distance between us is overwhelming, but I know that he is receiving the absolute best care possible. I am able to video chat with him every day, and I travel to New York as often as possible, spending days on end with him. Eventually, I will move to New York in order to be by his side as the disease continues to steal his life away.

The Love and Support That Keep Me Going

The love that I have for my son is beyond words. I still haven't given up hope that maybe someday soon there will be a cure for my beautiful son as well as all for the other courageous warriors battling Huntington's disease.

Through this whole ordeal, I have had the undying love of my husband, who has stuck by my side through thick and thin, even when I'm at my craziest. I love you, Rudy! Thank you to my parents for your never-ending love and support. Thank you to my amazing sister, brother-in-law, and nephew for all that you have done and continue to do for Luke and me. Thank you to my best friend, Debbie, whom I have known since I was seven years old, whose tremendous love and compassion for both my son and me are infinite. Thank you to my brother-in-law and sister-in-law who gave us a peaceful refuge when times got really rough. Thank you to my cousins, my nieces, my nephews, extended family, and all of the wonderful people who have so generously donated their money, time, and efforts to help ease the burden in moving Luke to New Jersey, then to New York. Thank you to our wonderful friends from the Church of Christ in Palatka, Florida, and Corona, California. Your prayers, love, charity, caring, and selflessness are truly a great blessing. Last, but not least, I have been blessed beyond measure in meeting some of the most wonderful people in the world . . . my HD family. Thank you, Sharon, for getting me through some really tough times, especially in Florida, and for continuing to support and encourage me when I'm falling apart. Thank you, Katie (my rock), Katrina, Daniel, and Denise for always being just a phone call away, always willing to listen and to help in every way possible. Thank you to the numerous friends that I have made at support groups and through social media, who share their HD stories, encourage me, lighten my load, and brighten my day.

I will continue to fight for my son, and I will stop at nothing in order to make sure that he receives the care he needs and deserves. Although there are days that I think I will not survive the heartbreak of losing him, I will keep going . . . one step at a time, one day at a time. And I will never, ever forget the words my son recently said to me . . . "I love you, Mom. Be strong."

About Georgia Porter

Georgia Porter currently lives in Yamba on the picturesque north coast of New South Wales, Australia with her husband, daughter, father-in-law, and their two dogs.

Georgia and her husband have careers in hospitality, although Georgia currently stays home to provide her father-in-law with the care he needs.

Georgia studied business management and hospitality during her high school years, aiming to travel and work in the hospitality industry. She learnt Italian and French, excelling in her language studies, and travelled briefly as a student to Italy, where she developed a love of travelling and learning about other cultures. Georgia also enjoys stand-up paddle boarding, playing piano, and loves a game of pool.

In the future, Georgia hopes that her family can travel, learning more about culture and cuisine. She wants nothing more than to experience life's simplest pleasures, good food, good people, and good music.

4

Hoping for the Best, Preparing for the Worst

When I first heard the term Huntington's disease, I had no idea what it meant or that it would be such a huge part of my life. I knew it sounded serious, but it was explained to me like Parkinson's Disease, a movement disorder. "I've seen that before," I thought. "I know what to expect."

My Introduction to Huntington's

My boyfriend brought his dad into the restaurant we worked at together, for lunch. He told me to take extra good care of him, that he had Huntington's disease, and that he had involuntary movements, not bad, but I would be able to tell. I kept this in mind when serving him his Coke, taking care not to put it in a soda glass which would topple over easily, and sat him in an easily accessible table where he could sit and enjoy lunch while watching his son cook for him. I could see that he had some movements, noticing what my boyfriend had warned me of; his knees dipped when he walked, affecting his stride, so he walked with a swaying motion, but he seemed otherwise okay. This was my first introduction to Huntington's disease.

As a young couple, we were such a dynamic duo, working together non-stop, my boyfriend running the kitchen, myself in front of the house. Work was our second home, our first home, even, as we spent so much time there. Life was busy, but brilliant.

We thrived on the energy of hospitality, the regular customers, the staff that were our best friends. My boyfriend was still an apprentice chef but had the passion and talent of a seasoned chef. Customers loved him and his food. We served the local elite, who would come into the restaurant and simply say, "Let him surprise me," allowing him to be as imaginative and creative as he liked.

His father always pushed him to be the best version of himself, wanting nothing more than for him to finish his apprenticeship and become a qualified chef. So my boyfriend left the restaurant we worked at together, onto bigger and better things to further his career.

Fast forward a year or so, and I fell pregnant. We knew my then boyfriend had a 50/50 chance of inheriting Huntington's from his father, but being young and naïve, we hoped for the best. We had a wonderful new baby girl, happy, healthy, and thriving. When she was young, we would visit her daddy at work, and all the staff would fuss over her endlessly, calling her the restaurant's mascot. We married when I was 22 years old, and he was 25. We enjoyed our new family life, doing what any young couple does. Life was just getting started for us, and we were blissfully enjoying it.

Moving to Singapore

My husband had always said that when his dad was unable to live alone, he would be there for him and help him, which I admired. He was such a devoted son, despite not having a close relationship during his childhood. We visited his dad on his day off every week for lunch, without fail, for three years, until we had the opportunity of a lifetime to travel to Singapore for work. One of the customers from the restaurant where we used to work together had a friend who was opening a restaurant in Singapore and needed some Australian staff. They both knew that the job was perfect for us, knowing what an adventurous and hardworking couple we had been. We jumped at the chance, this being something I had always wanted to do, live and work abroad. My husband had never been overseas and was thrilled to have this opportunity. His dad was so proud and excited for us, until about a week before we flew out. He was worried he was going to be lonely while we were gone, us being the only people who were part of his life, outside of his motorbike-riding friends, whom he saw roughly once a month. He would miss our weekly lunch visit. We didn't have a definite time frame of when we would return, expecting about a year, if all went well. We assured him if he needed us, we would be back, and that it was too good of an opportunity to pass up. He understood that if we didn't take it, we would regret it for the rest of our lives.

His dad did come to visit over Christmas and New Year's, spending two weeks with us in Singapore, making some cherished memories that we all to this day love reminiscing over. He told us then he would move there, too, seeing how much we loved it and obviously missing his son. We knew that it would never work out, him living there with us, because there was little support for the disabled there, and he needed to receive the disability pension he received in Australia to support himself financially. Him living in Singapore just was not a viable option.

Deciding to Return to Australia

While Singapore was a blast, we returned to Australia sooner than expected. The restaurant closed, and we declined other work opportunities, so we could return to his father, who missed us dearly. We stayed with him in his unit while we looked for a new place to live. We had noticed his dad's decline when he came to Singapore, having not seen him for over a month after seeing him so regularly in the past, so we knew his movements had worsened, but what we returned to was not what we expected. We knew his dad was a bit of a hoarder, and his house was always cluttered, but we did not expect to walk into the room the three of us would share to find he had done nothing to prepare for our stay. There were boxes piled up on the spare bed, which had been placed there when he moved into the unit ten years prior—he just never got around to unpacking them—a lawnmower, paint tins, piles upon piles of newspapers, more than ten years' worth to be exact, all his clothes hanging on a clothes hanger in the room, nowhere for us to put down our bags, let alone lay our jet-lagged heads. I got straight to work, trying to sort through it all, cleaning the dust, rearranging, while my husband kept our three-year-old occupied. His father was very concerned about her touching his belongings, so it was necessary to keep her busy and supervised.

The next three weeks were hard. All of us struggled to settle in, four of us in a two-bedroom unit. We realised that his dad needed help around the house, as he was not coping with the housework, and, of course, his movements were much worse than we had initially thought. We worried about him walking across the busy four-lane road he lived on to get his lunch at the local club he frequented. After living with him for those few weeks and seeing his rapid progression, we decided that it would be wise for all of us to move into a larger house together, rather than rent a unit for my husband, daughter, and me. We had always agreed that we would take him in with us when the time came; we just did not foresee that it would be so soon. We had been married only three years at this stage.

We found a three-bedroom house and began the packing. My father-in-law was on board with moving, agreeing that it was time to prepare for his decline, but not with downsizing his large hoard of belongings. He had a collection of motorbike accessories and his camping gear that he had accumulated over his years of going away on monthly rallies with his riding club. Everything he had was in multiples, never parting with his old, well-worn belongings, using his go-to set, but keeping the newer, still in the shopping bag with receipts and tags still attached, stored away, just in case he would use it 'one day.' We just would not have the room to store everything with all of our belongings, which were currently in storage. For a few days, we tried to urge him to begin to pack some items, things he didn't use daily, so that we could begin to move boxes to the new house. He just did not know where to begin. He paced the unit, picking up something, looking at it, then putting it back in the drawer or cupboard to sort another day. We knew it was not going to happen, having him pack, same as he couldn't sort out the spare room when we came to stay, so we took on all the packing and sorting. We ended up packing his belongings into boxes according to their usability or sentimental value, donating whatever he would agree to part with.

Parting with the unusable caused my father-in-law to become agitated. He would give many reasons why he wanted to keep certain items, reasons that did not make sense, trying to justify why he needed something when he probably didn't even know why himself. The process became incredibly stressful for both my father-in-law and us. He was visibly overwhelmed. Movements that were usually slow but definite became fast and erratic, arms flailing, and he began stuttering his words as he tried to put back items we had begun to pack, undoing whatever progress we made. His stress was palpable. We felt him growing increasingly distressed over the dividing of his items. It felt like feeling a storm brewing; the whole atmosphere changed. We tried our best to keep him calm. It was not a good time for all involved. We didn't realise at the time that this was all part of the Huntington's, that he mentally did not know where to start with packing and, of course, did not want to part with any of his belongings. In his mind, he probably wanted to do more but just wasn't able to help. It was the beginning of accepting his fate, the first of many losses to adjust to. We still, four years later, have boxes of items he would not agree to donate that he has not asked about or used ever since.

I Become a Caregiver

Finally, we were in our new rental house, ready to get settled and into a new routine. *Routine.* Who knew this word would become such a huge part of our lives? My father-in-law went from living independently to then, about a week and a half after the move, saying that he had not yet showered. Baffled, we asked why. He said that he did not know how; he didn't know where anything was or what to do. How could this be? This man would ride his motorcycle away on weekends to go camping with friends but could not work out how to shower? Nothing was making sense to me. I reluctantly agreed to assist him, not wanting him to struggle alone, and knowing my husband's hours at work meant that I was the only one who would be home at the time he requested to shower. He had been self-sufficient in his own unit, living independently, we presume showering regularly. He was always tidy and well kept, getting his own lunch and dinner every day, then went to completely relying on me to assist him with showering, cook and serve his food, and clean up after him. I thought he had just presumed that it was my job to do it all, being the "housewife." He seemed to just let me do things for him without a second thought.

My husband's incredibly demanding job required him to be out of the house doing split shifts six days a week. He was at work from mid-morning to prepare for lunch and dinner service, until late at night every day. I was trying to balance being the mother of a bouncing, exuberant three-year-old with my father-in-law micromanaging every aspect of our day. Our toddler was a joy to be around, but my father-in-law was still obsessively concerned with what she did, what she touched, and with the mess she would make, none of which he was used to dealing with. I was becoming increasingly frustrated, isolated, and exhausted. My husband did not see the daily demands I was under, nor did he understand the stress it was causing. Months passed of this constant catering to my father-in-law's needs whilst trying to make our lives work in cohesion rather than totally clashing. I was failing. I was confused, angry, and overwhelmed. This was not how I saw my life being at 25. We were all struggling in the chaos. Our daughter needed some normality, so we increased her preschool days from one day to four days per week. This kept her occupied and happy, whilst minimising the stress on his father at home, but also made our finances tighter, as preschool care is rather expensive.

One day, whilst our daughter was at preschool, and I was desperate for answers, I googled Huntington's disease. Why I had not done this earlier, I don't know. What I saw astounded me. I read:

Huntington's disease is a genetic neurodegenerative disease. This means that it is a disease of the brain that is passed down from parent to child. It typically starts in a person's 30s or 40s and has a life expectancy of 10-25 years. Huntington's disease results in progressive movement, cognitive, and psychiatric symptoms. No cure exists, but drugs, physiotherapy, and speech therapy can help manage some symptoms.

Cognitive. Psychiatric. This is why my father-in-law can't manage some things, I realized. It is no movement disorder alone. It is a complex disease that affects all aspects of a person's life. The more I read, the more I understood why he had changed what appeared to be so suddenly. He was 52 years old. I knew he was diagnosed at 37. He had been dealing with Huntington's for 15 years, of a possible 25-year progression. It wasn't a sudden change; he just could not initiate the task of taking a shower because we had disrupted his normal routine in his unit, where he had lived for ten years prior and had established a good routine and managed relatively well. He was now lost and confused, being taken away from his comfort zone.

I spent the next few weeks and months endlessly and tirelessly researching, learning, connecting with others on Facebook who were dealing with HD. I met some wonderful people online, a wealth of knowledge at my fingertips. Everything was beginning to make sense. All his behaviours and little quirks were, in fact, symptoms. The rigidity of timing of his meals, times of the day when he would agree to shower, the way he would get overwhelmed with noise when we had people visit, his inability to cope with anything that disrupted his routine. It all made perfect sense. Then it just kept getting worse. I met people whose children had HD, known as Juvenile Huntington's disease or JHD, even as young as four years old. Our daughter was about to turn four. My heart sank. There was so much even this family who had known of HD all their lives, four generations that we could trace, did not know. How could this be?

Advocating for IVF-PGD

With my new-found knowledge, I felt like I had to do something. I had to help bring awareness to this disease that no one knows about. I was like a woman possessed. That feeling of impending doom just kept growing and growing. I learnt that HD could be prevented from being passed down to children via IVF (In-Vitro Fertilization) and PGD (Preimplantation Genetic Diagnosis). That's it! It's not a cure, but it's the next best thing, I thought. Why hadn't I been told about this? Having made a close friend in the media industry, I did a news report, hoping to persuade the government to allow Medicare to fund or partially cover, at the very least, the cost of IVF-PGD to help families at risk of or with an HD diagnosis afford the procedure which would ensure the end of Huntington's in their family. It was well received, getting huge response from viewers country wide. I spoke with members of Parliament; I threw myself into campaigning, only for it to fall on deaf ears.

They heard me, yes; it just was not a priority for the government. I felt deflated. Why did no one care what the HD community is facing? Why did no one want to help? This is the closest thing to a cure we have at this point. It was very disheartening to see our plight go unanswered. I now know from more research and networking that HD can appear to be spontaneous, meaning that families with no apparent history of

HD can suddenly have a person diagnosed, the first in their genealogy. This meant that what I thought was the answer to curing HD was not to be. It would only make it even more rare for those 10 percent of cases known as a new mutation, making their fight for awareness even more difficult than what we face currently. We couldn't end HD that easily. I felt even more deflated, coupled with even more of a burning desire to help.

In the midst of all my researching and campaigning, my father-in-law had a motorcycle accident. We knew it was getting dangerous for him to ride, but he had been doing his yearly tests and medicals to ensure it was still appropriate for him to ride, and we thought it wasn't up to us to stop it. It is now clear that the roads and transport agency did not have a sound understanding of Huntington's. I believe had they known better, they would have taken his license long before this point. He lived to ride; it was literally his life's passion. He always said that when it was time to stop that he would have nothing to live for. He managed to convince all the powers to be that he could still ride safely for around four years.

Well, a month before what would probably have been his last examination, he went off on another one of his regular rallies. He, being so set in his ways, would pack the day before his tent, his pillow, and his sleeping bag. He'd plan out his trip with the map, making a list of directions to memorise and keep in his jacket pocket for reference along the way. Everything was planned to a T. The time he would leave, the roads he would take, the toilet and meal stops on the way. When he didn't return at the planned time on the Sunday afternoon he was supposed to return, I knew something was not right. Two o'clock came and went. Four o'clock came and went. Dinner time, I knew in my heart that something was wrong. I began calling every police station between our house and his destination. Every hospital. I was told by police that he'd probably decided to stay another night. No way. I knew through knowing him over the years that that was not his personality. He did not just decide on a whim to change plans, EVER.

I became increasingly frustrated at not being heard and taken seriously. I knew he'd had an accident. I begged the police to just hear me out. I was told that if he wasn't back by the next day to call back. We lived two streets over from the hospital in

Wollongong, so we frequently heard helicopters arrive and depart. One went straight over me as I was calling around, trying to find him. It wasn't until nine o'clock that night that I had a phone call from a hospital in Sydney, informing me he had been involved in an accident. Ironically, he was on that very helicopter that took off and passed right overhead, being airlifted to a Sydney hospital for emergency surgery. Had my fears been taken seriously earlier in the afternoon, I would have been able to be by his side, in the hospital, prior to him being airlifted.

He had a compound fracture in his leg, a broken thumb, and needed skin grafts on his knees. Luckily, it was a single-vehicle accident, and he did not injure anyone else. Witnesses said they thought he was drunk. We knew that there was no way he would ride after drinking; he only ever had one drink with dinner, never more. It is a common misconception for Huntington's patients to be perceived as being intoxicated. Yes, some choose to self-medicate with alcohol in an attempt to numb the emotional turmoil they experience, often years before any physical signs set in, but my father-in-law had witnessed his own father do this, so he was never a big drinker, out of fear of ending up the same way.

He spent weeks in hospital and then rehab, learning how to walk again. The accident caused him to progress very quickly, not walking for so long, being bedridden while his skin grafts and injuries healed. Any progress he made recovering from the accident was overridden by the decline caused by Huntington's. It was one step forward and two steps back. The rehab hospital arranged for us to meet with a social worker. She was so helpful. She understood how hard this was for us as a young family to handle alone, and she listened to my concerns with me being the one who would provide the care he would need when he returned home. I was not a nurse; I was not equipped to be providing this level of care; I was so young. She organised a meeting with an aged care provider to get us some in-home assistance. Why didn't we know about this sooner? I had been showering, preparing meals, cleaning for my father-in-law, collecting his mail from his post office box, assisting him with paying his bills, and running myself into the ground for months, juggling the roles of mother, housewife, and carer, yet had no idea we were entitled to this type of assistance until he had a near fatal accident and ended up in hospital. I was sensing a huge disconnect in the care Huntington's disease patients were receiving.

Yes, he saw a specialist team consisting of a neurologist, speech pathologist, occupational therapist, and dietician. We had accompanied my father-in-law to his yearly appointments for a few years at this stage, but none of these people would physically see how the person copes, or doesn't cope, as the case usually is, at home. They just take their one hour with the patient in their office and provide their advice based on what they see, a literal blink of an eye compared to the daily life of someone with HD. Huntington's patients tend to have a way of convincing specialists that they are okay. They put on their best face for others, showing how well they can walk, talk, eat, and often behave, whilst letting all their walls down at home, living in squalor if living alone, or relying totally on their families, usually their children, as their parents have often already passed away; that's if they're lucky enough to have children who will take them in, trying to make sense of it all, practically alone.

We Begin to Get In-Home Care

Once we had the in-home care established, it changed our lives. It did take some time to teach them how he liked things done; his routine was very strict, but once they developed a relationship with my father-in-law and knew him and his quirks, it took so much pressure off me. I felt a weight had been lifted; there were other, trained professionals to witness what we had been doing all alone for the best part of a year. They saw our daily struggles, the difficulty we faced in juggling our family's needs; they were there to help. They took on all his showering, taking that stress off my shoulders. My father-in-law is very particular about the time of day he takes a shower; it's at the same time in the morning that I need to drive my husband to work. I was finding myself rushed, and often, if I returned later than he wanted his shower, he would refuse and become angry that I had not done what he wanted at the time he wanted. I began to have panic attacks whilst driving if there was traffic, or if I ran late. I had never experienced anxiety like this before in my life.

They would assist him with his exercise regimen the rehab hospital had created for him, to help regain strength and attempt to slow any muscle loss whilst maintaining his current level of ability. They would vacuum and tidy his bedroom for me. At times, depending on which caretaker was in that day, they would do our dishes. They saw how overwhelmed I was and just did whatever they could to try and take a load off me. Not only did they provide my father-in-law with some companionship, giving him someone else to talk to, but I was also able to confide in them and looked forward to the days they would come, knowing that it gave me a chance to go do the grocery shopping or run errands without having to worry that he was waiting on me to return and that all his needs were being met. We had them come in three days a week. I arranged the days and the times of the day they would come in to coincide with my husband's day off, so we got some family time. With my daughter's days at preschool, I had a day to myself and could run all the errands we needed. I learnt quickly how to juggle my time and his care so that everyone had their needs met.

They made it possible for me to be the mother I had been before my caring role. I was no longer overwhelmed and short tempered. Our marriage had been under such stress with us having a young child, a disabled father-in-law living with us, and the toll that HD takes on the whole family when you don't have support. We could breathe a little, for now.

We were under a lot of financial pressure, my husband being the sole wage earner, with the huge rent we were paying, the costs of preschool, the financial aspect of having his father living with us, and all the fees for his care. I also had to learn very quickly how to handle finances and juggle his father's funding and budget. We knew if we were going to care for my father-in-law at home long term, we would need to change something. We couldn't keep doing it the way we were. Our daughter was starting school the next year. I was hoping to be able to go back to work once she started school. If we were going to move, now was the time. His father sold his unit, we got a house loan, moved north, closer to my parents, where we would have more support, and we built a house which would be safe and HD-friendly for my father-in-law. Also, if worst case scenario were to happen, my husband and daughter inheriting the faulty gene, we knew we would be in the right place, both geographically and financially, to face those challenges. It was a gamble, as the city we lived in was close to the HD specialists, whereas the town we were moving to was a small coastal town, remote to any specialists, and I knew that there wouldn't be any other Huntington's patients for hundreds of kilometres. We did, however, have my family as informal support and knew that my daughter would benefit from having them be able to help out when needed. We would never have been able to afford to build a house where we were living before, and my husband and I knew that it was now or never.

Moving to a New Home Once Again

It has not been easy, by any means. If you think moving to a new house is hard, try doing it with an HD person, strict on his routine, who requires assistance with most aspects of his daily life. That, along with facilitating the transition from one care provider to another, from one end of the state to another, was a juggling act. I still, to this day, don't know how I made it happen. I am eternally thankful we did make it happen; looking back now, I know it was the best decision we have made. I could not foresee the impact the move would have on us all. The gamble paid off. Financially and emotionally, my husband and I are in a much better position. Better than we could have ever imagined. It took a great deal of determination and support from my family. We rented my father's small unit while our new home was being built, blessed that we had this available to us, as it alleviated the stress of finding temporary housing and paying expensive rent while we waited for our house to be finished. I will be forever grateful to my father for his never-ending generosity. It took one hurdle and made it much smaller in this process for our family.

Having both my parents just being there for us, sharing our journey, our daily struggles, and including my father-in-law in our family, welcoming him in, has made this whole experience so much easier. They see how hard it is for us to devote our time and energy into my father-in-law's care, but they support our decision, knowing it was not the easiest choice to make. My parents are both older than my father-in-law, so they understand how hard it is for him to be losing so much of himself so young and why he doesn't want to go to a nursing home. Both my parents have expressed how they hope that the HD stops with my father-in-law. They, of course, only want what's best for me and my family, especially their granddaughter. They try not to think too far ahead, always reminding me to be positive and have faith that things will be okay. I get my strength, determination, and faith from my mother and my problem-solving skills and critical thinking from my father. They have both instilled in me a solid foundation to face life and all that it can throw at you. I am forever thankful for their support and guidance.

As time went by after our move, our daughter was settled into kindergarten at school. I tried to go back to work, at first, just for the social aspect, so I had some time to myself, and to feel like I was contributing to the family the way our friends, family, and society expected. It was short lived. By the time we were settled into the new house after it was built, one year exactly after we moved into my dad's unit, my father-in-law had progressed more and relied even more heavily on me for his every need. We still had the in-home carers come in whilst I was gone. They would do his lunch and personal care, but the funding we receive from the government to help with the costs just did not cover having someone there for my father-in-law for the entire day while I was working. They were only able to be there for two hours a day, max, and I would come home to him being agitated and angry if his routine was disrupted in any way, and there would be repercussions.

The moment I walked in the door, he would come to me with a list of issues; no matter how seemingly easy to overcome they were to me, they were unacceptable to him. It could be as simple as if the carer didn't dry his hair enough after a shower, or if they didn't give him the right cutlery to eat with. If he didn't get all the exercises done, he would say that he was now constipated and that he couldn't eat his dinner as he felt sick from bloating. He knew that he needed to eat a full meal, as weight loss was an issue for him, and we had added meal supplement drinks to his diet to try and maintain his weight. If the carer arrived later than rostered, he would be unwilling to do any of his exercises. He began to favour some of the carers over others. He would tell one carer not to do something, part of his usual routine, then tell another carer that they refused to and get them in trouble with their manager. He had decided which people he liked and disliked, so the list of people he would allow in got smaller and smaller. If he spilt his drink after they left, and he was home alone, he would not know how to clean it up and would leave it for when I got home, then say he couldn't get up and walk to the bathroom, as there was water on the tiles, and it was slippery. He would say that he had been needing to go for hours.

That agitation would radiate from him, movements becoming erratic as he explained his issue, and I was always feeling his emotions weighing on me. He had not become aggressive or violent, mainly just yelling and a few harsh words, but I found it increasingly hard to face this behaviour and remain calm whilst trying to reassure and reason with him. It was impacting my mental health, coming home to someone who was visibly upset, and he always held me accountable for things, no matter how out of my control it was. He didn't really do much throughout the day, mainly watched some tv and completed his routine of showering and exercises, but he didn't like being left alone. It was hard to justify me being home all day when he barely interacted with me outside of his need for assistance with tasks, keeping to himself while I was there but then being angry he was alone if I wasn't there. I swallowed my pride, accepted that I needed to be here at home to ensure he got the care he needed and that our lives were running smoothly. What I am contributing to our family is more important than money right now. My family's well-being and happiness is our number one priority. My husband has had to continue to work full time to make all ends meet. He is a dedicated worker, having inherited his dad's strong work ethic, and it also helps him to keep his mind busy to cope with all the stress of building a house and caring for his dad. It is this strong work ethic that saw him promoted to head chef, and all his father's encouragement and hopes for his career paid off.

On my husband's half-hour lunch break at work each day, I would join him for a coffee, being the only real one-on-one time we had together. One day, as I was leaving after our morning coffee, I had a phone call from the manager at the care provider agency. She told me that my father-in-law had verbally abused a worker and that the worker had to leave, as my father-in-law was becoming increasingly agitated with the worker. I rushed home to diffuse the situation. My father-in-law's moods had been changing over the previous few months, with him becoming even more obsessive over our daughter and her movements around the home, about timing and his routine. It had been a long time coming, this breakdown of sorts. We lost that worker and were down to a small handful of carers my father-in-law would cooperate with. We knew it was a gamble moving so far from the specialists who would be able to assess him and prescribe the right medications to help alleviate these issues, but we did have access to local respite options to give everyone a little break from the daily stress. We used respite quite regularly, until the National Disability Insurance Scheme (NDIS) was introduced into Australia and changed all our funding options. While yes, on one hand they increased our home care funding, giving us the option to have four hours, six days a week, so I can try and find a job which fits in around those hours, they, on the other hand, cut funding for respite.

With the new scheme in place, it brings all sorts of new issues to a system we thought we had handled, and it is still something we are attempting to navigate to this day. Most families in Australia trying to access the scheme are in the same situation, having needs not being met and having to fight for access to life saving respite options and services. We still are uncertain about what this means for our future, as far as caring for my father-in-law goes. It's another aspect of caring and living with HD that weighs heavily on families, funding, paperwork, accessing services, and finances. It is incredibly stressful pleading your case to an agency, trying to prove your need to access certain services, and often they are declined, due to a lack of understanding about the disease. Appeal processes take months to complete and often do not get the intended outcome. Our entire lives revolve around a system which can be changed or completely removed at any point in time, based on what government we have elected and their priorities.

Trying to Navigate More Changes

Despite the increase of in-home care funding we get, it is becoming increasingly stressful on all of us, myself trying to government agencies and funding, difficult behaviours and new symptoms with my father-in-law; for our daughter, sacrificing aspects of her childhood and dealing with her grandfather's declining health and increasing obsessiveness about her actions, often causing many disagreements and tears; and for my husband, working so hard, managing a team of chefs and all that comes with running a kitchen and the emotional turmoil of witnessing his father's decline and his own fears about HD.

Being at risk is so terrifying. Watching your father decline is one of the most difficult things to face in life, let alone the prospect of inheriting the same disease. The stress of watching your potential future play out before your very eyes day in, day out, is sheer torture. The fear he lives with daily is enough to drive a person insane. He always has HD in the back of his mind, even though he doesn't want to discuss it. That makes it all too real. HD has tainted every decision and milestone he's reached in life. Turning 32 is one step closer to the scary age when his dad became symptomatic. The promotion brought on feelings of, do I really want to work that much? Should I be spending those extra hours with my wife and daughter? What if I get sick, and work becomes too stressful? Should we travel now while we can afford it or save that money towards paying off our home loan, in case I do get sick and we have less income? Those what ifs aren't just playing on his mind.

The fear of the unknown is what I find hardest. I felt like the more I learnt, the more well equipped I was to handle this monster. I tried talking to my husband, only for him to shut down and not want to talk about it. I couldn't understand why we couldn't have a conversation about it. It drove a wedge between us, not seeing eye to eye. This has been one of our biggest challenges as a couple. "Knowledge is power," I would preach, trying to convince him that him getting tested was the best option for our family right now. If we knew he did not have HD, we could have another child, which he so desperately wanted. I just couldn't bring myself to have another child potentially at risk of inheriting HD. If he did, God forbid, have HD, we could think about how we would spend our time. Would we spend what could arguably be the best years of our lives together caring for his father and him working huge hours to make it possible? There was so much we wanted to do as a couple; what if our years were numbered? What if we continued the way we are, only to have him get sick once his dad passes away, and we don't get time to realise our dreams? What if I end up caring for three generations of loved ones with HD? What if, what if!! I was beside myself.

Learning to Compromise

What I didn't realise was that knowing it all is not what's best for some. It only helps if you can handle that knowledge, put it to good use, and not have it eat you alive. How would my husband cope if he knew for sure he would go the same way as his father, while watching what it was doing to his dad every day? He wouldn't. It would take away any hope he had for his future. If we found out his fate, our thoughts would also then shift to our daughter, and that's something neither of us can even bear to think about at this point.

The hardest part of having Huntington's isn't dying. It's living. It's making it through every day, knowing what is to come and navigating the changes in your personality and abilities. For some, not knowing is unbearable; for others, that knowledge can be severely detrimental to their well-being. I have learnt that people have different coping mechanisms, and that's perfectly okay. Some people throw themselves into advocating, raising awareness and fundraising. Some enroll in trials and studies to help find the cure everyone so desperately needs. Others prefer to live life without giving HD too much thought, sticking their heads in the sand, if you will, and dealing with it when the time comes. No way is right or wrong; whatever helps you get through each day and sleep at night is right for you.

In marriage, you must learn to compromise, and that's even more so when faced with the prospect of Huntington's. We've learnt to balance each other; he lives with hope, which helps me to have hope, and I handle the logistics of finances, in-home care for his dad, and general day-to-day household duties. His boss often jokes that I am the brains behind the operation, which is an accurate description of our relationship. We are so close as a couple; he is my rock, as I am his. Despite what I've learnt during my countless sleepless nights researching, whatever we will face, we know we have the tools to face it, even when he can't bring himself to do so. Our motto has become, "Hope for the best, but plan for the worst."

We've come to realise that not everyone will understand the choices you make as a family while facing HD. After much heartbreak, an online friend and I decided to create a support group on Facebook for carers who were lost and confused like we often were. We needed a safe place for us and others we knew who were facing many difficulties in their role of caring for a loved one with HD, a safe place for us to share our journeys and gain support and understanding, often not getting that understanding from friends who cannot empathise with our lives. While we were already members of other Facebook groups aimed at the entire HD community, having HD yourself is very, very different from being the main carer for someone who has HD. Both are incredibly difficult, but both come with a different set of complex emotions and very different roles.

Over the years of sharing my own experiences and being there for others in their experiences in the group, I have witnessed many relationships and friendships crumble under the pressure of trying to make sense of HD. I've seen women so consumed by their fear of losing their loved one to this monster, being so hypervigilant, symptom watching, that they drive themselves nearly to insanity, whilst simultaneously driving a wedge in the relationship, making matters a thousand times worse. It does become all consuming, witnessing the person you love struggle daily or change his or her personality right before your eyes, but constantly watching for changes can take over every waking moment. Precious moments slip past as you are so fixated on a recent change, a new symptom. Partners deny or are not aware of any changes and can be easily frustrated with not having their own fears taken seriously. They often do not want to discuss this thing that will rob them of everything that is good in life, all day, every day. It's so incredibly hard to find a balance between being an advocate and a carer and being a loving spouse or parent. Yes, be vigilant with any changes that may be helped with the right medication but be conscious of not being so hypervigilant that you get lost in the abyss of carer fatigue. This is the wedge I felt in my own relationship. I was so consumed by what I thought could be early symptoms that I thought having the genetic test and finding out my husband's status would fix all our problems.

Our problems fixed themselves when I took a moment to step back and look at things from his perspective. I heard his fear; I heard his desire to not live a life consumed by HD. Yes, he would always have his father's HD in mind, and there will be sleepless nights when his fear of inheriting it will keep him tossing and turning, but he needs so desperately to live his life. To be allowed to live with hope, before HD could become an undeniable reality that he cannot escape. As long as that is possible, I will strive to help him achieve all his aspirations in life. It is his decision whether or not to get tested, and I do not want it on my hands if I push him further than he is capable of going, and he ends up regretting finding out his fate.

That is how we've learnt to be strong in the face of HD, not just to survive, but to thrive. Without the carers group, I would not have been able to gain this life-changing insight. We would still be drowning, just trying to keep our heads above water, but fighting against each other, him swimming against the tide and me pulling him down as I tried to persuade him to go in the opposite direction. I call this realisation my epiphany, and I truly do owe this awakening to the online group we created. The members of our group, I now consider my extended HD family. They've been there for me, and I them, when we didn't know how to navigate this journey. Together, we've formed a great alliance in our fight to navigate this HD journey, and I could not express in words how grateful I am for them being there and for sharing some of the most intimate details of our lives with each other, things that only other carers and loved ones of HD patients would ever comprehend.

We've confided in each other when our "real life" friends that we thought could be there for us did not understand the difficulties we face and the choices we are forced to make. Sometimes, we put our loved ones before ourselves and put up with behaviours which, without the HD diagnosis, would be a total deal breaker. Friends can often find it hard to understand why we would make the decision to stay, when we are so clearly struggling, when the caring takes precedence over coffee dates and girls' nights or outings. It can be hard to deal with their ignorance about why we make the choice to stick by our loved ones, but this is honestly one of the hardest journeys in life, and they simply cannot possibly understand without experiencing it themselves. If you have a "real life friend," as we call it on Facebook, who supports you and understands your life as a carer and spouse of a person with HD, cherish them! It is rare and hard to find! Without our little online HD family and my best "real life" friend, I don't know how I would have survived up until now.

Caring for my father-in-law, as challenging and isolating as it has been, is also one of the most rewarding things we have done as a couple. It is a selfless act; it is not easy to devote every day to caring for another, handling his medical care, managing his finances, witnessing his daily struggles, often putting his needs before our own, but it has inspired a great amount of personal growth within myself and my husband to push through the hard times and make what we thought was impossible a reality. I will always fiercely protect my family and the decisions we have made for both my father-in-law and for us. Every decision and sacrifice we have made has been made with careful consideration, weighing up pros and cons, months of angst and research (and legal advice!) to ensure it is the right choice for us all.

Deciding Whether to Have More Children

At this stage, my husband and I have made the devastating decision not to bring another child into the uncertainty we face. I have heard it likened to playing Russian roulette with your children's lives. I understand others do not share our concerns, and they perhaps have more faith than I that their children will be spared, but the odds are not stacked in our favour. My father-in-law is one of three children, all of whom inherited HD. No survivors. Sadly, his oldest sister passed away as this was being written. She was only 59 years old. She leaves behind a husband, two children, and three grandchildren. We thought that we would have a long time before HD could potentially rear its head. Even "30s or 40s," as per the average age of onset, is not a long time. That is the prime of your life. My husband is now 32. That is now for us. The peak of his working career. To have to face the possibility of onset of a severely life-limiting disease in the prime of your life is gut wrenching. But it doesn't always happen that way. You cannot accurately predict the onset. The gene can expand during conception and cause a huge jump in the number of CAG repeats. It can start earlier, much earlier.

Learning about Juvenile Huntington's disease and seeing a friend's child at four years old be diagnosed with JHD is utterly devastating. These children will never have the chance to have a career. They will never get married or even get to consider having children of their own. They will likely not even grow mature enough to comprehend that they are terminally ill. They will only know what life is like, battling each and every day.

Every child is a blessing, but this disease is a curse that I cannot put any future children at risk of, knowing what I now know. I campaigned for IVF-PGD to be covered by Medicare, not so we could utilise it, but for other families who are beginning their lives together and can alter the course of their future with the amazing technology. We don't believe it is the right option for us to have a child and ensure there is no HD risk, as we already have one child who is potentially at risk. While her father remains untested, she has a 25 percent chance of having HD. We have to consider how she would feel if she had a sibling who did not have the same risk status she may have to face. What if she does, God forbid, have the mutated gene? How would she feel, like she was replaced? Like we gave our second child a chance at life she would not also have? I just could not live with myself if she were to have these feelings due to the decisions I've had to make. It has not been easy to have to make these tough choices, and I have considered many options and possible outcomes. I just hope she knows that both her father and I have always had her best interests at heart. These are the things we have to consider in an HD family. In time, perhaps our opinion may change. As she gets older, we may be able to ask her how she feels as we tell her more about HD. If I get the chance to return to work, and it is in our financial reach to utilise IVF-PGD, there may even be a viable treatment in the near future which could change everything. But until that point, we have to use the information at hand to make informed decisions about our future.

We do not know what the future holds for my husband and our daughter, and that's okay for now. We have enough to deal with, losing my husband's father more and more every day. He now requires round-the-clock supervision. He falls over many times a day. We can barely understand what he says because his speech has become so strained. He struggles to swallow his food, coughing and choking regularly, despite being on a fully puréed diet. He has lost a lot of weight these past few months. He is losing control of his body. We see a change in him weekly now. It won't be long until he is no longer able to walk or talk at all. He has been battling this horrible disease for nearly 18 years, and we see that he is growing weary. To see such a proud and determined man wither before your very eyes is not for the faint hearted.

As our daughter gets older, I know there are going to be some tough questions to answer, but for now, I answer her questions with honesty and age-appropriate information. She knows very well that her poppy is sick, that his brain is not working how it should, and that it makes him lose control of his muscles and not think clearly. She knows that it makes him say mean things sometimes when he gets overwhelmed or frustrated and to not take it personally. She was only five years old when she asked me if "she will get wobbly like Poppy." I choked back tears as I said that I didn't know, which is the truth. She knows she doesn't have a normal childhood. That is hard for her, but she has grown to be a very kind and courageous girl. She shows such bravery, more than I ever did at her age. She is the biggest blessing in both mine and my husband's lives, bringing us joy and laughter each and every day. She's an outgoing, confident and talented little girl, a natural performer and leader. I will forever be grateful that she came into our lives when she did. She is truly a gift from God.

While Huntington's can cut a person's life span in half, there is a long journey to face in the progression. When you first learn of HD, you just want to do so much, a burning desire to change the world, so to speak, to help raise money to find the cure, to raise awareness so you don't feel so alone and isolated, to change your fate. The true strength of those who face Huntington's, either directly or indirectly, lies in the longevity of the battle. It is a marathon in every sense of the word, a true test of endurance. To get up each day, knowing the struggle you could face, losing another ability, becoming less independent as time goes by, or witnessing the love of your life, your parent, siblings, or your children losing everything, but continuing to be their voice and stand by them, that is true strength. I myself have periods of a burning desire to advocate, to be heard and to make a difference for the HD community. Then there are times where I just want to live my life, unplug from social media, have a normal, uneventful life, craving to have those first-world problems that seem so trivial in comparison to what we face with HD.

Belonging to a Carers Support Group

Being so involved in our Facebook group, "Huntington's Disease Carers Support Group," also has its difficulties. Just as our HD family there has given me strength and understanding I didn't know I was capable of, I have witnessed a lot of heartache, suffering, and death in the few short years of its existence. We have lost members' loved ones, children, both to the disease itself and to suicide. Suicide is something that is difficult for people to discuss and understand. People with HD can feel like a burden to their families and not want to suffer the horrible end stages of the disease nor have their families see them that way. Some are left with no family support and feel like there is no other option. Some try to take control of their death as they lose control of everything else. Some have such intense psychological issues that they make decisions they would not have ever made prior to HD.

Carers often feel like they are at their wit's end with undereducated medical professionals who know nothing of HD other than what they learnt in a textbook during their studies, to families who don't make themselves present in their lives to offer support, being so isolated and burnt out that they can't face another day. Some have to endure the grief of losing their partner to HD, and then being left to care for children with JHD and HD alone, it can become too much to handle. Please, if you are a friend of someone with HD, be there not only for them, but also for their families. Their carers are very often struggling more than you could imagine and need just as much help as the people with HD themselves. We in the group can only do so much, not being physically close enough to wrap our arms around them and tell them everything will be ok. Or that they at least aren't alone in the fight.

I just pray that my family and I and the HD community from which I've drawn so much inspiration and strength continue to fight with the vigour and sheer determination we have up until now.

Hoping for the best, while deep down, planning for the worst.

Dedicated to the women who inspire me every day to be a better carer, wife, mother, and advocate. My strength is passed down to me from those who walked this walk and learnt the hard way before we had social media to connect with others. They did this with little to no support or guidance from others, and it is their willingness to share their stories with us who are new to HD that has inspired me to do the same. There are too many to name individually, but if we've ever chatted online and shared our fears and secrets, know that you're a cherished part of my journey with HD. Without you all, I would still be lost and confused.

To Lisa, my worldwide wolf pack comrade, my first friend in the online HD community, I will always cherish the times we had together online. Wherever life has taken you, I hope you think of me as often as I think of you. HD may have stolen your ability to communicate online, but it hasn't stolen the memories and friendship we share.

About Jean Miller

Jean Miller lost her daughter, Kelly, to JHD in 1998, at the age of 30. Since Kelly's diagnosis in 1983, Jean has fought to educate herself and others, including doctors and other healthcare workers, about Huntington's disease. Jean was one of the first people to use the internet to connect with others in the HD/JHD community, beginning with a small group she found on AOL in 1985. She asked questions and shared lessons she learned from her own experiences with Kelly. She has a huge network of friends that she has made online and in person through the years and shares every tidbit of information she can find about HD/JHD through her extensive mailing list.

In 2000, a group of kids approached Jean at the HDSA convention and asked her if she would be the adult advisor for a new youth group that they wanted to form. Jean agreed, asked Susie Hodgson to join her, and the National Youth Alliance was born.

Jean says, "HD gives us the greatest gifts of all: the importance of love, patience, understanding, compassion for others, and gratitude for life's littlest joys. Look at how many in this world never even scratch the surface of understanding that these things are really what life is all about. Yes, there is pain and heartache, tears and sadness . . . and although we can't see it when we are experiencing them, they are the ones that eventually teach us the real meaning of life. I have yet to meet one person touched by HD who doesn't have a beautiful soul/heart full of love."

5

The Kelly E. Miller Huntington's Disease Story: Our Personal Experience

The Early Years

Kelly Elizabeth Miller was born January 28, 1968, in St. Louis, Missouri. She was a very normal, intelligent, and beautiful child. In preschool (Montessori), with an IQ of 156, she was doing algebra!

Early in her school years (public) the teachers thought Kelly was hyperactive (now either ADD or ADHD), and she was treated for that up until the age of 12, for a very short time with Ritalin. That medication changed my sweet child into a monster, so they switched her to Dexedrine.

I had a very abusive, both mentally and physically, relationship with Kelly's father, Larry, for the six years we were married. It was when this abuse started to be directed towards Kelly, when she was five, that I finally left that marriage in 1973. We stayed in the St. Louis area another three years before moving to Florida because I thought having contact with her father would be best for Kelly. It wasn't.

The discussion of abuse in an HD marriage is another subject; however, it is something that should never be ignored, and if you are in such a relationship, RUN, don't walk, to get help. In the 70s, there weren't any "safe" homes, nor were the police willing to get involved in domestic problems. It took me years to get over that abuse, but I know that it had a significant impact on Kelly for many years.

We moved back to Clearwater, Florida, in 1976, to be near her grandparents George and Jean Steffens and so that I could transfer back to Honeywell's Space facility because the opportunities for growth were better.

The Horrible Pre-Teen Years

The years between 12 and 15 were THE hardest years in both Kelly's and my life! I had had several promotions at work and was putting in between 50 and 70 hours a week and traveling on business a lot. Although my parents cared for Kelly when I traveled, we thought a lot of problems she started showing were normal "adolescent" growing pains.

Kelly had always been mature for her age, and I trusted her completely. We had talked about drugs, drinking . . . the whole gamut of normal parental discussions when trying to protect a child.

When her grades started to drop, and her behavior became more bizarre, I questioned if she was experimenting with drugs and believed her when she told me no. My own ignorance kept me from being "aware" of the signs of alcohol or drug abuse. She became more sullen and disrespectful, totally out of character for Kelly. Then she started running away, or threatening to run away (which was just a ploy to stay out later than her curfew most of the time). There were threats of suicide almost weekly, which you can never take lightly, sneaking out at night while I was sleeping, even "stealing" the car and taking great pains to park it where I couldn't tell she had taken it.

She first wrecked my car when she was 12 . . . that was my lesson in teaching her to drive when she was younger! When she was taking the car more frequently later on, I kept taking my car to the mechanic and telling him something HAD to be wrong because my gas mileage was terrible!

We went through these years very painfully. To have to even consider the "Tough Love" methods of kicking your child at such a young age out of the house and ignoring them is very difficult.

To have to, at some point, sign an "Out of Control" order with the state to protect my being arrested for her actions and having her placed in a Juvenile home for delinquent girls for months is, I thought at the time, one of *the most difficult* things a parent would have to do.

To later have to have your child committed to a mental hospital for intense treatment because her behavior was endangering to herself and others (she threatened me with a knife) rips your heart out of your body. But it was there, finally, after almost four months and $30,000 later (in 1983) when I finally got "my Kelly" back. Daily one-on-one counseling, group sessions, alcohol and drug therapy, etc. returned her to me on her 15th birthday.

Loving Kelly didn't help her; counseling did because it helped her develop love for herself, which seems to be lacking in so many JHDs, no matter how much love they get at home. And it wasn't just one magical counseling session either . . . just one that worked, out of several attempts. You need to find someone they "click" with. Kelly happened to find one counselor who could see clean through her bullshit because, God love her, she knew she could con everyone, including me.

When I signed Kelly out-of-control, did normal school/parent-child counseling, sent her to the runaway clinic, tried parts of tough love which almost killed me, none of these phased her until the treatments at the psychiatric hospital. But that took her almost a month to accept, too, before it sunk in that Mom was not bailing her out of this one, based on their recommendations. She had to EARN the privilege of even visits home.

All the cries for help in suicide attempts, stealing from me, drugs and alcohol, were heard by me. But kids rarely listen to their parents or understand that some of the things you try to do for them is to help them vs. punishment.

Her poetry written during this time speaks of the pain she felt yet kept inside. Most of these weren't shared with me until years later. If you'd like to read them, there is a link to them at the end of this chapter.

After the intense treatments, Kelly knew who she was and liked herself, HD or not, and finally understood I was there and would always be there for her. Before then, Kelly would cry and plead her sorrow when she did something wrong, and I know she meant it with all of her heart, but that didn't stop her, or, I should say, she couldn't stop herself. It wasn't until she put some value on her own self/life that it all stopped . . . there were a few minor setbacks, but she came through those, too, which made me very proud of her!

I think JHDs have a hard time having self-respect even before knowing they have the disease, and it's just amplified after finding out. So maybe that is the answer. We all know a lot of teenagers go through periods of not liking themselves for one reason or another. Maybe with our JHDs this feeling is tenfold or more. It is bad enough to live through your teen years, but to have a physical or emotional situation brought on by HD must make their lives a thousand times harder. Years of mental and physical abuse by other kids at school taunting them and calling them names, years of parents and teachers not understanding (before realizing HD's ugly head is there) . . . all of these can add up to someone lacking in self-respect. After all, "Can all those people be wrong?" they must think.

Kelly told me she felt she was going crazy because she couldn't understand why she didn't remember tasks or assignments, or why everyone thought she wasn't trying, when she was.

Kelly got drunk quite easily and then would have blackouts and not remember a thing. Drugs made her hostile and angry, booze mellow and sloppy drunk. Was it a form of self-medication? Perhaps. After we found out about her having HD, I realized it was no wonder she tried to escape through alcohol and drugs. At least during those times when she was high or drunk, she didn't have to think about those feelings or feel the pain and frustration and fear of why all those things were happening to her.

What Is Wrong?

Shortly after Kelly's 15th birthday, she started complaining about everyone in school making fun of her because she was having these involuntary movements. Kelly was 5'9" and very beautiful and naturally drew attention to herself from her looks alone. Having the kids call her spaz and all kinds of derogatory names cut her to the core.

I'd study her, especially at night while she was sleeping, and couldn't see anything unusual and thought maybe it was all in her mind.

Sure, periodically she'd spill things or stumble, but I attributed that to her always being in a hurry with everything she did. But to ease her mind, I took her to see a neurologist. They ran every test imaginable on her and couldn't find anything, when the doctor suggested she have this *new* procedure done (1983), an MRI. It showed a small amount of atrophy in the caudate nucleus area of her brain. Based on this, the neurologist made an "educated guess" that she had Huntington's Chorea. "Say what?" we asked. This doctor did not have any bedside manner, was abrupt and not very communicative. He just blurted that it was a terminal illness and that he couldn't help and that when she got worse, come see him, but that she was going to die. Then he gave us a prescription for Haldol.

Kelly immediately went to the school library and looked up Huntington's Chorea and Xeroxed the only description they had of it . . . needless to say, it scared us. This article stated that the disease was hereditary, and we had no known history of HD on either side of her family that we knew of. This all occurred before the accurate genetic testing for HD was developed in 1993. The little information I could find on the disease wasn't very encouraging, either. So we spent the next four years taking her to a whole battery of specialists who evaluated what the initial doctor had done (and advised me that although he didn't have much of a bedside manner, he was thorough), then ran their own inconclusive tests. They were all stymied by the fact that there was no known history of the disease on either side of the family.

I had done extensive research on my family, and the data

obtained from her paternal side turned out later to be "non-truths." Two neurologists said it was wrong for the initial doctor to have said the atrophy was HD when she could have been born with the atrophy. Or, the atrophy may have been caused by a nasty fall down the basement stairs when she was one. Or, from other head trauma from a fall at age three (first stitches). Or, from hitting her head on the windshield of a car when she was five. Take your pick. The Chief of Neurology at Shands Medical Hospital in Gainesville (at that time, it was Dr. Greer) called it *"Kelly's Disease."* In the interim, Kelly's HD had progressed a little at a time, which was more noticeable to people who hadn't seen her in several months.

Kelly quit school at 17 and signed up for GED classes. They tried to get her skill training through PVTI (a technical school), which determined she wasn't "trainable," due to her inability to follow multiple directions and her dropping things. They were the ones who had her re-tested at the original neurologist's and had another MRI done, which showed the atrophy had progressed, and, all with our permission, had her declared permanently disabled and placed on SS disability before she was 18. However, we both still weren't convinced it was HD without a family history.

By this time, thanks to my employer, I had a computer and access to the internet and spent hours searching for information on HD. The Internet had very little information back then, but I found a small group of people on AOL who were connected to HD.

When the gene was found, and the testing became 99 percent accurate, we had Kelly tested at the University of South Florida. When her diagnosis came back [her CAG count was 16 and 56, low for JHD], Kelly shocked them by actually being *happy* about her positive results, saying that now she could tell people for sure what was wrong with her, and hopefully they would quit accusing her of being high or drunk (ha! people are ignorant).

The disease progressed fairly slowly the next several years. As she was robbed of one precious ability to do things on her own, we'd figure out another way to compensate for that loss. Since there was very little information available on the day-to-day care of people with Huntington's (pHDs), I learned you can be very resourceful when the need arises! The most important thing was to let Kelly know, constantly, that we would not give in easily and that, as a "team," we could face any obstacle this disease threw in our way.

Caregiving - A Choice Made

Being a caregiver was a choice I made. It was given a lot of thought and consideration, fully knowing my career would suffer and that I could lose my job, my friendships would suffer (but didn't) because I wouldn't have the time to spend with them, and any relationship was out of the question because Kelly and my job would require 101 percent of my time.

Family and friends tried to persuade me to institutionalize Kelly when she was about mid-stage and were putting a lot of pressure on me. My father, in particular, was trying to approach our situation without emotion, he said. In reality, he didn't want his child to have to suffer through what he knew was in our future.

To be honest, I did look into possible facilities that could care for Kelly. They are still, almost 20 years later, few and far between that have experience in HD care. The only one I found at that time was Jim Pollard's facility in Massachusetts, and after weighing the consideration of moving or sending Kelly too far away, I made my decision.

Maybe my choice was 99 percent easier because I was dealing with helping my daughter/only child. But once that choice WAS made, I could live 100 percent with it, and those that couldn't were told to keep their opinions to themselves from then on out.

Thankfully, they all honored that, and I never felt a need to complain about being a caregiver because it was a conscientious decision. I would verbalize about how difficult it got at times, and why, but *never* reconsidered the decision to care for Kelly at home.

The "Contract"

Once this decision was made, I promised Kelly that I'd always take care of her AS long as she was my partner in her care, which meant she had to help me wherever she could, for as long as she could. I sat her down and talked to her about it with my best friend, her Godmother Janis, as a "witness." I wrote up this "contract" that both Kelly and I had to sign. For as long as she could, she kept up her part of the agreement, but there were a lot of times, too, where with the pure stubbornness that seems to be inherent with HD (plus she came from a long line of stubborn people), she'd rebel and refuse to do things (laundry, dishes, etc.). I'd try rationalizing . . . of course, to no avail . . . then would calmly start looking up nursing homes in the phone book, telling her how sorry I was that she would rather move to one of those than to keep our agreement. She'd give me "that" look of not knowing if I were serious or what . . . until she heard me talking about whether they had a "bed" and what would the cost be and how soon could I move her there (I'd call my mom, who would just lay the phone down while I played out this scenario) . . . then Kelly would start hollering, "NO, MOM, NO," and we'd have a good cry, and she'd start helping again.

Am hopeful she's looking down, laughing . . . now . . . at how I duped her, but it worked! I should say that I took Kelly to several local nursing homes/assisted living facilities, as she did want to move out and be on her own, which was natural for any young adult. However, after seeing that not only would she be a good 50 or 60 years younger than most residents, she would have to share a room and TV with someone, abide by the home's rules/hours, etc., she decided living at home was much more to her liking! (She had Mom wrapped around her little finger and knew it!)

When Total Care Was Needed

In the summer of 1994, I was faced with the decision of having to quit work and go on welfare in order to continue caring for Kelly at home. I had remodeled our townhouse in late 1993 to make it "Kelly friendly" by putting down thick carpeting and removing all furniture that could hurt her if she fell or moving it to the outward walls of a room. I then enclosed the 12' x 22' patio in our yard and made it into a room downstairs for Kelly.

Kelly would have a fall at home at least once a month, sometimes calling me (ten minutes away at work) or calling EMS down the street because (according to her) they were all young, good looking guys.

Threat of Arrest for Abuse

The last call from EMS at work greeted me not only with the Fire Department and EMS but also with an officer from the sheriff's department. He, very kindly and with compassion, told me that he had been called in by the EMS because of the frequency of their visits due to Kelly's falls. In his opinion, he stated, it was obvious that Kelly was getting excellent care at home, and it was also fortunate I only worked ten minutes away. However, since I was *aware* of her disease/condition, he said, by law, he should *arrest me* for neglect/abuse for leaving her unattended. He then went on to tell me that, as a minimum, I had to post an emergency phone number where I could be reached 24/7 on the front and back doors and make this notice visible anywhere in the house where Kelly might be. The first thing I did after he left was get a cell phone and plaster the numbers all over my house and outside!

Our Regimen

At this time, Kelly looked very healthy and only had a mild chorea. She could still eat normal foods and hadn't had any choking experiences. She learned what she could eat and not, and had a strong sense of self-protection, refusing anything she knew she had trouble with. She was very nocturnal, staying up till all hours, watching TV, and sleeping until noon each day. Our regimen had been I would go home at noon and get her washed and dressed, feed her lunch, then get her settled into the living room, where she had her cache of food and drinks. The phone, with very large buttons, was pre-programmed for calling me at work and calling the EMS, her TV was programmed to her favorite channels, etc.

Kelly was still able to transport herself from the couch to a dining room chair on casters that she used in the house, into the bathroom with grab bars, and back into the living room. She used those chairs with casters for years vs. a wheelchair! However, if she missed the couch and wound up on the floor, a lot of times, she wasn't able to get herself back up, so she'd either call me at work or call EMS.

After the first couple of times of getting herself worked up into a panic, having near seizures, etc., I told her if she wasn't hurt to just lie calmly on the floor and watch TV until I got there. After that, she usually didn't panic *unless* she couldn't reach my secretary or me immediately; then she would call EMS anyway.

Help at Work

Naturally, what the sheriff said shook me to the core. I had been working for Honeywell for 33 years at that time. I went in to work the next day and spoke to my manager about the situation at home, explaining how I felt I would have to quit work. Honeywell was very compassionate and changed my work schedule to where I went into work in the mornings, then worked from home via computer in the afternoon. I had a very challenging position of managing multi-million-dollar subcontracts and also had twelve direct reporting people, so I'm not indicating that this was easy for me to juggle, but hey, aren't all HD caregivers superhuman?

Later Stages Starting

In October 1995, Kelly had her first bout of pneumonia. She was asphyxiating thin liquids into her lungs. The motor capability for normal reflex in choking was affected, and Kelly couldn't determine when something was going down the wrong pipe. Instead of listening to her doctor trying to force a feeding tube at that time, we just modified how Kelly ate. All of her drinks were thickened with Thick-It, which is an overly priced thickener you can buy at most pharmacies. We eliminated all dairy products since they have the highest bacteria, which, once ingested into the lungs, can cause aspiration pneumonia within 24 hours.

Doctor Ignores Advance Directives

Kelly's primary care physician, at that time, was "college educated" on Huntington's disease and knew the course of the disease. We had discussed with her several times Kelly's wishes about not wanting a feeding tube. When she ordered one, *without our consent or knowledge* on this hospital emergency, I was outraged. It was then I learned you need to ASK your physician whether they will HONOR your advance directives because many *will not* because it is against their code of ethics. This doctor was fired as Kelly's primary physician, and complaints were filed against our insurance provider (Blue Cross/Blue Shield), my employer Honeywell (self-insured), the state board of medicine, and the AMA (American Medical Association).

The Hospice Decision

While in the hospital in 1995, the doctor recommended physical and occupational therapy for Kelly, which would be fully covered if she were transported directly from the hospital to the rehabilitation facility. By this time, Kelly's chorea was much worse, and she was having difficulty even maneuvering her electric wheelchair.

Their "plan of action" included looking into making a method of converting her wheelchair with a straw type device to allow her to operate it by blowing into the straw and several other things that sounded very promising and positive for Kelly. After a week there and spending every spare minute there with Kelly, I could see they weren't doing anything but collecting insurance money. *What was their final recommendation?* Kelly loved clowns, and they thought I should take her to clown training, where she could be a clown, visiting hospitals!!

A Serious Decision

The very serious outcome of this whole episode, however, was that I had to finally face the facts that Kelly could no longer be alone, even in the mornings. Kelly was down to about 100 pounds. At that time, it was recommended that Hospice become involved in her care. That had been recommended two years before then, too, but we had declined. This time, I felt the need was real, as I could no longer care for Kelly at home and work full time without some help . . . it had become too dangerous to leave her alone.

There is no way of knowing how our lives would have been affected if the Hospice of the Florida Suncoast hadn't sent their "angels" in to help with Kelly and if my employer, Honeywell, hadn't been compassionate and caring enough to allow me to telecommute from home half days. Like everyone else, your first reaction to "Hospice" is "death" is imminent . . . oh, God, does that hurt, especially when it's your only child. I won't say it went easy at first because when Hospice first visited us, we got into a huge fight because of their perception of Kelly as someone young, looking "healthy," and not needing their care. After an education in Huntington's disease, and their going back to find out more about it, Kelly was accepted.

Talking It Over with Kelly

Before Hospice came, I had to discuss this with Kelly. Naturally, she was upset, too, thinking she was going to die in six months or less until I explained it to her that ONLY God could make that decision, and we just needed to think of Hospice as someone to help us at home in her care, so Mom could continue working and paying the bills. Once Kelly understood this, she welcomed their care because no matter how much someone with HD might tell you they don't need it, they are *relieved* to know someone is nearby 24/7.

The Disappointment and Personal Losses

June 12, 1996, after three years of being on the list to be the first person to have the fetal transplant procedure done at University of South Florida (USF) and placing every HOPE we had of stopping the progression of HD in Kelly, we were advised that they were finally approved to do this procedure. BUT [why do I hate that word?], they had changed their requirements and no longer wanted someone in middle to late stages of HD, but someone recently diagnosed. This was one of the most devastating times for Kelly, as well as for our whole family. After explaining this all in medical technological terms to Kelly, who was so excited about hearing WHEN she would have this operation done . . . I sat there shaking and crying and said to the doctor, *"YOU explain this to her in English."*

Kelly was getting upset, seeing how upset I was, and her chorea worsened. The doctor just responded with, *"You're becoming way too emotional over this,"* when I said to Kelly, very calmly, *"Honey, what Dr. H. is saying is that they won't be able to use you for this operation right now,"* and she started crying, *"NO! NO!"* and trying to say, *"I want to drive. I want to LIVE!"*

Then he said, "It's obvious you are both overreacting," and started to walk out of the room. I lost it. I started screaming at him what an insensitive b**** he was, etc., etc. Every patient in there heard me. We never went back there again.

Two days later, my dad, who was very healthy at age 76, dropped dead of a heart attack. Two days after that, Kelly became incontinent, and her physical condition started to deteriorate more rapidly. But being the survivor she was, she still never gave up hope that the researchers would find SOMETHING that would help her. I read her every new piece of research that looked like it could help one day. After my dad died, we moved my mom back into the area to be closer to my brother, sister, and me. Although she was healthy, she did have a drinking problem that was eroding her health.

The Feeding Tube

Further Decline in Health

On August 11, 1996, Kelly was admitted to the hospital after her fever reached 104.9 degrees. She was totally dehydrated, her oxygen was at 60 percent, her potassium was depleted, and she had developed pneumonia and was close to death.

The doctors said that Kelly must be one hell of a fighter, since she should not have survived the fever's ravaging of her body. He told me she would have been gone in 12 hours if I hadn't ignored the nurses and doctor and brought her in. He chewed me out for letting the nurse tell me Kelly wasn't dehydrated because when she pinched her skin, it came right back. He said even idiots knew the "pinch test" doesn't work on young people!

Listen to Your Instincts

I knew then that I would never listen to a professional again nor take everything they said as the gospel. I would follow my heart in caring for Kelly. They had been treating her with the wrong antibiotics at home and hadn't taken proper tests, etc. The hospital was surprised that irreversible damage had not been done to her already ravaged brain from the high fevers. By this point, Kelly had a new primary care physician through Hospice who was an oncologist. I truly feel an oncologist has a better understanding of a patient's care during the end stages of life. After she almost died, Kelly's doctor placed a "stat" in her medical file that ordered everyone to "*do as Mrs. Miller suggests.*" He admitted to me that I knew more about my daughter and Huntington's disease than he was able to learn. This was after several different medications had been ordered by the nurses for Kelly at different times which would have caused her more harm than good. The doctor and the nurses had good intentions, but they really didn't know Huntington's. After I researched any medication they recommended, in most cases, I would tell Hospice never to give them to Kelly [*ever*] and threw them away. They were not allowed to start her on any medication without my permission.

Wrong Medications

Speaking of medications, when you're under Hospice care, remember that typically, they order the medication through their pharmacy. In this area, Hospice handles thousands of patients; at any given point, quite a few of them have the name Miller. Twice, the wrong medications were delivered for Kelly, and if I hadn't been home to receive them, and look them up, the nurses would have given them to Kelly. Both would have caused her immediate death because they were for another Miller with a different health problem.

Questioning "Competency"

Kelly's doctor told us in the hospital that Kelly had to make a choice. She needed a feeding tube to live. Even though Kelly had lost her ability to verbalize, her feelings, her eyes and nods spoke volumes!! At this time, the doctors had to question Kelly's competency for her to make her own decision. They were amazed at her awareness and understanding and decided she *was* competent to make her own decision about whether or not to have a feeding tube. What I had to explain to them is not to ask *the standard questions,* like what year it is or who the president is. Since, at this stage of HD, the person's world usually revolves around TV, family, etc., I told them to question her on those things. She could tell you every TV show, time, and station but didn't give a damn who the president was!

Kelly's Choice to LIVE

After explaining the choices Kelly had, and the procedure for the feeding tube and how, in someone so young, having the tube could possibly give her many more years to live, we left Kelly alone in the room to make her decision. I went outside and cried my very soul dry. No one or no words could comfort me. I was also torn with leaving Kelly alone to make that decision because I knew she depended on me; therefore, I knew I could not be in the room with her to influence her choice in any way. It was God and I alone in that parking lot with my praying that He give Kelly the guidance to make the decision that would be best for her.

After 30 minutes had passed, the doctors and I returned to Kelly's room. I don't remember breathing for the past 30 minutes, but the minute we walked through the door, Kelly had this huge grin on her face and said, as clear as a bell, **"I WANT TO LIVE!"** . . . and I could breathe again.

Re-ask "The" Question

I know there are many pros and cons about having a feeding tube. The only thing I would like to add is that (especially in young people) if they are cognitive and aware, even though they may have previously been adamant about not wanting a feeding tube, when the time comes where it is a life or death situation, they should be given the right to reconsider that choice. Like Kelly, there have been other young people with Huntington's disease that, when faced with this final decision, have changed their minds. Also, please see my articles on feeding tubes. They really aren't difficult to care for.

Saying Goodbye

To have to tell your child that it is okay to let go, if they want to . . . that you'll be with them again one day . . . is THE hardest thing any parent has to do. And yet, we must when the time seems near. The first time Kelly and I discussed this was three years before she died. At first, she was a little angry and upset and asked me if I wanted her to die. She had been delirious from dehydration and was seeing angels all around her. Kelly fought hard to live then, and boy, did we both have a good, long cry over that first discussion.

Having this discussion with your loved ones lets them know you understand that fear staring them in the face. It lets them know you are there, which they like to have constant reminders about. During this time, they may be experiencing deep fears of abandonment, even from those that love them. No matter what stage of the disease, we can never know for sure how much time someone has. That's why it's so very important to remember to count each and every day as its own entity and a gift to treasure.

You can never say **"*I Love You*" too often**.

Seizures and Night Fears

Kelly didn't have seizures towards the end but had them in her early 20s. They were usually brought on by her hyperventilating by becoming overly excited about something. After the first grand mal seizure, I learned to see the signs and 98 percent of the time could stop them before they went into full-blown seizures by getting her calmed down.

Pre-Seizure Signs

In Kelly, the signs were sweating profusely [especially from her knees], chorea became much worse, body clammy and cool, but the key thing was her eyes would dilate until the entire color was gone, and then, the split second before having the seizure, would shrink to the size of a pinhead. She would go into a trance-like state right before having the bodily movements of a seizure.

Stopping Her Seizures

If it got that far, typically I could "bring her back" by yelling, calmly, soothing words into her ear until she began to focus again. Well, I don't know if they were soothing—mostly just calmly and LOUD, *"Kelly, Kelly, Kelly, you're having a seizure, honey; calm down. Calm down, honey. Mom is here, and everything will be all right."* Her eyes would start to refocus, and she'd smile and say, *"I was having a seizure, wasn't I, Mom?"*

Seizures and high fevers scared the hell out of me more than anything else with HD. Both can do more damage to the brain, which isn't good, especially for someone with HD. Twice, when Kelly had one of her very high fever bouts, she went into multiple seizures. The nurse was shocked, as she had never seen anyone have so many in such a short time nor be "pulled back" out of one by coaching.

Night Fears

Seizures are scary and frustrating where you feel at your wit's end. It dawned on me that if seizures were making me feel this way, just imagine how Kelly felt! Kelly was very scared; her body had changed, and she didn't have the ability to communicate her fears. Lying there, especially in the dark, they are more aware of, and scared of, dying.

Kelly's eyesight was also affected in the later stages of HD. Although I couldn't get her in to have them examined, I would test her myself by holding up fingers, etc. at different distances. During the last six months, if TV became harder for her to see, I bought a larger set!

Shadows in the room can be very scary if you don't know what they are, and you're helpless and alone. We learned leaving a light on in her room eliminated those "shadow monsters" that were coming from shadows cast by the TV light!

I had a long talk with Kelly when she started to become afraid at night, talking to her about her fears and asking different questions for her to nod her head to. She cried when she realized I understood.

Even with baby monitors and constant checking on her, in the later stages, Kelly was more at rest when she could physically see me. That's when I started sleeping in her room at night, so she could rest. Her voice had become almost inaudible, to the point where her moans or cries for help could not be heard on the monitor over the sound of the TV in her room, even though the monitor was in the bed, near to her head.

Another Tragedy

On June 3, 1998, after not being able to reach my mom at

noon or for the next several hours, I called the Hospice nurse back in to watch Kelly so that I could run over to my mom's apartment and check on her. I found her dead with a broken neck from a fall in her bathtub. She had apparently had a stroke, leaning over the tub to hang some underwear that she had washed by hand sometime very early that morning. I had just seen her the afternoon before, bringing groceries over to her place before going home after work. My other "rock" in life was now taken from me.

"WHY, WHY, WHY, WHY?" I kept screaming in my head, over and over. I knew this would devastate Kelly, and although she saw the sadness in my face and swollen eyes later that night when I got home, I lied and told her Grandma had fallen and hurt herself badly but was in the hospital. I wanted Kelly to get a good night's sleep. Kelly woke up during the middle of the night, calling for me. She was sobbing and looking upward towards the sky and trying to say, *"Grandma, Grandma." She knew,* and she wanted to know the truth. Had Mom come to say goodbye to Kelly? Hopefully one day I will hear the answer to that.

A Crack in My Veneer

Apparently, a crack developed in my veneer of "super woman/saint" who could handle just about anything, and I just sort of started to unravel at my seams! "Depression" was not a new word in my vocabulary but definitely one I'd been fortunate enough not to have to deal with personally in what seemed like a zillion years ago (my 20s). After my mom died, Hospice firing our beloved steady nurse, then having to make Mom's, Kelly's and my funeral plans, and Kelly's declining health, I guess it all became a little too much for me to handle. I was intelligent enough to know the symptoms of depression and knew I was building up a classic full-blown case but imagined this would be just another one of those things I could "handle." Shying away from getting involved even with the online HD support group, or even friends, letting things go around the house to the point of disaster, slacking off on my job responsibilities, lack of sleep/too much sleep, sobbing at the drop of a hat to a certain song, etc. became all too familiar to me.

The week after Mom died, I took an "unplanned" week vacation (a day at a time). I just couldn't face anyone and am so fortunate Honeywell understood because during that week, they never knew from day to day if I was coming into work or not. I spent the seven hours the nurse was here each day attacking my house like Mr. Clean, without a break, thinking the physical labor would shake me out of these doldrums, plus I would accomplish getting an organized house. Well, my house was spotless and looked beautiful, Goodwill was richer, and I used muscles my body had forgotten it had! But, after that week, I still found myself quivering all over when I drove into work, and then again driving home, with periodic bouts of shaking and crying in between.

When I recognized I was causing physical damage to my own body (heart palpitations, hyperventilating, etc.) I finally admitted to myself that maybe this was something I *couldn't* handle on my own and sought help through our employee assistance program. At my first visit with the psychologist, I was told I'd probably been in a "severe" state of depression since my dad died and all the major changes in Kelly's health. My mom's death and other things were just the final inevitable straw, which broke the veneer.

The next few months were a blur to me. Kelly's will and spirit seemed to diminish more each day, but I still had hope in my heart that she would rebound as she had so many times before.

The "Kelly Mobile"

In October, we got the chance to take Kelly to her most beloved place, Clearwater Beach, as we were given a free weekend at the Sheraton after a newspaper article appeared in the *St. Petersburg Times* on Kelly. The students at the University of Florida's Mechanical Engineering department had completed their project for Kelly. The "*Kelly Mobile*" was a portable gurney that I could use to take Kelly out of the house that fit into the back of our 1993 Taurus station wagon. It was just like an ambulance gurney, where the front wheels collapsed to place the device (and Kelly) into the back of the wagon. I had gotten the idea after seeing some baby carriages made out of PVC piping that could be taken apart.

When all the newspapers and TV stations came to our house in August to write the story about the "*Kelly Mobile*," Kelly's stamina was better than mine. She loved every second of all the attention, and the gleam in her eyes showed in every picture!

However, although Kelly loved being with our family and friends who all came with us that weekend, her heart really wasn't in this trip, and it took too much of her energy with all of the excitement. It was two months later now . . . where did the shine in my baby's eyes go? Was I too tired and worn out to notice it had gone?

Kelly's Battle Ends

Kelly gave up her battle with HD on November 15, 1998, at the age of 30, two months shy of her 31st birthday. God came and gently took her hand. She left in peace and with the biggest smile on her face.

Kelly's Lessons

This disease robbed Kelly of the chance to experience the gifts of life, like independence, the love of a husband and children, lasting friendships, things that too many of us often take for granted.

Kelly is my most profound joy and love in this life, and she gave me, and everyone who knew her, a great sense of pride in her continuous fight to "live."

The lessons Kelly taught people were humility and unselfish love. She found *joy* in almost everything, gave from the whole of her heart, and forgave all injustices human beings had been capable of inflicting upon her. She was, without a doubt, a beautiful angel on earth. Even when she could no longer verbalize her feelings, her eyes were the windows to her soul. Kelly's cognitive abilities remained very intact throughout the course of her HD.

Would I Do It Again?

We would all like to turn back the hands of time, if even for a few precious minutes, but I don't think very many would ever want to change anything in their lives because everything is a lesson if we learn from it; we'd just re-live the special times. Even if I knew about HD being in Kelly's father's family, I am so *thankful* that I was given Kelly's love to share that the only thing I would want to change is for a cure to have been found in time. If given the chance to do things differently, knowing about HD, life might have been easier for Kelly. Would I have had Kelly, knowing the risk of HD? That's something I can't answer, but I know I could have never been given as much love, or learned so many of life's lessons, if she had not been my child.

I used to tell Kelly God knew she would be a special child, so He looked long and hard to find the mother who would be there and help her in her life before He chose me, that we were a team assembled in heaven that no human being could break or shatter. Then I would tease her about how, in our next lives, our roles would be reversed, and she would be caring for me. Sometimes she would get this mischievous grin on her face, like she was thinking of all the things she could do to me, but then she would shake her head "*yes*" and say, "*I love you,*" which was the only thing besides "*Mom*" that she could say fairly clearly up until her death.

Choices and Lessons HD Teach

"*You have choices. You either change your attitude or your life.*"

You know, when you hear this, you immediately think, "*What a joke! Easier said than done.*" When you're confronted with a life situation like a terminal or serious illness, you learn, finally, that there are things in this life that you . . . no matter how much effort/heart you put into it . . . *cannot* change.

The Serenity Prayer

"*God grant me the serenity
to accept the things I cannot change,
the courage to change the things I can,
and the wisdom to know the difference.*"

Then one day the wisdom to know the difference dawns on you. "*When the student is ready, the teacher appears.*"

Unfortunately, most of us usually subject ourselves to months and years of anger, doubts, frustrations, pity, etc. and are usually on our last rope before we allow this very simple truism to be known to our conscious mind. Once accepted, you learn to adapt your attitude/your life. That IS survival. You learn to trust your own instincts, and most importantly, you learn to laugh at yourself.

Living with HD has taught me what God has wanted all of us to learn, and that is that *"love is the answer."* It's so simple, it's sad how we spend most of our lives chasing answers when they are all in our hearts to begin with, if we'd only open our souls to see.

HD gives us the greatest gifts of all: the importance of love, patience, understanding, compassion for others, and gratitude for life's littlest joys. Look at how many in this world never even scratch the surface of understanding that these things are really what life is all about.

Yes, there is pain and heartache, tears and sadness . . . and although we can't see it when we are experiencing them, they are the ones that eventually teach us the real meaning of life.

I have yet to meet one person touched by HD who doesn't have a beautiful soul/heart full of love.

Love IS Endless

During the last fifteen years of her life, Kelly taught:
"forgiveness"—towards those who demonstrated hostility against her because she was different;
the joy of *"laughter"*—even in the face of impossible adversities;
"humility"—in knowing that there are some things in life over which we have no control;
"faith"—in seeing her acceptance that a greater being was in charge of her life;
"compassion"—towards all things living; and
unending *"love"*—which shone in her eyes, every waking moment of every day.

The last week of her life, I had to tell Kelly that if she wanted, it was okay to let go. That in heaven she would be free of Huntington's and be able to sing and run and talk again and be surrounded by her loved ones that were waiting for her. Normally, in the past, she would look at me angrily when I talked of this, as if to ask if I wanted her gone. This time, she just looked at me with eyes so filled with love, as if to say, "*I know, Mom, and please know how much I love you.*"

I then kidded her that after the holidays would come her 31st birthday, and she shook her head, strongly saying, "No." At first, I thought she meant she would be some other age, but then I remembered her always saying she would never live past 30, even when she was young. The first time she said this was at age five, when I turned 30. She looked at me, matter-of-factly, and declared, "*You know, when I'm 30, I'm going to die.*" Then I teased her about 30 not being old. However, Kelly made this prediction many times during her life. Somehow, in my heart on this November day, I felt that Kelly did not want to go during the holidays but had no intention of waiting until her birthday!

The emptiness in our home and in my heart cannot be described, but early that Sunday afternoon, all of a sudden, my whole being was filled with a sense of peace—Kelly telling me she was so happy and free. Even in my pain, I could not deny her final happiness. Kelly was in such a deep sleep the Saturday night before she died, and so very many family and friends told me that they had either dreamt of her Saturday night or awoke very early Sunday morning thinking of her and wanting to call. I feel that Kelly's spirit was going around saying her good-byes to those she loved.

Her love will continue, and I know she will be an angel of caring for anyone suffering, just as she did in her life. Her compassion for others knew no boundaries, and her abundance of love, and love of life, was felt by everyone who knew her.

A few days later, after taking care of some paperwork at the funeral home, my friend took me to dinner at Dervish Brothers on Sand Key, which we hadn't been to in years. The dining room overlooks the Gulf of Mexico, and the water was so tranquil, with the waves gently breaking against the shore, similar to Kelly's final breathing. I felt such a sense of pain and loss and anger that she couldn't be there . . . then the sun started to set. Never in my life has there ever been a sunset so amazingly pink . . . Kelly's favorite color! The most vivid shades of pink threaded throughout the scattered, wispy clouds and spread over the whole horizon for miles. Everyone was exclaiming how exceptionally beautiful the various shades of pink were!

All of the tables had white candles in various stages of height. Our candle was only burned about one-quarter of its height. Suddenly, the waiter appeared with a brand-new PINK candle at our table and lit it. Janis, Kelly's godmother, and I both gasped, and I asked him why was he changing our candle, and why did he choose pink?? He replied he really didn't know, that he saw a pink candle among the others and thought he would put it on our table. To us, Kelly was smiling down and showing us we were surrounded by her and that she was happy for me to be there.

My life has changed somewhat since then. I continue to carry forth Kelly's love and compassion into my everyday life by trying to help others living with Huntington's. Is there any mystery to the fact whenever I bring my camera to the beach that the sunrises and sunsets are drenched in various colors of pink? To some, probably not. To others, these are a gift from Kelly, letting me know that love is endless. In my heart, I know it is my Kelly saying, *"Hello, Mom, I still love you!"*

Goodbye, My Child
By Jean Elizabeth Miller

Child of my womb,
my heart......
my most profound
heavenly joy.
I watch you go
wrapped in arms of love
and my heart breaks,
shatters.
There is comfort
in knowing you
are whole and at peace
once again
and will welcome me
with love one day.

With love,
Jean & Kelly Miller
(*in heart/in spirit*)
Clearwater, Florida

Note: If you would like to read any of Jean & Kelly Miller's poems, they can be found here: *http://www.renettedavis.com/jean.html*

If anyone would like a copy of any of the articles listed below, please email Jean at *jemiller@tampabay.rr.com:*

A Letter from My Heart – *by Jean on coming to grips with what matters in life*

Coping at the End – *advice from Jean to another mother of a child with JHD*

Two of Kelly's Poems – *"Without You Mom"* and *"You Are Always There"*

"If I Can't Talk, Am I Still Here" – *a poem written by Jean when friends stopped coming to visit*

About Stacey Sargent

Stacey Sargent lives in Douglasville, Georgia, with her husband, Terry "Santini" Sargent. Stacey earned her LPN from Chattahoochee Technical School and works for Visiting Nurse Health System/Hospice Atlanta.

An active member of the JHD community, Stacey lost her son, Cory, to JHD in 2015. She is also the proud mother of a daughter, Kristen, who is not at risk for HD.

Stacey and her husband are also very active in their local Legion. Their commitment to JHD and to the Legion came together in 2010, with the help of a friend, in the form of "Cory's Crusade for a Cure for Juvenile Huntington's Disease." The event has continued annually, raising thousands of dollars, first for Cory's medical expenses and then for JHD research.

Life Interrupted, Volume 2

6

Cory's Crusade for a Cure

I was young when I decided to marry and start having children. Young and in love, at the age of 17, family history wasn't important to me; he was my high school sweetheart. We had a rocky relationship, on/off again, dating other people. I got pregnant at 16, by another boy, but he was the one who stayed by my side, claiming my baby as his, a beautiful daughter whom I named Kristen. We married when she was a year old, and I immediately got pregnant again, even though I was on the pill (which he kept throwing away).

Right after our marriage, he changed; he became angry, abusive, verbally and physically. He couldn't hold a job very long, so we ended up living with parents or friends. He was a high school dropout who cared more about playing sports. I thought a baby was going to fix everything, especially being a boy, but it didn't. I was a senior in high school and had an early curfew, a car he wouldn't allow me to drive, and I couldn't talk to my friends.

When Cory was born, he was three months premature, due to my husband's abuse of me, and weighed only two pounds. While in labor, pumped full of steroids to develop his lungs, one of the nurses even said, "Poor boy," because girls have a higher rate of survival. I was furious with her, then even more scared than I already was. No one thought he was going to make it. In his little incubator, attached to a ventilator, feeding tube, and numerous other machines, he was propped on his side, trying to push himself over. I knew then I had a little fighter on my hands, and he was going to be fine. Cory came home after a little over two months in NICU (neonatal intensive care unit), about three weeks earlier than expected. What did those labor nurses know about survival?!

For two years, he was on a heart and lung monitor, and we had to see a specialist every three months, on top of his regular checkups. I barely graduated high school, having been out for a month after Cory's birth, but thankfully, I had some caring and understanding teachers who took extra time with me to ensure I did. Six months later, I ended the marriage. I could no longer take my husband's alcohol and drug abuse, but most importantly, I could not take his abuse towards my children. During our 14-month marriage, I had called the cops numerous times, but this time, he was gone, and I was determined to have a better life for my children. He ended up in prison for armed bank robbery because he couldn't afford to pay $60 a week in child support. He was sentenced to six years.

Two years later, I remarried a man who loved me and my kids, and most importantly, my kids loved him. On our wedding day, Kristen said, "Yesterday he was Terry; now he is Daddy." Four years later, my husband sent me back to nursing school, I became an LPN, and he joined a band. Four years later, Terry adopted the kids legally.

Searching for Answers

I knew that due to Cory's premature birth, he would always be developmentally delayed. When he started school, Cory had some learning difficulties and a slight speech impairment, but he still seemed pretty much like all the other kids. After first grade, a student under the supervision of the special education department at his school tried to diagnose him as autistic. We finally went to a neurologist, who decided Cory had ADHD and wanted to put him on Ritalin. I refused to give medication because I felt that he was still being a typical boy, full of energy, and decided to try diet modification. We cut out all sugars, artificial coloring, ate fresh vegetables instead of store bought, thanks to my wonderful grandmother who lived next door and agreed to help. We noticed an improvement in his ability to concentrate, and he wasn't as hyper as before.

A year later, we moved, and we noticed a decline in his abilities at school, but we had strayed from his diet quite a bit. Then one day, we noticed a drooping in his face and a drastic decline in his ability to speak. After an MRl, we were told by a neurologist that Cory had Encephalopathy . . . a big word for brain degeneration of unknown cause.

In order to get insurance to cover therapies, and to attach a label everyone would understand, Cory was diagnosed as having spastic cerebral palsy. After some intensive speech therapy, Cory improved. By the time he was in the third grade and had failed his end-of-year testing, summer school, and he failed again, I thought he just wasn't good at testing. We finally decided to try meds for his ADHD, and after repeating the third grade a second time, and summer school, I had to appeal to the board of education, arguing that keeping him with his peers was more important than retaining him. Besides, he was smart; he just couldn't test and retain information well. I thought the medications were working on his ADHD; he wasn't as hyper and did well when we tested him at home. We even saw a psychologist, who, at that time, just saw a child who was small for his age, who was slightly immature, probably due to my overprotection because of his premature birth.

At age ten, Cory started walking on his toes. Again, we took him to therapy; he got braces for his feet (which he hated), and he improved. Then, at the age of 12, he had another decline, this time affecting his posture, his ability to walk, his speech, and his ability to eat/swallow. Cory would often hold food in his mouth like a chipmunk, or he would vomit after meals, losing weight. We took him to the pediatrician, who showed no concern. Cory was placed on medication for nausea as needed, and he continued to vomit, eat very little, and lose weight, even though I was feeding him high fat, high carbs. Then we noticed as he was feeding himself, he would have the fork in hand, looking at it like he was telling it, "Go to my mouth." He was getting stuck all the time. Usually the first to get dressed and at the breakfast table, he now needed direction from me on how to get dressed. He was falling all the time. His body would just get stiff as a board, and he'd fall flat on his face. It was time for a new neurologist.

This new neurologist didn't speak English very well, and we spent so much time clarifying each other, that I decided there was no way in Hades she was treating my child. The next neurologist, number three, looked at me like I was crazy and changed Cory's ADHD medications. A doctor whom I had dealt with in my nursing career via phone and had thought highly of, the next neurologist, number four, saw that something was not right, and was probably the first of many doctors whom I let know that I was in the medical field.

It was during this time that Cory started having trouble sleeping. He would start kicking like a horse, get upset, complain of itching, but Benadryl and lotions didn't help at all. I told the doctor it seemed like an exaggerated case of restless leg syndrome. The medication at the time for RLS was new and not tested in children, so the doctor put Cory on a Parkinson's drug, and it helped. After numerous tests of urine, stool, blood work, and another MRI, the doctor finally admitted to me, after about a year with him, that he didn't have a clue. He sent us to his mentor at Emory, who noted Cory was thin and pale. He asked me why we were there and not in a hospital. I broke down. I just cried and told him how he was our fifth neurologist in Cory's 15 years of life. I told him about all the things we had been through with doctors, therapies, alternative therapies. He personally made some calls and then escorted us to Children's Healthcare of Atlanta on March 30, 2009. We skipped the emergency room and were taken straight to the neurology floor. The next day, we were being seen by every specialist known to man . . . neurology, gastroenterology, orthopedics, therapists, counselors, dieticians, and with every specialist came at least 15 students. No one there believed me when I told them that my son had once played like other children.

During this time, they didn't have all Cory's medications, and I had to send my husband home for them. It was here that they recorded Cory's legs with and without the Parkinson's medication. After almost a week, when yet a sixth neurologist was making rounds, I turned off the cartoons and played our home movies, one of Cory and his sister climbing rocks, running and chasing each other around me. She asked who was in the home movies. I told her it was Cory. She then asked to borrow the videos, said her husband was a neurologist, and she was treating him and our referring doctor to dinner and a movie that night.

Getting a Diagnosis

The next day, as the doctor made her rounds, there were no students. I already knew it was bad news. On April 9, 2009, the doctor brought an aide and asked if we could talk in another room. I was given the diagnosis. She handed me some papers, explaining Huntington's disease. As a licensed practical nurse of nine years, I knew about the disease and had one patient with HD in the skilled facility where I worked. I remember reading over the papers, wondering if I had missed something when I was doing my own research. He was way too young! In my haze, I remember the doctor saying, "At least we figured it out before he had kids and passed it on."

Talk about being kicked in the gut when you're already down! Then came the devastation that there was nothing I could do to help my baby boy. That I would never see my son marry, have children, or have a normal life. I excused myself to go get some fresh air. The ride down in the elevator, the rage came. I screamed inside. Once outside, I walked to the garden. The first person I called was my father, who was in a hospital himself, having back surgery.

"Hello," he said as he answered the phone.

All I could say, or actually scream, was, "My baby is dying because of that (many explicit words) ex-husband, and I am going to kill him!"

After he calmed me down, I explained what had just happened. My daddy is Superman; back surgery was his kryptonite. I know he would have been there if he could have been. I am sure he felt so helpless. Then I cried as I dialed Terry's work number. A coworker answered. Knowing I never call my husband directly and that Cory was in the hospital, he asked if all was okay. I remember saying, "No," and the tears came again. He immediately got Terry to the phone. All I could say was, "We have an answer; our son is dying."

Terry said he was on the way. He returned my call from his cell, we talked, and I cried some more. He called his mother; I called my grandmother, as I knew she was probably about to leave her home for my daily relief. She visited daily, so I could go eat, walk, and get out of the small room alone. I told her to go get Kristen and come, that I was calling my mom, and I would tell everyone at once. I called my mom and told her we had news and that she needed to come to the hospital immediately. I called my best friend, the one person who knew my deepest and darkest fears. I cried some more. Everyone arrived slowly and gathered in the small room with not another inch to spare, oxygen being depleted as I took deep breaths to try and hide my fears and tears in front of family and friends, but most importantly, in front of Cory. As I told our families the news, there were questions about how, how far along is he, how long do we have. You could hear a pin drop between the few answers I had and my sobs. Cory just sat in his hospital bed, watching TV, and so strong.

My daughter wanted to get tested. I told her she wasn't at risk and why, and at the age of 17, she realized I had lied to her her whole life, letting her believe my first husband was her father. Devastation hit again, along with panic. Her father hadn't wanted to be a part of her life, getting another girl pregnant when I was three months pregnant with her. I guess I didn't want her to feel rejected, and the boy I married had stood by me when the other boy didn't, so I had lied. As a mother, I am supposed to kiss my children's hurts away. Because of Huntington's, those hurts are so much more profound than I had ever imagined.

During the two weeks before the devastating news, it was discovered that Cory had many throat and stomach ulcers and a hiatal hernia, probably caused by the poor posture. He also had mild scoliosis, caused by the dystonia. We had already decided on a mic key button (a feeding tube for children, shorter than the traditional tubes, more flush to the skin), but he was going to have a nasogastric tube placed first, until the medication could heal his ulcers, and his weight improved. At the age of 15, he was skin and bones, weighing only 58 pounds. He was also very anemic. The children's hospital was great. They brought in a counselor who showed him what the tube looked like, let him "try it on," and decided he was going to be able emotionally to handle it.

After surgery, the doctor came to the room with a small brown bear and told us he did great. Cory woke up, and like anyone, his hand went straight to the tube coming out of his nose.

We distracted him; he was still very groggy from the anesthesia. At first, he seemed mad about the tube, looking at himself in a mirror. Then he noticed the bear, asked where it came from, and when I told him the doctor, he sighed, then seemed okay with the idea of the tube since he got a bear out of it. We were expected to sit around for two or three weeks, until the mic key surgery. I said we wanted to go home so that we could rest better, and I requested they order him a wheelchair. At first, they didn't want to, but I demanded one for his safety for long distance walks. One arrived, and home health was arranged to teach us about the feedings.

While at home, I applied for Family Medical Leave, started my research, but kept putting it off. The geneticist said she would see us in three months, instead of her usual six months. Maybe it wouldn't be HD; maybe it would be something else. I was still too devastated. I applied for social security disability, and other state programs, again. (I had been asking for help when insurance ran out and kept getting denied.) We went to the wheelchair clinic, and the man wanted to give us an electric wheelchair, which, personally, I am completely against. That, and I knew if it was HD, I was going to have to eventually stay home with him. I had just bought a new car, needed to buy my daughter a car, and didn't want a minivan just yet. I needed to get out of debt fast. We also have a split-level home that I knew we were going to need a ramp on, as well as a handicapped bathroom. And I could just see Cory trying to chase people, mainly the girls, in the school hallways and running over people. So we decided, or rather Cory decided, on a bright orange wheelchair that the man said would grow with him as Cory grew, and even gave him front wheels that lit up in different colors when he moved.

At the age of 15, instead of getting a learner's permit to drive a car, Cory was learning to use a wheelchair. When he was 17, we did go to an HDSA convention in Minnesota, and even though he was in a wheelchair, the other guys were a little jealous that Cory was the young man of the night with the ladies, his lights on the chair lighting the dance floor.

In August, we finally had our appointment with genetics and got our answer. Positive. CAG 85 and 21. But what did it mean? I had a lot of research to do and suddenly felt overwhelmed. We went to Emory Department of Movement Disorders, this time a different doctor who specialized in HD, and she reassured me of JHD's rarity, telling me that Cory was the third JHD case they had ever seen in that clinic. We ran into the doctor who'd escorted us to CHOA, and I stopped to hug him, thanked him for saving my son and giving us more time with him. I know I cried, and I believe he did, too, when he left the waiting area.

Finding Support

During my research on Juvenile Huntington's disease specifically, I saw that there wasn't much. Very little information, no support. I decided to see if there were walks for this disease, and I discovered a walk in my area. After we confirmed Cory's diagnosis, I signed us up. Immediately, the chapter president called me, wanting to learn more about Cory and Juvenile HD; she, too, was at risk for the disease. We talked, and next thing I knew, I was talking about Cory and our struggles at the walk. She and I became close friends. As with anyone who had met Cory, it was love at first sight for both of them. We attend the walk every year, and only twice have other JHDers arrived.

I then found an online support group based in England, and there was where I met another young man who was at risk and knew of other children, some in the USA, and he helped us make contact through social media. I at least had a few people who could relate to our struggles. I went to a local support group meeting once, and it was mainly older people, caregivers, talking about caring for their spouses. There was a young couple there, maybe mid-twenties, that had just discovered HD ran in their family and were debating starting a family of their own. I cried inside for them and prayed that if they had children, they would be fine. I felt out of place; my problems were so different from theirs, and none of them had ever met a child with JHD. Cory was their first, so I didn't return. I kept to my online support groups, those with experience, and people I now call family.

Cory was starting high school in the fall. I went to the middle school and informed them of his new diagnosis because over the years, they had shown genuine concern. I also wanted everyone to know about the new diagnosis, just to show the school that sometimes we have to fight for the correct diagnosis in order to treat properly. At our last meeting of the year, I'd yelled at them, saying, "I can't make the doctors put him in the hospital to figure this out! I know that's where he needs to be!" and left the room.

I went to the high school and demanded a meeting with all his teachers, therapists, and even the principal. We had already been to Emory, an HDSA Center of Excellence, and the social worker there had already contacted the school, sending them information on HD and what little she had on JHD. The middle school had been refusing to increase his therapies for a while because, since he could access the things he needed to at school, home life was not of their concern. This time, I was about to make sure we got all the help we needed. They had already done some reading and had lots of questions and were very helpful in getting me all the help Cory needed.

His speech therapist from third grade was present and could confirm to the others just how much he had declined over the years. I felt I finally had someone on my side! She wanted to get communication devices, which I refused, because I wanted to hear him speak as long as possible. I didn't want him to get lazy. Now I sometimes wish I had, so he could have been more social with family and friends, though his ninth-grade teacher said he could say a million words with just his eyes and smile. I wish I'd recorded his voice for the days I miss him, just to hear him say, "I love you, Mom," one more time.

Cory's Crusade is Born

In April 2010, Cory's Crusade Against Juvenile Huntington's was born. My friend had seen us struggling financially and me stressing over the honey-do list. The biker community gives more than anyone can imagine, always doing rides for charities. She organized the ride; we came up with the name, booked the local bar for the day, booked bands for the day, and 100 bikes showed up. We raised enough money to pay Cory's unpaid medical bills, and one of the bands ended up building and donating the ramp. During the event, another friend whispered to me that she knew we would always need more help and needed to have the ride annually, so we did. Moneys went to help with Cory's needs, and after those were met, any money left over went to research. We did poker rides, then scavenger hunts, and last year, a memorial ride, raising over eight thousand dollars for JHD research, and we will continue to do so.

The following year, Cory was a sophomore in high school, and our family was contacted by a local organization, The Georgia Dream Factory, that grants wishes to sick children. Cory loved to watch hockey and wanted to be a player when he grew up, along with owning his own McDonald's and being a fireman. His physical education coach at the school had even ordered him a special hockey stick to fit across the arm rests of his wheelchair so that he could still participate. He had been in a firetruck before, so he decided he wanted to be a hockey player for a day.

The organization contacted the local NHL team we had at the time, The Atlanta Thrashers, the local news, and his school. His school did a small pep rally for him, the football players pushing him through the banner just like they do at their games, the band played, and the cheerleaders loved on him. When the dream organization told him what all the commotion was about and asked what he thought, Cory looked at me and said, "I love you." This was the last time I ever heard his voice, words that I have learned to not take for granted because you just never know if they will or can be said again. At the game, the Thrashers manager put him in a jersey and a suite, and he let him start the game by lighting the giant Thrasher heads at the top of the arena. His big sister got to ride the Zamboni since Cory was already too weak to hold on and sit up straight. He got to meet Thrash, the mascot, and all the beautiful Thrasher girls. And we were playing his dad's favorite team! Thrashers won! Just Cory's luck.

Calling in Hospice

The disease progressed so quickly that by age 17, his junior year, Cory was unable to speak, unable to attend school, bed bound and completely dependent on us for his every need. He received home-based education. The therapists, upset that they weren't going to have Cory anymore, agreed to see him after school if they had to. At the age of 18, when he was supposed to be coming into manhood and choosing a college, we were choosing which hospice agency to use. The doctor, putting it ever so gently, suggested we get some much-needed help. Being a nurse, I knew it didn't mean Cory was going anywhere soon, but it wouldn't be a surprise if he did.

My main hurdle was convincing the family, which I did, and he was on services two weeks after turning 18, in a pediatric hospice program. We had been approved, then denied social security disability for Cory, told we had to pay them back. I was only working part time, even though I had family support in caring for Cory. I did, with the hospice social worker's help, find an affordable attorney, fought for two long years, and we won our case. A few short months after going on hospice, Cory started having seizures. We both had seen seizures in friends before, but when it's your child, it is the scariest, most helpless feeling on earth. I blamed his hospice nurse for not checking with his neurologist about a medication increase, but it could have been timing. (Please check side effects and read all pharmacy information about medications when giving them to any loved one!)

Cory's second year as a senior (because even the school knew we needed help and was going to keep him until he aged out at 21), I decided I wanted to see him graduate and that he needed to accomplish something in his short life. He needed something he could be proud of himself for. He did manage to graduate at 19, and all our biker friends and our Legion escort truck gave him an escort to the graduation, and during the ceremony, nothing could be heard over the sound of a dozen or more motorcycles and a standing ovation from his entire school and staff! Even today, I meet new people in my community, and they have heard of his grand graduation.

At age 21, Cory was less alert, less aware of his surroundings, and unable to order his first legal alcoholic drink. He never had a real girlfriend, his first kiss, or a prom.

Now, during this time, there were times I had issues with Terry being in a band, feeling like his hobby came first. After Cory's first seizure, he quit music. Having a special needs child is very stressful; adding the not knowing what is wrong is even more stressful. I had told Terry when we got the Juvenile Huntington's diagnosis that I wanted him to leave, that I didn't want any stress in Cory's life. I had promised Cory when we got the news that there would be no more yelling, name calling, or getting mad. Terry wasn't going to let me deny him of Cory's last days, so he stayed. Things got better for a while; then every time Cory declined, it seemed like our relationship did, too. I was asking for help and felt alone. We had no sex life, no couple time, so again I asked Terry to go to counseling or leave. We both went individually and as a couple. I can say that counseling saved our marriage. It helped us to better understand that we each have different needs and grieve differently. I think it was at this point that I realized we were already grieving.

Losing Cory

Two weeks before Christmas, 2015, Cory's big sister was graduating from college. My little sister, his aunt who is only three years older than Cory, had a baby in July whom he really wanted to hold. The first time he saw the baby, she was six weeks old, and his dystonia was in overdrive, so I told him, "Not right now," words he wasn't used to hearing! He had a small seizure, and it was time to come home. For weeks before Kristen's graduation, I kept telling him about the baby and how she could hold her head up and that he should be able to hold her. He was awake and alert for the entire graduation, smiling with pride for his big sister. He was happy that his big sister was showing him off to all her friends. At my sister's house, we had planned a private family lunch. He and the baby were in the living room, and I heard them both cooing back and forth, a sound from him that was music to my ears. He was happy to be with that baby! We finished lunch, and he held her, with help, of course, and he was again beaming with pride and love. Two days later, at home, surrounded by family, our legion family, his high school teacher, and neighbors, he passed away.

Four years of hospice care, and I still wasn't prepared for that day. I could literally feel and hear my heart shatter as Cory took his last breath. I remember feeling numb as Cory's nurse had us sign the paperwork, dressing Cory one last time in my favorite red shirt and his black flannel pajama pants and long white socks. The funeral home referred to Cory as my son and not "the body" or "the deceased" (which I am deeply grateful for). Then I panicked as Terry took him down the ramp because he didn't have his house shoes on, and weeks later, I was in a panic because I couldn't find them. Something so trivial to most, but it was something I had decided I wanted to put up to remember him by. We wouldn't allow the funeral home to bring the stretcher inside our home. Terry had said long ago, he would carry him out because it was the only way Cory had left this house in years. I was completely fine with that.

My first memory of death, when I was about five years old, my great grandmother wouldn't wake up for breakfast; the next thing I knew, men in black suits came and took her away, and I never saw her again. Although our daughter was a young woman of the age of 23, I didn't want her to have that memory of her brother. To us, it was to symbolize to her and our family that we knew his fight was over, and we willingly gave Cory up. As Terry placed him on the stretcher, and they covered his body (not his face) with the velvet blanket, I had my second breakdown of the night. I watched with tear-filled eyes as the Legion escort truck and the bikes led the hearse to the front of the subdivision, Bob's lights a blur from my tears, the siren and bikes, one of Cory's favorite sounds, bringing a slight joy to my heart. Cory would have been so happy. My family left, and my Legion family stayed with us for a while, and the feeling of complete exhaustion, on every level, physical, mental, emotional, spiritual, set in.

For months, it was hard to sleep, not hearing the machines that we were used to hearing for years, or to wake up and not hear those machines or Cory himself. Certain times of the day, his normal wake up or med times, nap times, and bedtime were also hard. We had had such a strict routine for so many years. I miss our Emory trips, as well as all the nurses and students who would find us to flirt with Cory. I miss the homebound education team; I even miss our Hospice team; though we have kept in touch, it's not the same as our visits.

The last three years have been spent remembering Cory and the years before and how he was doing physically and emotionally. I hope time continues to fly until it is my time to join him. Don't worry, my faith will not allow me to do something stupid, and for those who don't believe, don't stomp on my hopes/dreams. If there were no Heaven, how could he leave me the rocks that I find or send messages of love through other children? Since he has passed, I have felt extreme heartache, on a physical and emotional level. I have felt joy, then felt guilty for having fun or taking a trip and relaxing. I have felt anger, at his biological family for never telling me about this dreadful disease, about all the milestones he has missed out on, and about the new family or people in my life who never got to meet him.

Then there is also guilt. Guilt over things said (before his diagnosis, calling him lazy, being so strict, yelling) and things not done (wishing we had known and taken more vacations as a family). This is the roller coaster of emotion that I will have to ride for the rest of my days, and for those who stick around, thank you. My worst fear is that people will forget him. Thank you for buying this book. Thanks to Help 4 HD for helping me remember my son. I love you all. God has brought us together for a reason, and I am so thankful to Him as well.

In loving memory of Cory Sargent
February 16, 1994-December 12, 2015

About Kinser Cancelmo

Kinser Cancelmo is a financial aid assistant director by day and an HD/JHD warrior by evening and weekend. After losing her daughter Meg to JHD in November of 2015, she started a nonprofit organization in her memory: Meg's Fight for a Cure, Juvenile Huntington's Disease Foundation, Inc.

After losing her husband to HD in February of 2016, Kinser became a board member for Massachusetts for HDSA (Huntington's Disease Society of America). Between working, volunteering for different HD/JHD events and encouraging her older daughter on with her grad school program, Kinser is a force to be reckoned with. Always up for a challenge, and always willing to lend a helping hand or an ear to listen, she lives, eats, and breathes HD and JHD.

You can follow Meg's Foundation on Facebook to learn more about the most current events.

Life Interrupted, Volume 2

7

Meaghan's Story

November 18, 2015

Not an important date on most calendars, but for me, it was to become a day I would never forget. While most people were still in sugar comas from Halloween and gearing up for the joys of spending time with loved ones on Thanksgiving, I was saying goodbye to my daughter, Meaghan.

*****

Meaghan's story starts back when I was in college. I met a handsome man; we were both students at UMass Amherst, and John was the roommate of a friend of mine from high school. He was a year ahead of me and majoring in Business Management. He was cute, smart, kind, and he made me laugh. He seemed to have his future mapped out and was the kind of guy you just knew would be successful. Within a short period of time, it was clear: I wanted to be part of his future.

We were like all young couples in love; we talked about marriage, children, and a future that included grandchildren and growing old together. Little did we know how few of our dreams would come true. Our future would be filled with illness and heartache. How naïve we were.

But for the time being, we were young, having fun, and making memories. We spent the next few years completing our bachelor's degrees, and, after his graduation, John moved from New Jersey to Massachusetts so that we could be together. In just two short years after that move, I graduated, and we got engaged and were married. We both secured jobs we loved, life was on track, and we were both so happy.

John worked for GMAC in the Finance Department, and I was at Springfield College in the Financial Aid Department. Our jobs were demanding, and we worked long hours. We didn't let that detour us from our motto, "Work Hard, Play Hard."

We had a great group of friends in those early years, young couples and singles who enjoyed dinner parties and socializing. We would try to outcook each other, going so far as having annual Chili Cook Offs, complete with elaborate scoring processes and prizes for the winners. John made his own beer, and we loved to entertain. Our house was a gathering place for our social group, and we were proud of the life we had built together. We were also very health conscious in those early years and were in great physical shape, spending a lot of time at the gym and running many miles together. We were working hard, playing hard, and keeping ourselves healthy. If you'd asked me then, I'd have told you we were doing everything right.

We often visited his family in New Jersey, spending time with his mom and siblings. John was from a large Italian family; his five brothers and sisters were scattered around the U.S., and his mother, a widow, still lived in New Jersey. John's father had passed away years earlier at the age of 51, when John was only in high school.

We both loved New York City and would make a point to visit whenever we were in New Jersey. John loved football and was an avid Jets fan. His siblings and high school buddies were all Giants fans, so football Sundays could be wild and raucous—with a lot of screaming, good natured ribbing, eating, laughter, and love.

Since John's father had passed away when John was a teenager, I never had the opportunity to meet my father-in-law. I was told he had passed away from complications from

Huntington's disease; in fact, he had choked to death while eating a late-night snack. Though I was horrified at such a tragic story, and as odd as it seems now, there wasn't much more said about it, and I didn't ask.

After about seven years of married life, we were one of the few couples who had not yet had children. Most of our close group of friends had already had at least one, and we agreed it was time for us to join rank, so to speak. We saw the joy our friends got out of their children, and we wanted the same for us.

At the time, I knew nothing about Huntington's disease, and though I felt awful for all John and his siblings must have gone through to lose their father that early, I didn't even think of researching the disease. It was never presented to me as anything I'd have to give thought to. We didn't have Google or the internet then, and so I just filed "Huntington's disease" away in my brain under "what John's dad had" and didn't give it much more thought. I had no idea how much I didn't know and how much I would soon learn. Thus, I had no idea what was at stake as John and I started to discuss having children. I was young and in love and so excited to be thinking of starting our family. How would I have even known to think that kind of horror would touch my husband or my family? Since the gene wasn't even discovered until 1993, at that point, in the late 80s, even John didn't know his odds or that the odds were against him.

Becoming Parents

Our first born was a beautiful baby girl we named Alyssa. Alyssa gave us quite a scare by being born eight weeks early. At 24 weeks, I went into labor and was put on bed rest and labeled a high-risk pregnancy. Even with all the extra care, that little girl wanted to be born early. We were so lucky with her because she was born healthy and with no major complications. Even though she was eight weeks early, she only needed to stay in the NICU for three weeks before I could bring her home.

Like everything we did together, John and I jumped head first into parenthood. After seven years of "just us," it was a huge change, but we were happy, and John was a great dad. He was never afraid to tackle anything, taking on diapers and midnight feedings with the same energy he put into everything else in his life.

Alyssa was a sweet, easy baby, hitting milestones on time and growing up to be such a joy. We enjoyed watching her navigate the world, and we just loved our new little family. So when four years later, on March 29, 2000, we welcomed Meaghan into the world, we were ecstatic and felt our family was complete. This pregnancy was full-term, and Alyssa was thrilled to be a big sister, helping us wherever she could and doting on her baby sister. As they grew, our two little girls became best friends.

Though it sounds cliché, it's true. I had my best friend by my side, and we were raising two beautiful girls. Life was as I had always dreamed it would be.

However, all was not as perfect as it may have looked on the outside, or as I was pretending that it was. One night, while I was pregnant with Meg, my John, who was just 37, came to me and told me he wanted to get tested for Huntington's disease. I listened in shock as he explained he'd been experiencing what he thought were symptoms of the disease and felt he had to know if he was sick, or if this was all in his head. Looking back now, I understand that he knew. He knew because he had seen his dad's slow deterioration from the disease and was seeing some of the early warning signs. Oh, how hard it must have been to come to me and tell me his fears that day. To tell me he was dying. And though I didn't hear that at first, had not witnessed the devastation of the disease, I think I must have had some inkling I had smacked away and hidden very deep. Denial allowed me to overlook small things I had noticed, like how John's eyes would roll as he was watching TV at night. I thought it strange, but he told me it was just because he was tired. How he was forgetting things at work and at home, behavior we wrote off to being busy parents with two young children. We'd tell each other it was hard to retain all the information we had to keep straight, though I knew I wasn't struggling like he was. He also started getting angry at little things, which was odd because John was the gentlest, most even keeled man I'd ever met. We figured he had a hormone imbalance, which was easily solved by a trip to his doctor for some medication. While I was actively avoiding connecting the dots, John had come to realize he was ill.

Deciding to Test

We talked for hours that night and realized we could not avoid the inevitable. John had to be tested. Even then, I had no idea what could be ahead, no idea just how much my life would change because of this disease about which I had so little information. I just wanted him to get tested so that, again, we could be given the magic fix and move on, get back to our beautiful, messy, noisy, busy normal.

Things would never be normal again.

At that time, we lived in Connecticut, and the University of Connecticut (UCONN) had an HD program that was free for Connecticut residents. With me still not thinking he was ill, we made an appointment. I think even John was, on some level, doubting this could be happening. He continued to try to convince us both that all would be fine. Again, I smile at how naïve we were. So willing to believe it would work out.

John's testing wasn't just one appointment but a series of meetings with doctors, a social worker, and a genetic counselor. The test itself was a simple blood test; however, the results would take months to come back. We simply had no idea what we were getting into. We were shocked when we were advised to, while waiting for the results, get life insurance and long-term care policies. Why were they telling us to plan for John's death? To have insurance policies to care for him long term? We were young; we didn't have to think about that yet. However, we did as we had been advised and got the coverage in place. As it turned out, the information was a Godsend, and, when we needed it, we were blessed to have that protection in place. I have no idea what we would have done without it.

Several months later, the test results came back. We had tried to live life as normally as possible while waiting, but it was stressful, and we were relieved to finally receive the call to come in and discuss the results. As John had suspected all those months ago, he tested positive with a CAG count of 46. We learned that the CAG count is the determiner for the Huntington's gene, with anything over 39 being a strong indicator that the disease will develop. Unfortunately, there is no average age and no way to know when it will hit; the afflicted person will just start to see or feel symptoms, and it will progress at varying rates from there.

John did well for a couple of years after being diagnosed. While I had no idea what to expect, I was not seeing any major changes or sensing anything earth shattering was happening. His mood was even keeled for about a year, initially, and, if he had a bout of anger, it was infrequent and short lived. Odd things began to happen, things that, by themselves, seemed innocent enough, but together started to add up to the harsh reality that his disease was beginning to take over, and he was losing more of himself every day. He'd go grocery shopping and forget which cart was his, often being confronted by a confused shopper who wanted his or her cart back. He'd go out for a run and get lost, calling me to come get him but not knowing where he was. He'd have to read road signs or give me landmarks so that I could find him. He'd decide, while vacuuming, that he needed to take the vacuum apart but then not be able to put it back together. I'd come home from work, and there would be vacuum parts everywhere. Some days, it was so hard not to get frustrated with him, but then I'd feel guilty; this wasn't his fault. I told myself that I was human; it was normal to get upset at the crazy situations he got himself into, that I could only take, could only give so much. I felt like I had three children and had lost my partner. Some days, it was more than I could bear. Then I'd look at John, see him slowly disappearing, and I'd put my game face back on and take care of my husband.

One day, he came to me and handed me the car keys. He was losing his ability to drive and told me he never wanted to hurt me, the girls, or anyone else. He didn't fight this loss, just seemed to accept it. I know it was so hard for him to let go of that piece of independence, and my heart broke for him. I admired his strength and willingness to make the hard decisions and to reduce the friction between us that fighting over his driving would cause. By now, I was in a support group and was hearing horror stories about those with HD being unwilling to give up driving and the subsequent fights and accidents. I took this small hurdle as a blessing from the devil disease that offered none.

Life went on. Believe it or not, because so little was known, neither of us even gave thought to the kids being sick or having the gene. In our minds, there was no connection. John was sick, and that was it. So much so that, even as strong, clear signs were given, we failed to see them for so long. We allowed ourselves to move forward, blissfully unaware that our girls, our precious girls, would ever get sick like Daddy.

Meg's Struggles Begin

As Meg grew into a toddler, we could not believe her energy. We joked that she was non-stop and would keep going strong until the very minute she fell asleep. She was always busy, and we often used the word "feisty" to describe her. She could be defiant and fight hard when she wasn't getting her way, but we just wrote it off to "spunk" and agreed she kept us on our toes. She was our Meg, and we would not have had it any other way. Preschool was tough for Meg; she had trouble conforming to the routine and to the idea that she was expected to behave and follow the teachers' directives. At three, even though my friend was the director of the school, Meg was asked to leave her Child Development Center School because of her behaviors. Meg would throw chairs or major temper tantrums when things didn't go her way; she could be aggressive with the other children and was a disruption to the classroom. We were sad, but we knew that CDC was within their rights to ask her to leave, and we found another school. We knew something wasn't right; we just didn't know what. We told ourselves that she had ADHD and hoped that age and maturity would help. We pinned our hopes on kindergarten and rode out the rest of her preschool years, stepping in when needed and hoping beyond hope she'd grow out of these behaviors.

When it was time for kindergarten, Meg was accepted into a local charter school through the lottery process. We were so excited, as the waiting list was several years long. Our initial joy dimmed a little when, after a few weeks in school, it was clear that Meg was going to have more difficulty in school academically than her older sister.

Meg brought the same energy and spunk to school that she shared with us at home; unfortunately, that level of energy didn't translate well to school, where she was expected to follow a stricter schedule and to gain concepts that seemed unusually difficult for her. Whether it was her defiant nature or her difficulty with the educational concepts, Meg started spending time in the disciplinarian's office; in fact, eventually, she was there more than she was in her classroom. Our girl was struggling, not only academically but socially, as well.

John and I discussed our concerns with each other and the school and, based on what we were all seeing, we decided to have her tested by the Curtis Blake Center at American International College. We were worried what this testing would tell us, but, at the same time, we knew we needed to find out what was going on and to do whatever it took to help Meg be successful.

We scheduled the testing, believing the results would provide the map for us to navigate Meg's educational journey and felt some hope that we could fix this and move on. For three days, Meg spent three or four hours a morning being analyzed by professionals who would then provide her educational team the tools to help her learn. Each morning, I'd drop her off, and she would happily skip into the testing room, ready to hunker down with the testing staff. The staff quickly fell in love with her; she was so easy to love, making it difficult to be cross with her when she acted out. We found ourselves moving between laughter and frustration often with her, but Meg was happy and lived her life to the fullest, like her dad, so we accepted that life with Meg was a bit of a roller coaster, and the testing staff saw evidence of this, too.

After testing was complete, we set up an appointment to meet with the professionals to go over the results. It was at this meeting that we learned Meg had a language-based learning disability. Unfortunately, based on these results and Meg's behavioral issues, the Charter School informed us they could not accommodate Meg's needs. To say I was heartbroken is an understatement, but I didn't have time to dwell on it. I had to find a public school for her, and, in Springfield, where we lived, the schools were known for being less than ideal. There were problems with bullying, gangs, and an overall deficiency within the school system. We were terrified and very unhappy at the prospect of our little girl being immersed in that world. Luckily, I was able to choose from three schools that could best accommodate her needs. I met with the teachers at the school closest to our home and was so pleased with them. I chose this school for Meg, knowing, for at least the next two years, she'd be in her neighborhood school with teachers who were dedicated to her educational success and that we had her in a program best suited for her specific needs. At the time, I was not aware of the similarities between learning issues and Juvenile Huntington's disease. Honestly, JHD was not even on my radar at that point in time; I didn't even know what it was! At this point, I was satisfied that I was doing the best for Meg, and we'd get these issues ironed out, never even dreaming this was the beginning of something much larger.

Around that same time, Meg joined a soccer team with a few of her friends. They were so young and could, sometimes, be found picking flowers out in the field and paying no attention to the game; however, they were learning, having fun, and, when Meg focused, she was on fire. She loved the game and would tear down the field, kicking and jostling for the ball along with the other girls.

While many children can still be physically awkward at that age, we did notice that occasionally Meg would carry her arm in a funny way. She would run with it bent in a 90-degree angle with her hand in the air, almost like she was using it to balance herself. We made note of it but didn't give it a whole lot of thought. She seemed fine, wasn't in any pain, and loved to play soccer. So what if she looked a little goofy when she ran sometimes? We were certain she would grow out of it.

Unfortunately, this awkwardness when running was one of the first signs that something far more sinister than we could ever fathom was beginning to take shape inside our Meg. This awful disease was giving us signs that it was there, taunting and teasing us with tiny clues we could never have been expected to find, no way to make those heartbreaking connections.

In 2002, John had to 'retire' from work. He could no longer hide how sick he was becoming and was unable to perform the duties of his job. I continued to think life would stabilize, and John and I would find a new way of living that would work for us. He was still getting lost or forgetting things, but it had become a part of our days, and we coped as best as we could.

Our days fell into predictable patterns, with no major upsets or further issues with Meg. Both girls were doing well in school, and John and I continued in our new normal. We didn't work out as much; we didn't have time, and John wasn't as strong as he had been, but we still spent a lot of time with family and friends. Blissfully, for the few years following Meg's transfer to a new school, life truly was grand. Back to the American Dream where I could breathe easy, knowing we were happy and basically healthy, our kids were happy and healthy, and all was right with the world. Or so I thought.

After he left work, John was okay for a few years, but slowly he lost the ability to take care of himself, and I could no longer do it alone. He was home with a part-time CNA that helped him make lunch and do physical therapy to keep his muscles from tightening. Again, we adjusted to our new normal and kept going. He was still my John, and I could still pretend this was just a physical impairment, and nothing more.

By 2006, I could no longer deny the severity of our situation, could no longer write off the little oddities I'd see with John or ignore the losses he was suffering almost daily. He could not function without full time, around-the-clock care, and I could not do it alone anymore. I needed help. The doctors told us he was in stage two of the disease, and I made the heart wrenching decision to have him placed in an assisted living facility.

While on some levels, this was devastating, I found I was able to refocus all the energy I had been spending on taking care of John and divert it to our Meg, who greatly needed my attention.

I was now completely alone at home with the girls, and, as Meg's disease progressed, my life went from typical to nightmare in what felt like the blink of an eye. I worked full time, came home and ran Meg to doctors and therapies, regular appointments in Boston, and tried my best to provide a normal life for my older daughter, Alyssa.

No easy feat.

My World Comes Crashing Down Again

While Alyssa continued to progress and gain skills, Meg was losing skills, and it was suggested she have psycho-social testing. We were referred to a psychologist from our area who was highly recommended. Meg was tested, and as I sat and discussed the results with the evaluator, I'll never forget what he told me that day, how hard it hit me. He said Meg's results could be indicative of Juvenile Huntington's disease. I felt like I had stopped breathing, like the world had stopped turning. How was this possible? I was angry at myself for not realizing this had been a possibility or that it had taken so long to figure it out, but, as in the past, I didn't have time to beat myself up or wallow in self-pity. I had to act.

I went right from that meeting to a library where I started researching Juvenile Huntington's disease. What I found terrified me. Meg fit into every category.

Every.

Single.

One.

I stayed in denial just a bit longer, but our Meg was digressing in school, her motor skills were declining, and when she finally was unable to write legibly any more, I gave in and had her tested.

Meg was tested, and she was clinically diagnosed with Juvenile Huntington's disease (JHD), and, in a nutshell, my life was falling apart. No, it had already fallen apart when John moved to assisted living; my life had just crashed and burned. I think I operated for a period after her diagnosis on a combination of shock and sheer determination. I had no choice. To say the next few years were a struggle is an understatement, and it was only going to get worse.

When Meaghan was in sixth grade, she started to really digress, and the progress her classmates were making was in stark contrast to Meaghan's development and behaviors. The school was amazing, and we agreed to place Meg in the Language Based Learning Disabilities class. By eighth grade, she had moved to the Life Skills class, where she would stay for the next two years. She had a full-time paraprofessional, and it truly was the best placement for her for those last two years of her formal education.

In January of 2015, Meaghan suffered a fall and hit her head.

I had had a stair lift installed in anticipation of Meg's ultimate decline. Meg would ride up the stairs, and either Alyssa or I would unhook her and help her off. One afternoon, when I did not immediately respond to her requests for assistance, she unhooked herself and fell down the stairs. She cracked her head, and from there, her neurological digression progressed much more quickly. I was told that head trauma could quicken the progression of the disease. It was like I was being told a very bad joke. Meg had fallen, and now, because of that fall, she would get worse faster. How much more could we take as a family? The cruelty of our reality seemed beyond human limits.

After that incident, Meg started to fall more, had more headaches, and could not be left without medical care. I had to find a CNA so that I could go to work, even though my insurance did NOT cover that necessity. God bless my brother-in-law, as he helped me through all of this.

Again, as a family, we found our new normal, and I went to work, visited John, and managed Meg's home medical care, doctors' appointments, therapy appointments, and CNA schedules. I grocery shopped and tried to keep in touch with friends, and, most difficult, I tried to give Alyssa the best life I could, considering all the obstacles in the way.

The Battle with the Hospital Begins

Life went on like this for several months, until finally, in July of 2015, I knew I had to take Meg to the hospital in the hopes she'd be admitted, and the doctors could provide some relief. Things were getting bad, and I couldn't seem to fix everything as I had been able to in the past.

Meaghan had been having a rough time, more difficult than usual, and that was saying a lot. She hadn't been sleeping, could barely eat, and had developed a rash that was causing her immeasurable pain. I had done everything the doctors had told me to do, but my girl was suffering, and I simply could not tolerate it any further.

Thinking of nothing but helping her feel better, I finally, in the early hours of the morning, abandoning all thoughts of anything else—work, Meaghan's support dog, Dixie, my other daughter, and the fact that I was running on fumes from sheer exhaustion—I put her in the car gently, made sure she was as comfortable as possible, and prepared myself to fight to get her the help she needed. As I started to close her car door, I told her it was going to be okay. Such empty promises, but they were all I had. Meaghan wasn't fighting me tonight. This was unusual. Maybe she was in too much pain, or maybe overwhelming fatigue had robbed her of her moxie, but we made eye contact, and I smiled at her. I loved this little girl, and, as futile as it felt, I was going to make sure the doctors listened to me tonight.

I put my key in the ignition and started both the car and an ordeal that would dominate the next four months of our lives.

We arrived at the ER, and I explained my concerns and Meg's issues. The ER doctor listened and examined her skin ulcer and told me there was nothing he could do for her. He said she'd have to wait until she could get an appointment with the wound specialist at the wound clinic. I was so frustrated. This was NOT why I had brought her to the emergency room in the middle of the night. Her skin ulcer, though troublesome, was only one of the medical concerns she was exhibiting and that were causing her such pain. Meg had a doctor at the wound clinic, and he was aware of her skin ulcer. Meg was also itching to the point where her skin was red, torn up, and swollen. She was not sleeping at all and had been awake for days.

I had told them that her neurologist from one of the Centers of Excellence had requested that she be observed and checked out. I explained she had Juvenile Huntington's disease and that she was suffering with some symptoms that were debilitating, and, at this point, out of control.

I asked—and then demanded—Meg be admitted for observation. The doctor was hesitant and didn't seem to agree with me that she needed to be hospitalized. Up until this point, I had been doing my best to help Meg maintain calm; however, if I was going to have to fight to get her admitted, I was going to need to let them see this was serious, and so I let her become her uncontrollable self.

I stood back and watched as it took four nurses to hold my daughter down to draw blood. At times like this, her strength was almost inhuman. They were having a hell of a time being able to hold her still enough to safely take her blood. The staff was amazed, but to their credit, they kept trying. Meg wasn't calming down, and the situation didn't seem like it would resolve any time soon. At one point, they tried to get her to sit down, but she was in such pain that she was unable to comply without writhing in agony. Between the itching and the neuropathy in her legs, she just could not accommodate the simplest of requests.

Finally, she was given Ativan, and she relaxed enough to allow them to safely examine her. She appeared to have a yeast infection from the antibiotics meant to help stave off infection from the skin ulcers. It was unclear if perhaps the antibiotics could be causing the itching, but the doctor agreed she needed something to relieve her obvious distress and started her on meds to help reduce her pain.

While the doctors were examining her, I called Meg's neurologist in Boston and left a message, letting her know where we were and what was going on. She was just an amazing doctor, so dedicated to Meg and all her patients. I needed her support, and, though it was now 4:00 a.m., she called me right back. She spoke with the doctors and explained that Meg really needed an overhaul, to take it down to basics, address her issues, get her relief, review her medical treatment goals, and have a plan for moving forward. I was so thankful that they not only agreed to speak with her, but also to listen to her advice and admit Meg. I was so happy—Meg would be admitted and get the help she needed.

Or so I thought.

At first, Meg's medical staff and social workers were all wonderful. Everyone seemed on board with the plan to figure out what was going on and to evaluate the best way to help Meg. A pediatric neurologist and a psychiatrist were called to assist her medical team, and I was repeatedly assured they would work together to get Meg relief. I was happy to know she would be taken care of and that I could take time away to get much needed sleep. I hadn't slept more than two or three hours a night since March because that was when Meg stopped sleeping.

Over the next days, I met with "The Team," as I called them, and it was explained what they planned to do and how they could help. I requested only that they coordinate with Meg's neurologist in Boston, as JHD was such a difficult disease, and no one on this team had experience with JHD. Being forever the optimist, I was certain the hospital, a teaching institution, would use this time with Meg to help educate their doctors, nurses, residents, and support staff about this rare and horrific disease. I could not have been more off base.

Over the next several weeks, Meg's meds were adjusted and changed to find the right medical concoction for her. The team met every Friday to share information, and I spoke weekly with Meg's neurologist in Boston to assure myself that the team was implementing her suggestions.

After the first Friday team meeting, I spoke with one of the social workers who would be contacting hospitals, on our behalf, to find one that could accommodate Meaghan's needs. JHD is so rare and the needs so complex, with no two cases being exactly alike, and needs varying so diversely that finding a good fit would be difficult, at best.

Meg's world was small; it truly revolved around me, her sister, and her service dog, Dixie. My world was not much larger. I'd go to work every morning, head home after work to pick up Dixie, and then drive to the hospital to be with Meg. Alyssa, now a sophomore in college, visited between classes and studying. Because of this, I hoped we would be able to find a hospital close enough to home where Alyssa, Dixie, and I could keep our routine with Meg, allowing her to have some sense of normalcy.

So when the list of hospitals able to accommodate Meg was finally presented, and most of them were near Boston, I was crushed. This just wouldn't work. I just couldn't let my baby be that far away, without family and Dixie to be with her every day. I knew it would break her heart, and she wouldn't do well in such a placement; I even feared her overall health would suffer. So I prepared myself to fight.

Over the next few weeks, the Admissions Coordinators would come to visit with me, Meaghan, and her team. After hearing of her intense needs, her monster list of strong medication, and her need for one-to-one assistance, many of the hospitals shied away from accepting her. In their defense, most had never handled a JHD patient before and were ill-equipped to offer a comprehensive setting to adequately help Meaghan. I would make sure to voice my additional concern that the distance would work against Meg medically, and that would seal the deal. The hospitals would politely advise the social worker and me that they would not take on Meg's case. The social workers and I were not the best of friends, but I had to do what was best for Meg and could not worry about their feelings or their agenda. I had my own, and it was focused only on my girl.

Not only was I working with Meg's team, her social workers, and meeting with the hospital administrators, but I was also in contact with the representatives from the various state agencies that were connected to Meg because of her condition. I was exhausted and overwhelmed. I wondered if we'd ever get this worked out and was beginning to lose hope that I would be able to find an acceptable solution for Meaghan.

I started to consider other places I had first investigated when I was trying to find similar placement for my husband. Once his illness progressed to the second, and final, stage of HD, I could no longer take care of him at home. I had found some great places near our home; however, for Meg, the issue was that she was only 15, and none of these facilities would accept a child. Only adults could be patients.

One such hospital was right in Westfield, where I had grown up and gone through school. Not only was it close to home, but this hospital had an HD unit, and I was thrilled when they offered to give me a tour. Unfortunately, once again, Meg was turned away because she was not yet an adult.

That was the beginning of my fight.

The State of Massachusetts runs Western Mass Hospital, which is where I wanted Meaghan to go, at least until I could get my house ready for her to come home. Again, due to her age and the laws that govern who can go there, Meg could not be a candidate. Given the fact that my health care advocate knew of some loopholes, he suggested we ask if the hospital could request a waiver from the State that would allow Meg to be placed there. Now, I knew that this was being actively entertained because I had contacted the governor's office and asked for such placement. It took a bit of time, but the answer that came back was still 'no.'

Due to the complexity of Meg's disease, there were several different doctors involved in her care. One, from the Complex Care division, had agreed to treat Meg in Westfield. I crossed that issue off my list.

Meanwhile, the hospital was making it clear they wanted to discharge Meaghan. They had taken away her 24-hour care nurse and moved her closer to the nurses' station in the hopes that a care facility would take her if she did not need the one-on-one assistance. This was heart wrenching for me and detrimental to Meg, as she loved and needed the interaction and really liked to stand. When Meaghan was lying down, she was uncomfortable after a short period of time. To help make her comfortable, she was removed from the bed and put on the floor, on gym mats that were covered with sheets. If she couldn't stand, this was the most comfortable way for her to spend time. She was being denied basic human needs to mislead a potential care agency and off load her care elsewhere.

My poor girl needed physical and occupational therapy, as well as speech therapy, but I was told that because she was on the adolescent urgent care floor, those services would not be provided. I was horrified, and I was not alone. This was a hospital, and no efforts were being made to help her maintain health; they were merely keeping her alive. Meg was also very skinny. She needed 5000-8000 calories a day to maintain her weight; the disease can alter metabolism, making it difficult for HD patients to maintain their normal weight. With feedings not happening as they should, and extra care not being given to her specific needs, Meg had lost weight and was very thin. I worried that her inactivity would cause further health concerns, and, as it turns out, I was right.

I regularly spoke with her neurologist in Boston, who maintained it was imperative to keep Meg up and moving as much as possible. While I was at work, she was just lying on her mats, and I knew I needed help. I could only do so much alone.

I contacted Meg's former CNA, who'd cared for her in the months prior to her admission to the hospital. The CNA and her agency agreed to allow me to pay her to be at the hospital every day with Meg while I was at work so that she would not be alone and would get opportunities to stand and move off her mats.

The nurses and nursing students at the hospital were amazing. They were as good to Meg as they could be and, like me, were appalled at the hospital administration for not only pulling her 24-hour care nurse, but at the lengths they were going to in order to get Meg out of their hospital.

And that was just the tip of the nastiness iceberg. We continued to meet on Fridays; however, now there was a discharge date assigned, and these meetings now focused not on Meaghan's care, but on Meaghan's departure. I cried in anger and frustration often, and my heart hurt for the way they were treating my daughter. I learned what was meant by the saying, "The strength of a mother knows no boundaries." If I had to rely on human strength, I'd have long ago collapsed, but this was my child, and I wouldn't stop until she had what she needed. I knew what was best for her because my love wasn't tied to budgets or laws or red tape; I merely loved this child, and she would get what she needed. It didn't cross my mind to think otherwise. And so, I kept fighting.

By this time, Meg had lost her ability to walk, was incontinent, and was in pain most of the time. It was becoming increasingly more difficult for her to eat. She couldn't come home like this, as I would be unable to properly care for her. Not only was I still working full time to keep my insurance and pay the bills, but Meg wasn't sleeping nights, and our home wasn't handicapped accessible. I was overwhelmed. If the hospital couldn't handle her care, how would I be able to do it alone at home?

However, it looked like that would be the result; the hospital would continue to fight until I had no resources left to fight with. I needed to start preparing to take my daughter home.

I continued the fight. My friends were invaluable, with many of them using their connections and money to assist me. One started a GoFundMe campaign to help raise money for the changes needed in our home; another had connections with the home builders' association and collaborated with a foreman to build an addition to our home that could accommodate Meg's need for specialized space; a local news anchor was contacted, and I was interviewed with Meg in the hospital, with the hope that Meg's horrible disease could gain some exposure, and I might find support in my local community.

And, as we knew would eventually happen, the hospital set a drop-dead date for Meg's discharge. I was told, regardless of Meg's need for hospitalization, she could no longer stay there. I was a mess. We were working on her transition plan but just were not ready to take Meaghan home yet.

My health care advocate advised me not to pick Meg up at the designated time. He told me they could not send her anywhere without me, her legal guardian, there to pick her up or help her transition. So against every motherly instinct, I was not there at the designated time. Meg's "Auntie" visited her, but I stayed at work. "Auntie" was my health care advocate's wife who had been in all the meetings with the hospital and cared deeply for Meg and would not allow Meg to be alone during this event. If Mom couldn't be there, Auntie could. It provided me with a great deal of emotional comfort in a time of high stress and anxiety.

Meg's discharge time came and went. The hospital called me at work to ask where I was, and I let them know I would not be there, that I disputed their plan and would not be there to assist them with turning my daughter out.

Things went from bad to worse in the blink of an eye.

The Hospital Charges Me with Neglect

When I failed to pick Meg up that awful day, the hospital filed a 51A against me for neglect. I was being charged with a form of child abuse because I refused to let the hospital deny my daughter continued care until a safe alternative could be found for her. I felt strongly they were the abusive party, and yet, here I was, charged with neglect.

A caseworker was assigned to Meg's case, and the interviews began. Meg's pediatrician, CNA, and any other person the State could find was questioned about my care of Meg. I was interviewed several times, and my every decision and action were put under a microscope to assure I hadn't been a neglectful and uncaring mother. How was this happening?

No one believed I would be found a neglectful mother; this whole situation was a power move by the hospital, and I was overwhelmed by all that was happening. My father wrote to the governor's office to try to get help, and my friends and family continued to work toward the inevitable, making my home ready to receive Meg, once she was discharged. We had to be ready for whatever the state agencies, hospital, and insurance companies decided. Regardless of what we felt was best for our Meg, we had to be ready for the final decision, no matter what that might be.

The Deputy Director of Mass Health called a meeting of all the agencies involved, the hospital staff, and me. The meeting would be held on the hospital's home turf, where in a cold, impersonal conference room, my daughter's fate would be decided. On the one hand, I was elated. So many months of upheaval, stress, fighting, sleepless nights, and the continued love and care of my daughter would culminate with this meeting, and I was hoping for an acceptable resolution.

The day arrived. Meeting at 11:00 a.m., in a room of no less than 20 medical professionals, to say it was overwhelming is an understatement. If these people were not on Meg's side, I was outnumbered and ill equipped to continue this fight.

The Deputy Director took the floor and demanded that each agency report on their plan for Meg's transition and long-term care. The Deputy Director was a force to be reckoned with, and there was no place, in her meeting, to provide less than a comprehensive plan. Each agency reported out; however, when it came time for the hospital to report out, their spokesperson seemed to trip over his words, starting and stopping and offering a less than ideal course of action. It quickly became clear the hospital had been the ones neglecting the standards of care for my little girl. It was discovered, through a hammering of questions by the Deputy Director, that Meg's stander was never provided, and she was denied vital Occupational and Physical Therapy that not only would assist her in her day-to-day activities but would also help alleviate the severe pain she experienced when her muscles went unused and further atrophied. It became clear, through this same round of questions, that I was virtually alone in searching for a place for Meg to live once she was unceremoniously dumped from the hospital. The Department of Children and Families (DCF) reported that they had found the hospital's charges against me unsubstantiated and that the report had been knowingly falsely filed. The hospital staff KNEW I was anything but a neglectful mother. Slowly, painfully, the hospital's failures were exposed.

After a long meeting, I was assured Meg would receive 24-hour care once she was discharged and sent home. I couldn't believe it!! My perseverance had paid off! I had WON! Meg would have what she needed! The representatives from Mass Health commended me on my advocacy and asked if they could give me a hug. It was one of the best hugs of my life. Meg would be okay. My daughter would have what she needed. They asked if they could meet Meaghan, and I was honored to introduce them to the little girl behind the big fight. I took them to the fourth floor, her home for the past four months. When we arrived on her floor, Meg was in rare form! She was in her wheelchair and wanted to go for a walk. I ran to her immediately to calm her down and give her hugs and kiss her beautiful face.

The representatives asked to see Meg's room and were appalled when they saw how she'd been living for the past months. We were all glad she was going home; this wasn't the way this little girl should be spending her time. I couldn't wait to get her out of there.

I went home and called every single person that had helped along the way. Everyone was thrilled; we had gotten our victory for Meg. There wasn't a dry eye in my life that day.

As was my routine, I went back to the hospital that night, and Meg's Auntie met me there. We hung out with Meg, sharing Ben and Jerry's ice cream with her and playing and laughing with Dixie, who was a gassy dog that evening! I was calmer than I had been in months; everything was going to be okay. I was so happy.

So happy.

We kissed Meg goodnight and promised we'd be back tomorrow. I was so tired and looking forward to a good night of happy dreams. My girl was coming home! It would be the first night I could sleep without worrying in a very long time.

A Phone Call Changes Everything

I woke up to my cell phone ringing at 11:30 that night. The caller was telling me that Meaghan had gone into cardiac arrest and that I needed to get to the hospital as fast as was possible. I was certain I was having a nightmare; this surely wasn't happening. Two hours ago, I had been eating ice cream with her; she had been laughing with her dog. This was a huge mistake.

By the time I got to her room, I was hysterical. In fact, the minute I arrived, the staff put me in a wheelchair because I could barely hold myself up. I was wheeled to the Pediatric Intensive Care Unit (PICU), where Meg was in a bed, intubated, with wires everywhere.

I wish I could provide more details for the rest of the night, but it's all a blur.

Over the next five days, Meg had so many visitors, they had to move her to a bigger room. Former nurses came and cried as they said goodbye to a child who had become more than a patient; they loved this little girl. Her family of aunts, uncles, grandparents, and cousins came to see her, as did teachers, school and neighborhood friends, my friends—it seemed that anyone who had ever known Meg came to share this time with her. She literally had people camping out in the waiting room, waiting to see my little angel, our little angel.

It was so hard to believe she was sick. She looked so peaceful, and it was easy to forget she had gone through so much, and so much was still unknown. On the second day, the hospital told us an MRI was needed to see how much damage had been done to her brain, due to the lack of oxygen she had suffered. The results from this MRI would help determine what the next steps would be for Meaghan's care.

The morning of the MRI, I asked my best friend's husband, who was also my health care advocate, to accompany me to the testing. On our way down to the testing room, we stopped, held hands, and prayed. We knew this was a defining moment in Meg's and my life, and I was overwhelmed with the headiness of the situation.

When we arrived at the room, we were given earplugs to help lessen the noise of the MRI machine. It was a monster of a machine, and it was difficult to see my baby girl in that large, rumbling monster.

The procedure itself took just ten minutes, and it took only a look and a brief shake of the head from the PICU doctor to have the world come crashing down. The damage was extensive, and my little girl would never be the same if she lived. To say it was the worst moment of my life is an understatement. Everything turned gray, and I just lost it. Thankfully, I was with a friend who could help me function until I could regain my composure and begin to process my new reality.

I went back to Meaghan's room, heart heavy, and explained to Meg's sister, Alyssa, that we had a decision to make. If we left her hooked up to life support, she would languish for an indeterminate amount of time, but we would never have our girl back. We could unplug her from all the wires and machines, and the doctors would keep her comfortable and out of pain, and that would allow her to live out her last days with us by her side.

The decision was nothing less than heart wrenching. Of course, selfishly, we wanted Meg with us, no matter what the circumstance, but we knew the reality was we needed to let her go peacefully, and our hearts would not allow us to keep her here, attached to machines.

We gave ourselves a day to process, pray, cry, and grieve, and, in the end, we made the decision we felt was best for our Meg. She was unplugged from all life-saving equipment. Meg would live – and die – on her own terms, when her body was ready. Our Meg was tough, even in death, and that little fighter held on for three more days. As she had been in nursery school, our girl was going to do it on her own terms. We had always said it would serve her well to be so strong. Alyssa and I were so proud of her for being herself to the very end.

Saying Goodbye

Alyssa and I spent those last moments in her room with her. We would take turns lying next to her in bed, holding her and telling her how loved she was. We whispered to her softly and let her know it was okay to go, and that, while saying goodbye was the hardest thing her sister and I would ever, ever have to do, we knew it was the right thing to do.

As life goes, Meg's dad, my husband and Alyssa's dad, passed away from HD less than three months later. Everything was surreal for the next year. Trying to find our new "normal," pull ourselves back into a place of functioning in the world again, this was a feat and a half.

When asked if I'd do it all over again, had I known then what I know now, without hesitation, I say yes. I loved John very, very much. I would not trade the life we had together for a life that did not include his love. It is far more difficult to answer whether I'd have children, but, as awful as it was to see my children suffer because of this disease, I can't imagine a world where they didn't exist. While our ending was not as we had planned, I can't imagine a life without him, without my girls.

We were forced to say goodbye to our girl and my husband, their dad, and now, now we will use the same energy we had used to fight for her to find a way to say, "GOODBYE, JHD, as well as HD, and good riddance!"

We need a cure NOW.

After Meaghan's death, I started a non-profit in her memory: Meg's Fight for a Cure Juvenile Huntington's Disease Foundation, Inc. You can visit us on Facebook. We have fundraisers, and this year, 2018, we added a golf tournament. I have a lot of friends and family that continually help with all of the efforts to assist research. Won't you check us out?

About Randy Thomason

Randolph Paul Thomason, Jr., was born in Lafayette, Louisiana, and grew up in Tallahassee, Florida, where he lives now with his mom, two cats, and a dog.

Randy is a musician, artist, avid reader, movie buff, and audiophile. He can trace Huntington's back at least four generations in his family.

Randy is in Enroll and has volunteered for other clinical trials but has not been accepted because of exclusion criteria.

He believes God healed him and that miracles do happen, and he believes that there's more hope in the world than just limitations on life. He believes that with hard work, you can break through any boundaries so that the best quality of life can be achieved. He also believes that the more peace, the better, and he strives to find that in his everyday life.

8

Growing Up in a Family with Huntington's

My childhood was insane. It was also magical. All the love in the world. My parents both had a deep value for life because of how much they had paid for it, and even though there was sickness, everything seemed fine for a while.

I first realized something was wrong with my dad when I was two or three years old. Somehow, everything seemed off. He'd grab me too hard, and he'd say things that other people didn't say. He just seemed a little rough with everything he did, and I was kind of scared of him. We started going to a support group in Thomasville, Georgia when I was three, but I didn't really realize why or what it was for. I didn't know what was wrong with my dad, just a vague sense that something was off. Much of my childhood is a fog. I do remember my mom and dad fighting, but not a lot.

My Dad Is Diagnosed with Huntington's

When I was three, my dad was diagnosed with Huntington's, but no one told me. I guess they thought it would hurt more than it would help, or that I was too young to understand. My dad started staying home and not working anymore. My mom worked all the time, and I went to pre-school and also spent a lot of time with my grandparents. I didn't know then that Mom was afraid to leave me with Dad because he had told her that even though he wasn't working, he couldn't take care of me.

When I was five, my parents told me they were separating. My mom says I burst into tears, but I don't remember that, either. Dad and my Uncle Steve, who'd been living with us, moved into a mobile home. My parents had shared custody, so I spent part of each week with Mom and part of each week with Dad. I remember accidents happening a lot when I was hanging out with him. One day, when he was picking me up from kindergarten, all the kids that were waiting for their parents were playing, and Dad started playing with us. He accidentally hurt one of the kids a little bit. Things like that had a big impact on me. I liked going to stay with him, though. I was a little bit spoiled. I remember him taking me to arcades, the mall, movies, and playing games, and I liked those things more than I actually liked spending time with him. Time spent with Dad was always "fun" time, even though it could also be scary. The conversations with Dad and Uncle Steve were kind of painful because they sounded kind of drunk, and things they said sounded kind of rough. Uncle Steve was gentler and softer spoken, but my dad could be hard to take after a while.

My dad loved to hunt and fish. One day, when I was five, my dad took me fishing. He decided to let me run the outboard motor. When I started it, I gave it too much gas, and it threw me out of my seat. My face hit an aluminum rod holder, and I had a long gash across my forehead. I remember there being a lot of blood and my dad taking me back to his trailer. He called my mom and didn't know what to do. She told him to meet her at the emergency room, so off we went. The hospital ended up getting a plastic surgeon to fix my injury.

After that, my mom went back to court and filed for supervised visits with my dad. He was so mad. He felt like he still had rights, and he wasn't going to mess anything up. His thinking was really skewed. He didn't realize that all this was going on because of the Huntington's, and he would tell me he didn't like my mom. That really hurt because it went against my heart.

I Begin to Learn About Huntington's

I don't really remember exactly when I found out that Dad

had Huntington's. I was about eight years old, and he told me I'd better be nice to him because he was sick, and one day, I might have the same thing he had. It made me sad . . . I didn't look forward to it.

At some point, Dad started traveling lots of different places and living out of his car. He finally ended up at Nana's (his mother's) and started living there. My mom would take me over there to see him, but he wouldn't even allow her to come in the yard, or sometimes she'd meet Nana halfway to drop me off. I loved going over there. I loved seeing my family and hanging out with them, and I felt very safe there. Once he got out of Tallahassee, things started to settle down. When his driving got too bad, he stopped driving, but before that, he would take me lots of places that were fun. I had no idea that his driving was dangerous or that he wasn't even supposed to be driving me anywhere.

I had two uncles, Steve and Joey, who also had Huntington's. I also knew that my grandpa, Randolph, had died from Huntington's. My dad had HD from his 30s on, and Uncle Steve had it from about his 40s on, but one of my uncles, Joey, had it a little bit earlier, and his symptoms were the worst, then my dad's, then my Uncle Steve's. Uncle Joey had a lot of physical manifestations, and they hit him early and very hard. He needed constant care. My dad was 12 years older than Joey, but he didn't need nearly the same amount of care because his symptoms were mostly mental. It was very hard to eat at the same table with Uncle Joey because he was so sloppy when he ate.

Uncle Jerry, the oldest of the four, didn't have Huntington's. He had a good business running, so he would take care of the family when they needed help. And my grandma was never short on money, and my step-grandpa, Hollie, was fantastic, one of the finest men I have ever known. He also helped out, and everything seemed comfortable all the time.

Somewhere in elementary school, someone in my dad's family told me that I was at risk for Huntington's. I don't really remember who told me or when, but I remember being sad but optimistic about it. I thought that I could handle it.

Good Times and Happy Memories

I have a lot of good memories of times with my dad. I loved hanging around my grandma's house and being with my family. He'd take me to shoot pool, to air shows, to yard sales, and out to the water. We'd play in the bamboo forest behind Nana's house, and I'd play with cousins and friends that were always stopping by there. When Dad got so he couldn't take me to arcades anymore, he'd buy me Game Boy games, and I'd play those.

Every June, we went to Third Sunday in Pleasant Home, Alabama. This was my grandmother's family reunion, and there were so many people I was related to that I didn't know. I just wanted to hang out with my first cousins, the people I knew. Having to introduce yourself to your own family is pretty embarrassing. We'd eat lots of good food, straight from the fields, and we'd go to the homecoming at the family church, where they had dinner on the grounds and Sacred Harp singing. We'd visit the graves where my grandpa was buried, then later, Steve, then my dad, then Joey. I liked going to the graves so that I could talk to them, especially to my grandpa since I never got to know him.

One of my favorite things to do was going out on Uncle Jerry's boat. One time, we went out on the boat to watch the Blue Angels do their air show. Other times, we went deep sea fishing. I got sick each time. I don't have very good sea legs, and I couldn't catch anything because the fish were too big, but I loved being out there with my dad, my uncles, and PaPa Hollie.

Getting in the car with Uncle Joey was always fun. I can't ever remember him talking—he lost the ability to speak very early on—but when we were in the car, if the radar detector went off, he'd say very clearly, "Beep!"

Uncle Steve was like my best friend. Once my dad started getting really sick, Uncle Steve became like a second father. He worked well with my mom to make sure I had what I needed. He's probably my favorite person I've ever known. We'd drive around town, get food, get whatever I needed for school, and he'd take me over to Milton to see everybody. He'd go to all the high school football games to watch me play the saxophone in the marching band. He gave me my first car. He never got angry; he was always very peaceful.

The Scary, Sad Times

Watching all the crazy things Uncle Steve and Dad would do was scary. They'd act irrationally, trying to do the right thing, but the insanity of Huntington's was sad. I couldn't really say anything because I didn't want them to snap. Uncle Steve was always buying lots of stuff that didn't make sense. He bought a very low-quality computer, expecting that it would solve all his problems with communication, and when it didn't work, he didn't know what to do about it. He bought furniture that he didn't have room for and just stacked it all in the dining room, floor to ceiling. Dad did the same kind of thing, and it seemed like bad decisions just followed both of them around.

When I was in ninth grade, my dad went into the first of three nursing homes. He'd been wandering out on the highway and was almost hit by a car. He'd also been wandering around neighbors' homes at night, scaring them, and he'd stopped eating because he was afraid of choking. He was placed in the psych ward of a hospital in Pensacola. Nana and Uncle Jerry decided that he'd do well with a feeding tube, so he got one. From there, he went to the first nursing home. It was in Panama City, so my mom and I would go visit him on weekends. By then, he actually liked her again, so we could visit him together. I liked going to see him because the care he was getting was appropriate. He needed it, and I was grateful for that.

Nana had him moved twice, each time closer to Milton, where she lived, but that meant he was farther away from us, so then I didn't see him as often. While he was in the second nursing home, in Destin, Uncle Steve killed himself. It was in January of 2003, my senior year of high school. I was at a church youth group, and my mom came and got me and told me. I can't remember clearly anything from that time, but I know we went to Nana's the next day. Uncle Steve had shot himself while at Nana's house. I believe that he did it because he was starting to need care, and he didn't want to burden anyone. Nana was already taking care of two sons with Huntington's.

I remember at the funeral, my dad was shaking so hard that we thought he was going to fall out of his wheelchair. My mom and I got on each side of him and held him. Uncle Steve was buried in the Pleasant Home Baptist Church graveyard, right next to his father.

Five months later, I graduated from high school. Uncle Jerry brought Dad over in the back of his Suburban. Mom gave him his tube feeding, and then we all headed to graduation. I graduated from the same high school where my mom taught, and she'd arranged for my dad's wheelchair to be down on the floor with the graduates instead of up in the bleachers. When it came time for me to walk across the stage, my cousin Jay wheeled my dad up next to the stage. My mom handed me my diploma, and then I ran down the steps to give my dad a big hug. Afterwards, he was able to meet a lot of my friends, and I was so proud. It was one of the best days of my life!

I Decide to Get Tested

I decided to take a year off from school before starting college since I'd already earned several college credits in high school, and I wanted to work and save up some money. I was going to a counselor, and after talking things over with him, I decided to get the blood test to see if I had the Huntington's mutation. I felt like I was ready to know and that I should find out, just to have an honest perspective on my life. If I tested negative, I figured I'd be happier for the rest of my life. If I tested positive, I'd approach life differently. I'd be more thoughtful about college and career choices, and I'd live life to the fullest. I just wanted an honest shot at life.

My mom and I went to the Center of Excellence at Emory in Atlanta, the same place where my dad had been diagnosed. The difference was that when he was diagnosed, there was no genetic test. When we got to my appointment, I spent about an hour talking to the psychologist, the same one who had worked with my dad. She decided that I was okay to do the test, so I had my blood drawn with the understanding that we'd come back in about a month to get the results. While we were waiting, I felt a little anxious, and I didn't want my dad to know I was getting tested. I talked to my best friends about it, and they said they'd pray for me.

A month later, in February 2004, we went back to Emory to get my test results. Two of my mom's friends went with us, and another one met us there. The psychologist took us all in a room, took out the results, and asked me if I still wanted to know. I said I did, so she showed them to me. She had tears in her eyes as she showed me the numbers: CAG 45 and 21. My mom started crying, and I just looked over everything. I was in shock, but I was fine. The psychologist said I should get some counseling when I got back to Tallahassee, but I never went back to my counselor. Once we got outside, I called my best friends and told them the news. I also told everyone that I didn't want anyone to tell my dad.

Hurricane Ivan Strikes with a Vengeance

That August, I started college. Then Hurricane Ivan hit in September. Nana's house was in the path of the storm, but everyone got out of the way and was safe during the hurricane. However, her house was covered by a 20-foot storm surge, flooding about eight feet inside her house from what was just a low-standing bayou.

Nana had just lost Steve; then the hurricane hit and destroyed the house and carried away a lot of memories. My granny had a lot of things around that she called her "pretties," and she lost a good bit of them. Later, I remember enough being salvaged to keep the rebuilt house like home, but it was still not the same. The love there seemed betrayed. My dad and Uncle Joey were in the same room in a nursing home in Milton by then, and they were evacuated farther inland. Unfortunately, the storm came in farther than expected, and the temporary nursing home lost power. Dad got pneumonia. They transported him by ambulance to a hospital, where he was given antibiotics and sent back to the temporary shelter. His pneumonia got worse, so they took him back to the hospital, and he was admitted.

I was going to college that September and working at a restaurant, and doing okay, but not doing so well in college. I'd been to see my dad in the hospital on the weekends, but around the end of September, my Uncle Jerry called me, and said, "If you would, come see your dad. I think it would be the time because it seems like he's not going to make it for much longer." So I got on the road, kept at a safe but quick speed, and got there in time to see him.

When I got there, my family was gathered all around his room. I walked in and sat by his side and talked to him. He couldn't speak, had no tremors, and just sat there looking back at me. I was his whole world, so he was complete.

Time passed, people made their peace with him, and then I talked to him to make ours. I told him that we all loved him so much, that we couldn't love him anymore if we tried, and then we just sat in silence. It was October 1, 2004.

Minutes later, he passed on, but he came back for one breath, and then was gone. Greatest man who ever lived.

I started crying, and everything after was done as it should be. With Uncle Jerry's, Nana's, and my mom's help, I planned my dad's funeral. I was 19 years old. We buried him next to my grandpa and Uncle Steve.

When I went back home, I had a few days off work for grieving, and I talked to one of my professors at the college. She told me I should take the semester off, and so I did, and it was well-timed because I hadn't really been keeping up with my assignments anyway, and I wasn't going to make a very strong start into that part of my life.

Two years after my dad died, Uncle Joey died on Christmas Eve, and everything was finally done for my grandma's loss. Three sons and a house were too much, but we rallied, and it was as good as it could be.

The Darkest Times, and Coming Back from Them

I got an inheritance after my dad died, and I won't even begin to tell you everything, but it was a very dark few years, and then the money was gone. I was diagnosed with Huntington's at the age of 24, retroactive to age 21. Prior to the diagnosis, I ended up in rehab for drugs and drinking. And I just basically bounced around for the next ten years from rehab to rehab, psych ward to psych ward, fix to fix, and finally ended up at the state mental hospital. I made the decision to stop drinking and drugs completely, got in touch with my higher power, cut off my so-called friends, got my chance back by staying clean for the year I was there, and it worked. Today, four years later, I am still clean and sober. I'm fully compliant with the medications I'm on for the psychiatric symptoms of Huntington's. I don't have chorea or any "twitching."

Looking back, knowing I had HD made me appreciate more and hate more than I realized. Complete enlightenment, even if it was just a gut feeling that I didn't identify. I said, "Hey, I'm broken right now, but in my heart, which has just a few stains on it, and is perfectly good, all I'm doing is building love."

Love, appreciation, gratitude, humility, etc. All virtues that grow from hurt. Sure, there were bad things happening, but I have full love, from a full heart. I'm glad I got tested; I don't count it as a mistake at all. But that's me. I'd encourage others to do what is best for them.

I believe God was getting the best out of me. Putting me through trials, so as I would fail, I believed that, in the end, it would be okay, even though the ground was slipping from beneath me. Now, I have years to go before I die, and I'm in perfect health (except for HD), I have my sanity back, I'm making good decisions, and everything is falling into place. And I took the path, every step, until I knew a way out.

Life takes what it takes.

About James Torrington-Valvano

James Torrington-Valvano lives in St. Cloud, Florida, with his husband, Ian, and his mom, Amelia. He has over twenty years of experience working with individuals with disabilities. James was diagnosed with Huntington's disease in 2009, and was a care provider for his brother John until his death in 2016. James lost his father from cancer and Huntington's disease in 2012. There are dozens at risk in his family.

James began WeHaveAFace in 2009, with the idea of producing a film that touched on sensitive topics in the HD community. In 2015, he completed the documentary, *The Huntington's Disease Project: Removing the Mask*, and entered it into the film festival circuit, where it won many awards.

In the meantime, WeHaveAFace.org received its Florida State Incorporation status and became a legal incorporated nonprofit organization in May 2015. In September of 2015, they obtained their IRS Letter of Determination - 501(c)(3) status. The mission of WeHaveAFace is to broaden global awareness of Huntington's disease and Juvenile Huntington's disease. James serves as president of the nonprofit organization.

In collaboration with Help 4 HD International Inc., WeHaveAFace.org produced two documentaries about JHD, *The Warriors, Fighting the Incurable Juvenile Huntington's Disease* (Help 4 HD) and *The Purple Road* (WeHaveAFace) in 2018. Both received numerous awards from film festivals.

James was also named as the Marjorie Guthrie Award Recipient in June 2016 by HDSA (Huntington's Disease Society of America). He is an Associate Member of the Huntington Study Group (HSG) and a member of the European Huntington's Disease Network (EHDN).

For complete information about programs and resources offered by WeHaveAFace, please visit *www.wehaveaface.org*.

9

When the Alarm Went Off ...

Summer 2000

I sat there in a sweating heap of panic and exhaustion. I was
on the floor, sobbing like an infant—hammer in hand, with the
walls closing in around me. A thick blanket of detestable blackness
ravaged me yet again, but it was the year 2000, and there was no
specific rationale for me to be this disconnected from myself and
so psychotically and emotionally dysfunctional. I was working in
Corporate America for an international technology company and
earned a very handsome salary. I was the regional manager for
the entire east coast and was lucky to work from my home office.
My partner (now spouse), Ian, had also been working for an
international petroleum company and traveled throughout the
southeast to train other managers.

Together, we needed or wanted for nothing. We had the
perfect house and fence to match; although it was not a white
picket fence, we had a fence. We decorated our home with all the
bells and whistles. All the bills were consistently paid on time,
with quite a bit of money left to spare. We hosted parties and
entertained family and friends; simply, we were happy. We could
buy whatever we desired and were able to travel anywhere in the
world. We traveled to many states in this beautiful country and
frequented our most favorite destination—Las Vegas. We reserved
catwalk seating in front of Siegfried and Roy, the German-
American duo of magicians and entertainers who became known

for their appearances with white lions and white tigers. We visited the Grand Canyon and went tubing down the Virgin River, which is a tributary of the Colorado River in the states of Utah, Nevada, and Arizona. We experienced so many stunning destinations. We made many sensational memories. However, do not miscalculate this description of the lifestyle we led. We did not live 'the life of Riley,' but our dedication and hard work provided us with the ability to live life comfortably. Everything was earned.

So why was I sitting there on the floor in a messy ball with a hammer in my hand? I am not yet ready to explain. There is more you need to know so you can understand. Honestly, there is too much to tell you, but I will save you from most of it. Over a period of ten years, I voluntarily sought counseling—there was something wrong inside of me. None of the five (yes, five) of the professionals I visited over a ten-year period could ever find out what was wrong with me. Ironically, I worked as a residential counselor for several group homes in Queens, New York, for Catholic Charities. I worked alongside physicians, psychologists, and psychiatrists, and aspired to be a psychologist myself. But that was so very long ago; it was all prior to having the hammer in my hand. Please bear with me.

2001

After the tragedy of 9/11, in New York City, Ian and I lost our jobs but quickly found new employment. This also came with a financial blow, and our lifestyle rapidly changed. I decided to return to work for individuals with disabilities and ran group homes. The field of mental health always gave me such an emotional reward. Ian became employed by another petroleum company, and life continued.

1992

Let me take you back to when I believe the monster started to plant its seed. In 1992, I was just 21 years old, working in Queens, New York, as a residential counselor. My training was serving people with disabilities; my specialty was adaptive equipment and behavioral modification. I was the youngest employee to receive my AMAP certification (Approved Medication Administration Personnel) and was attending Saint John's University in Astoria,

Queens. My plan—to graduate with a double bachelor's in psychology and film/communications. At work, I never had any issues and felt very confident in my role. But while attending college, I began to feel *weird* and began to shy away from people. At that time, I was interning under a wonderful psychologist and asked her for her advice. She said that it could possibly be SAD (Social Anxiety Disorder). Of course, I had heard about this, but I just did not see how this could be happening to me. My personality was outgoing and inclusive, and I was taking major psychology courses. Nonetheless, in the summer of 1993, my best friend Irene (A.K.A. Teddie) asked me to go out of a drink with her. We were two peas in a pod and were inseparable. We had met at a local bar which we frequented often. She began to tell me that her cousins were going through a very nasty divorce, and she was planning on visiting Florida to care for their children while the divorce went through. My first thought was—Florida? Who the hell lives in Florida? Being a hardcore New Yorker, we had a saying back in the day—Only old and retired people move to Florida. The joke would soon be on me.

Teddie left for Florida, and I missed her terribly. We would speak twice a week, and her original plan was to stay until the divorce was final. However, four weeks into her visit, Teddie told me that she had decided to stay in Florida and was going to attend school to get her National Massage Therapy License. My first reaction was shock! How in the world was I going to live without my bestie? We talked a few times over the next month, and she asked me to fly down to Florida and take a vacation. Seriously? Florida? I had accrued quite a bit of vacation time at my job, and after some convincing, I booked my tickets, and within two weeks, I was in the air, flying south.

I arrived in Jacksonville and got off the plane. As with the other passengers, I followed in suit to retrieve my luggage. I remember the feeling. I truly recall it—the moment I walked outside. The feeling was magical. It was literally the scene from The Wizard of Oz, when Dorothy walked through her door, into the land of Oz. I saw the colors . . . foliage . . . palm trees . . . the tropical environment. The heat and humidity filled me so quickly, and I fell in love with all of it in an instant.

Fast Forward

I was willing to throw it all away. I was willing to leave it all behind. Days after arriving in Florida, I decided to stay. The calls I made to everyone back in New York came with resounding shock! I left my job. I left my family. I left my friends. I dropped out of college, eighteen credits short of my degrees. As each day turned into the next, I knew I was finally home. Florida was where I was meant to be.

1994

Before the internet was the place to socialize and seek people via dating sites, the newspaper was our major source of connectivity. Yes, the personal ads. No, I am not ashamed to admit that I submitted a personal ad to my local newspaper in Jacksonville, Florida. Back in those days, being outwardly gay was still a very dangerous thing—especially in Jacksonville, Florida. But I had been living in Jacksonville for a year and was quite lonely. So the ad ran for a few weeks. I was very young and naïve then, but I really wanted to share my life with someone. I had never been in a relationship before, so it was time. Back in those days, you would dial a number and hear the voice and a short description of the people who are interested. After meeting several people, I became discouraged. All of them were not up to par—actually, they were not my cup of tea! Then, I met Him. I will not mention his name. Not because of permission, but because he is not even worthy of acknowledgement. I was so very naïve back then, very young, and inexperienced with relationships. He was a con-artist, but I did not know it at that time. Literally, after meeting him, I left our home and moved in with him. Inexperienced. Stupid. Age-typical. After seven months of verbal abuse, I packed my bags and returned to live with Teddie. This is the short version, only because this specific experience is too difficult for me to write about. But I will have to revisit Him one last time before never mentioning him again.

1995

The lucky number 17 brought me to Ian. I remember hearing the kindness in his voice. At that time, Ian still had a tad bit of his English accent. The night I called him was a night I will never forget. I literally sat with my back up against my closet wall and had my feet sticking outward. We talked for hours; okay, I will not lie, I talked for hours! Ian did talk, but he was a terrific listener! We spoke every night for a week and finally decided to meet.

A week later...

I had just finished my shift working at AT&T and was home my seven o'clock in the evening. Teddie and I had our own place on the west side of town, and she was happy that I had finally found someone to talk to. The doorbell rang about an hour later, and standing before me was a tall, black man. He had a smile on his face, and so did I. I invited him in, and we talked for hours. He was intelligent . . . a professional . . . beautiful inside and out. He was seven years my senior, which was one of my preferences. Ian and I talked all night long until the sun rose the next morning. At that time, Ian worked as the Director of Security for a huge entertainment arena in Jacksonville. He was educated and had his bachelor's degree in Computer Science.

More time went by...

Ian and I remained friends for over a few months. I know he had feelings for me . . . it was obvious. I, on the other hand, had constructed a wall since Him. Ian would come over every day and sometimes spend the night—separately. Ian knew about Him—everything. Ian knew what type of person he was and listened to me when I needed to vent. Then "that day" happened. I received a page from Him, stating that he wanted to see me again. Stupidity and tiny strings still existed at that point. It had been three months since I had seen Him. HE was the first.

I remember that day clearly. It was early morning, and Ian was at work, as was Teddie. I invited Him over and he rushed to my side of town. He knocked, and I opened the door. I turned away and walked into the living room. He followed behind. I will spare you the details and get to what really mattered. After two hours of hearing His excuses and the many "please take me backs," Ian walked through the front door. Although you might think that I should have been shocked, I was not. Ian often came by at different times during the day. Moreover, Ian and I were "just friends," and it was my home. Ian continued to walk into the

house and went to the kitchen. HE and I were sitting at the
kitchen table. Was it awkward? Yes. Each of them knew about one
another, but I was utterly caught up in His stupidity, so I just
remained quiet. Ian began making breakfast. HE continued to give
me looks and even tried to sit closer to me at the table. HE wanted
to mark what He considered his territory. Ian did not flinch, nor
did he say a word; he. continued to cook breakfast. More time
went by in silence until Ian turned around and put two plates of
breakfast in front of Him and me. At that very moment, I was
SHOCKED! At that moment, something inside of me blossomed. I
felt my heart flutter . . . warmth filled my spirit. I grabbed the plate
from Him and looked at Him.

"Get out!" I yelled. "I never want to see you again. You do not
deserve me!" I continued. He got up from the kitchen table and left
my home. That was the moment that changed everything—
changed me. Ian's humility and his unconditional respect for me at
that moment made me finally realize that I was in love with him.
Not Him!

On Valentine's Day of 1995, Ian and I made a lifetime
commitment. It was the beginning of something beautiful, but a
frightening stage for what would come was in construction behind
the drapes.

1996

We had been together for just over a year, and Ian was still
working as the Director of Security. I was working for AT&T in
Quality Control, overseeing hundreds of employees. We would
page each other throughout the day and even speak on the phone.
However, something inside of me wasn't right. Depression and
anxiety began to enter my life without any simple reason. I started
to get snippy with Ian and verbally aggressive. I would frequent
his place of work throughout the week to visit and to watch live
hockey games at the arena which he oversaw. People always
surrounded Ian—lots of people. Many people knew him, and at
that time, I began to get overwhelmed. I started to get jealous, and
it did not matter who it was. I was never that kind of person.
Never.

A Saturday night...

It was close to eight o'clock at night, and I wanted to check in with Ian, so I called him at the arena. He said that he would be working late that night and not to wait up for him. By eleven o'clock I began to stir, so I paged him—411. For those of you who remember, when you would send a 411 page, that meant 'what's going on?' I never got a return page or a phone call. I tried to call him at the arena, but he never picked up. It was now midnight, and the stirring turned into a panic attack. I paced the house and peered outside the window dozens of times. At one o'clock in the morning, he pulled in the driveway. He did his best to enter the house as quietly as possible, not to wake us up. He came into the bedroom to an all-out vicious attack from my inner core. I accused him of cheating and demanded to know who he was with. I called him every name in the book, including the "N" word . . . I was relentless. He stood there in front of me with an oversized box in his hands. He did not respond to any of my abuse; instead, he handed me the box. The monster quickly went back into its bottle as I witnessed the contents of the box. Ian had brought me home a kitten – our first child. The tears ran down my face, and the guilt and embarrassment from within was overbearing.

"I wanted to surprise you." Ian whispered. "I know you wanted to kitten, so I had to meet the family after work to bring him home to you." His words softly set me at ease. "I didn't call you back because I was hoping to surprise you," he continued.

There we were in our bedroom, and in my hands, I held the very first gift Ian had given to me. The most gorgeous baby boy I had ever seen. We named him Dusk, and he became my best friend for 17 years. Dusk was our first child, and I will never forget that terrifying and joyful night.

2004

By this time, I had become much more anxious and socially withdrawn. The anger was persistent throughout the early 2000s. I was always irritated but hid it from everyone in my life. The target was always Ian. I incessantly tested my relationship with Ian to the point that it almost destroyed us. I would lose my temper easily and would constantly accuse him of cheating. It did not matter where we were or what we were doing; the monster from within took over my spirit and body.

It was a humid night in Saint Cloud, Florida, and Ian was working overnight at a local petroleum station. The rule was set in stone: he was to call me at least five times per shift. If not, there would be 'holy hell' to pay. The fifth call did not happen, and it was close to one o'clock in the morning. After clock-watching for over an hour, I grabbed the cordless phone and dialed him directly at the station. Busy. Busy. Busy.

Twenty minutes . . . thirty minutes, I tried again. Busy. Busy. Busy.

The monster within raged and rattled its cage. The sweating began, as did the endless thoughts. I paced . . . and paced . . . I called repeatedly. Busy. Busy. Busy.

"911, is this an emergency?" the operator questioned. Although I would like you to believe that I was calling 911 because I thought something had happened to Ian, I would be lying. At that time, my thoughts were not associated by any concern for his wellbeing but that he was cheating (again).

"I apologize . . . It's not an emergency, but . . ." I began to explain to the operator. I wish I had a recording of the load of bull that the demon within spewed to the woman on the other end. I did my best to keep it short and sincere. I explained to the 911 operator that Ian was a diabetic, and I feared that something happened to him while on his shift at the station. I requested to have a police officer check on him, just in case. I pleaded my case, and she said that she would have someone dispatched to his location. Before letting her go, I made her confirm the address twice. I slammed the phone down on the kitchen counter and proceeded to rush into the bedroom. I emptied all the contents from each of his drawers—clothing, paperwork, miscellaneous items. I knew I would find something. I had to find something.

Thirty minutes had gone by, but it felt like hours. The phone rang, and I bolted to the kitchen, leaving our bedroom ransacked. Within seconds, the phone was in my hand. I grasped the cordless with a sweaty, forceful hand. The caller ID confirmed it was Ian.

Sadly, and shamefully, I cannot go into the gruesome details of how I reacted. However, I can tell you that I was hateful (again). I screamed and even used the lie that I'd told the 911 operator—that I was concerned. But my *concern* turned into madness and vulgarity. He was cheating, and that was the answer within my mind. It was the only answer I accepted . . . believed. I angrily disconnected the call once I was done with my rage. It was only when I went for a cigarette in the garage that I found enough silence to piece together Ian's words during my wrath.

"No, I'm not . . . no . . . stop . . . I'm okay . . . police came here . . . I accidentally knocked the phone off the hook . . ." Those were bits of Ian's words I recall. I felt shame. I felt internally disgusting and unworthy.

Summer 2007

The years came and went, and I could not shake the depression, anxiety, and madness. I had no explanation for what was happening to me. I continued to seek my doctor's advice and took so many different anti-depressants, which made me gain 35 pounds. I visited counselor after counselor, to no avail. Each time, I was told to seek counseling with Ian, but we never did. So why was I siting on the floor with a hammer in my hand? Let me move a bit further in this story; then I will let you know why.

Time quickly moved by, and I decided to fulfill a lifelong dream. Among my passions is the love of sea life. Living in Florida and having the opportunity to live in what I call "my paradise" affords me to visit gorgeous beaches and inlets—filled with God's most beautiful creations. Having an utter fear of sharks, I knew that it would never be possible for me to scuba dive and immerse myself within my friend Nemo's expansive and majestic world. Although I had always surrounded myself with aquariums throughout my life, I needed something more. I decided to leave my job and become a partner of a retail marine aquarium shop. In 2007, my dream came true. I was part business owner of "Open Oceans." Like many aquarium enthusiasts, I would visit many "fish stores" and witness the way in which they were run. You've probably walked into your local aquarium store and wondered to yourself—what died in here? That was not going to happen on my watch! Our store was going to raise the bar. It was going to highlight a true love for the hobby and show respect for sea life every day. Open Oceans was a success, and the community constantly reminded and praised us for our ethics and husbandry of the sea life we sheltered. The establishment was designed to look and feel like a salon. Every customer would be treated like gold and would receive education and quality services. We adopted and instituted a "chemical-free" policy within our practice. I researched marine biology and began to harness and use probiotics and autotrophic microbes: both photoautotrophs and chemoautotrophs, which are naturally found within our oceans. It was a dream come true.

Winter 2009

A very dark cloud was rolling in above Saint Cloud—above my family. I am the seventh of eight children, and growing up in Queens, the neighborhood always knew that the Valvano family stuck together. No matter what, arguments, fights, and the like, we banded together through thick and thin. By this time in history, all my brothers and sisters had moved to Florida and were here for quite some time. Just like in New York, everyone lived literally minutes away from one another. My brother John was the last to unite with the family and finally settled down here in Saint Cloud. We heard over the years that John had had multiple car accidents, but we never read into it. Simply, they were accidents. None of us could see the blackness which was about to shroud all of us, but it was coming.

I was still in love with my job and expanded our services to educate local schools. We often had field trips to our marine aquarium shop and taught children of all ages about marine biology. The only time the monster never showed his face was when I threw myself into my work at the shop. It was my haven, and I would get lost in the love of my passion.

The dark cloud finally settled above us in Saint Cloud, but the thunder and lightning had not sounded yet. When the family finally got to see John (it had been a few years), we noticed something very peculiar about him. His arms, legs, and fingers were "twitching," and it made all of us very concerned. John was one of the most independent individuals you could have ever met. He owned his own business throughout most of my life and was a professional dancer (and instructor) for two decades. But this person we'd just reunited with was not my brother. The entire family would question him, out of concern, but each time, he would deny that anything was wrong. He had his own place of residence as well as employment, but as time moved on, things got worse.

Spring 2009

John decided to come visit me at the shop. I remember that day as if it were yesterday. The store was packed with customers, but I immediately stopped what I was doing to greet my brother. His movements were worse, and his voice was a bit off. Before I could say more than a few words to him, a customer asked me if he could speak with me privately. I remember the customer's eyes— they screamed, it is an emergency! I walked over to the corner of the shop with the customer, and instantly, he pointed outside the front window into the street outside.

"Your brother parked his car in the middle of traffic," the customer whispered.

I remember the huge lump in my throat and the sinking feeling within my stomach. I quickly ran over to John and brought him outside the store. I took his car keys and bolted across the four-lane avenue. As I drove his car into the parking lot, I knew something was terribly wrong! John no longer wanted to stay at the shop. He took his keys from my hand and, within seconds, drove off to his apartment.

A few weeks went by, and the entire family was concerned. We were absolutely terrified! After many arguments and screaming matches, John finally agreed that he should admit himself to the hospital visit for testing. We were so relieved that he agreed, and we waited a couple of days for results to return. For the next day or so, John was quite submissive and relaxed. Seeing this made all of us calm and hopeful.

When the test results came back, the only thing the doctor found was that John had a vitamin B12 deficiency. I remember that exact moment very clearly. I turned to the doctor and told him without pausing that there had to be something more . . . it had to be Parkinson's disease or some other neurological issue. Although I knew that a vitamin B12 deficiency could indeed cause forgetfulness, a change in complexion, and imbalance, there was something more here, and I requested additional tests. The family agreed; so did John, as did the doctor.

Monday: Three weeks later . . .

John had gotten into a major car accident and totally wrecked his vehicle. It was time. John agreed to move in with Mom and Dad, and all of us were relieved that he was safe and under their watch. Following many arguments, John agreed to no longer drive. I would call Mom at least five times each day just to see how things were going. It was such a difficult time back then. John would get angry in an instant, and behavior manifested quite often. If he was told 'no' about anything, he would throw a fit. Mom would call me, and I would rush over to try and calm John down. He would throw chairs at Mom and Dad and demand anything and everything. Those times were so very rough on Mom and Dad. It was rough for all of us, including John.

Wednesday

The phone rang, and I saw that it was Mom. I quickly picked up the phone and immediately asked her if everything was okay. The dark cloud above Saint Cloud became heavier, and the thunder and lightning commenced.

"The blood test came back, and he has something called Huntington's Chorea," Mom reported, trying her best to say the terminology correctly. "I'm looking at it right now on the internet!" she exclaimed.

Right away, I ran to my computer and did the same. As I began reading the description of this thing that had just entered our lives, my stomach began to churn line-by-line.

Mom was crying heavily, and I did everything I could to calm her down. So much following that call blurs together. Instantly, the family fell into an emotional abyss. What were we going to do? What could we do? We had to accept that the monster had officially arrived in Saint Cloud.

Summer 2000

So, why was I sitting on the floor in a pile of myself? Why did I have a hammer in my hand? Let me tell you why.

As I mentioned previously, back in 2000, Ian and I were doing quite well for ourselves. When we bought our home, I began to experience panic attacks and major anxiety. Noise (any sudden noise) would set me off. I convinced Ian that we should have an alarm system installed in the house. He agreed, and the company came and installed one. I was committed to believing that an alarm system would make me feel safe and secure. It became my bubble of control. I did not have to check to see if the windows and doors were locked ten times before laying my head down on my pillow. I no longer had to get up in the middle of the night and check to see if anyone stood outside. Ironically, the only intruder I overlooked was the monster inside of me.

6:00 p.m., Friday night: 1 month later . . .

Ian was away on business, and I was out with a friend. Ian always returned home from travel each Friday night, so I wanted to be home before he arrived. My friend dropped me off at my home at six o'clock in the evening, giving me a few hours before Ian would walk through the front door. I waved goodbye to my friend and unlocked the door. Robotically, I walked over to the alarm control panel and punched in the code. Casually, I did a few chores and went about my business.

6:20 p.m.

Suddenly, the security alarm rang through the house. It startled the hell out of me and the cats. I instinctively ran to the panel to punch in the code. It stopped. I ran to every window and door in the house. Someone was inside. I continued to check every closet and space within the house—nothing. I checked under each bed—nothing. I peered again outside each window—nothing.

6:30 p.m.

"Screech . . . screech . . . screech . . ." The security alarm went off again. I ran to the panel and punched in the code. Nothing happened. The screeching continued, and I awaited the call from the security company, but it never came.

6:45 p.m.

The screeching continued, and the madness inside of me raged. I grabbed the cordless phone and called the security company.

"Hello!" I interrupted the representative before she could finish her sentence. "The alarm is not shutting off, and it's driving me crazy . . . please, what do I do?" I pleaded.

The representative asked me to confirm my password before answering me. I quickly did and was not expecting her response.

"Sir, your account is past due, and the service has been terminated. The alarm will sound, but we can't help you." She reported this news to me as I stood in the garage, trembling, with a cigarette in my hand.

I did not have the energy to continue the call. I hung up, and the reality hit me. I'd forgotten to pay the bill.

7:00 p.m.

The screeching continued, and the rage within began to overflow. How will I stop the screeching? I must stop the screeching!

7:15 p.m.

I stood there in front of the panel. I punched in the code several times—nothing. I did it again, but the screeching was unbearable and relentless. The monster came to the surface, and I was no longer in control. My security bubble had burst, and no one could help me.

7:25 p.m.

I did not realize it until I had looked down on the living room tile. Twenty or so feet of cable coiled at my feet like a snake. I had ripped the panel from the wall and pulled as much of the wiring as I could. The screeching continued, and I stood there, sweating and crying like a baby.

7:30 p.m.

The madness took me into the garage to search for it. I had to get it. After a few minutes, I found the hammer and wielded it like a madman from a horror movie. I ran into the house to find the control panel. In that moment of rage, I could not recall where the main control panel was hiding. I ran from room to room, checking every closet possible, but found nothing.

7:45 p.m.

I almost gave up, but there it stood. It was inside the small hall closet next to the air-conditioning unit. I swung open the door, and there it was—the silver control panel. I began to smash it with all my might . . . again and again. I tried to tear it from the wall. The screeching continued, no matter how badly I destroyed the unit.

8:00 p.m.

I ran back out into the garage and panned each wall—nothing. Then I saw the power something. It was a power pack unit plugged into the ceiling next to the garage door IR unit. I grabbed the ladder from the corner of the garage and set it just below the unit. I climbed to the top, and the rage continued. I swung the hammer and hit the power pack. With one swing, it fell from the outlet. I did not notice that the screeching had stopped until fifteen feet of the alarm cable entangled my body, as I stood on the ladder.

8:15 p.m.

So there I sat in a sweating heap of panic and exhaustion with the hammer in my hand. The silence was deafening, and, literally, I could hear my own heartbeat. I sat among the cabled snake in the middle of my living room, waiting for the rage to leave.

9:00 p.m.

The front door opened, and in walked Ian. His eyes said it all. He stood there, looking at me and the destruction I had caused. Through tears and heavy breaths, I explained what had happened. At that moment, I knew that he knew, something was terribly wrong. The only intruder who had entered the house on that night was the monster from within.

Afterthoughts

Looking back at that point in time, I realize now that the beginning of my own battle with Huntington's disease was occurring. It had been inside of me since Ian and I had gotten together in 1995, but it did not begin to manifest until years later into our relationship. When John received the diagnosis in 2009, the alarm bells went off in Ian's and my mind. Ian and I hid all the years of my insecurities, abuse, anger, and anxiety from everyone around us. Even this story.

In 2009, Dad decided to get tested, and we found that the gene came from him. Mom always suspected *something* wrong with Dad. He had movements of his feet and legs, and his balance was not getting better. I, too, decided to have the genetic test following my father. My primary care physician, who also saw John and Dad, wrote the prescription for the test. Off I went, and then I waited for the results. In my mind, it was just a formality. I already knew the results.

Ten days later, I was at my marine aquarium store, helping customers. The phone rang, and it was my doctor. I asked her for the results, and she requested that I come to her office for a meeting. She knew me . . . she knew me very well. I insisted that she tell me over the phone, and she did. My CAG repeat was 40, and Huntington's disease was confirmed. Was I surprised? Was I shocked? No.

My results shook the family, and my parents took it hard. Clarity came to me and Ian, and the healing and understanding began to rebuild the household I'd been destroying for years. By this time, I had to make a choice. I knew that I should no longer drive because I often got lost or found myself parked in a strip mall, wondering how I even got there. I knew that I was having problems with eye movements, so a decision had to be made. I decided to take my doctor's advice and leave my passion for sea life and proactively take control of my health and life.

Three months after leaving the store, I fell into such a deep depression. For those three months, I sat alone most of the time, rarely shaved or showered. Then the day came. I stood there, looking at myself in the mirror. I saw the reflection of someone I no longer recognized—I didn't have a face. I began to shave myself, and afterwards, I felt something within myself come to life. I needed to take control from the monster. I needed to take control of my life. I began a medication regimen which slowly grounded me. Ian and I openly talked, and I began to learn how to express myself calmly instead of raging. There were times I faltered, but Ian continued to support me at every turn.

I had so much inside of me, so I decided to write a book based on something a psychology professor asked us during class in 1990.

"If you could depict the end of your life, what story would you tell?"

I wrote *One with the Blue* in less than two months and provided readers with some fiction and some truths. It was a way for me to release pain, anger, stress, and so many more emotions. I then joined Facebook with the intentions of finding others who were affected by this disease. This was the beginning of my new life; the decision was oddly destined. I learned so much from thousands of my peers and built incredibly loving relationships over the years.

2009

It was time to join the advocacy train. It was time for me to do something—anything—to help our community. In that same year, I found some incredible people who were willing to join a small team to begin a project called "WeHaveAFace." Its sole purpose was to create the first film of its kind to bring very sensitive subject matter to the forefront. Back in those days, advocacy was strong, but there were too many stigmas existing. Many were afraid to come forward; I totally understood and respected their feelings. But my way of advocacy was different—it was unorthodox, to say the least.

The first decision I made was to enter a five-minute film into the NeruoFilmFestival (hosted by the American Academy of Neurology, or AAN). How was I going to do this? What was I going to create? I spend a few weeks thinking and writing and decided that I would create a silent film. There would be a soundtrack, but I would use visuals to show the world what it "looked" like to have Huntington's disease. The short film was titled: "The Faceless Faces of Huntington's Disease." It was raw, filmed in black-and-white, and had a very eerie soundtrack. I gathered my family and, with their permission, filmed several of them within the production. Within two weeks, I submitted it to the festival. I was scared. I was very scared. I did not know how my peers would react. Within the short film, I coined the word "Monster" to describe Huntington's disease. I utilized a silver mask and a black cloak whenever the "Monster" came into the eye of the camera. It was shocking and scary, but so is this disease.

It was time to share the link on Facebook and let the voting begin, via the AAN. Thousands of votes were cast by individuals in our international community. Although the short film did not win, it finished in the top five. Releasing this short five-minute film came with consequences—directly from the community it was serving. I knew from the onset that the film was going to have an impact, visually and emotionally. Within two days, comments via Facebook and email started to flow through my inbox.

I will admit that the majority of the correspondence was very positive and constructive; however, there were many to the contrary. Here are a few of the actual responses I received:

"How can you call us monsters? YOU are the monster!"

"We are not monsters! You should be ashamed of yourself."

"Your video was too dark, and it was way too scary."

"We are not animals or monsters, and I hate what you are doing!"

"We don't want you representing us like this. You are wrong for doing this to our families."

Truly, the list goes on. At that time, those responses (although within the minority), affected me the most. We had received hundreds upon hundreds of uplifting and positive replies, but I felt so horrible about the negatives ones. During that time, I had a Facebook page specifically for this production to facilitate conversation and to allow my community to get to know me. Looking back, I regret that I took that page down, but during that time, it was quite hurtful. I tried to explain in as many ways as I could the reasoning behind my portrayal of my film, but the pressure and drama it was causing was too much. I learned my very first advocacy lesson that year; you cannot make everyone happy. I needed to move on, so I did.

2010 – 2011

By this time, I had an amazing (yet small) group of advocates who helped me push onward. What were we going to do? How were we going to advocate? I had already created WeHaveAFace.org, and the plan was to create an international documentary which would cover a plethora of topics and sensitive subject matter. It was time to remove the stigmas of Huntington's disease. It was also time for our community to remove their masks and come forward and testify. It was quite difficult back then to find any financial resources to climb this very tall mountain; however, through T-shirt sales and direct donations from our international community, I could begin filming. The film was titled: "The Huntington's Disease Project: Removing the Mask." I traveled to many different locations and received many video testimonies from the international Huntington's community. In 2015, the film was completed and entered into the global film festival circuits. I had no clue what would follow; however, in a very short time, the film won several "Best Feature Documentary" awards and dozens of "Selections." We knew at that moment that the message was heard, as were the voices of our community.

2015 – 2016

The WHAF team grew substantial by this time, and we had expanded our mission into Canada, England, and Germany. We were setting the stage to broaden our reach to fill in gaps which existed. Our aim was to have WeHaveAFace nonprofits in these countries to better the lives of our patients and families. Although this was a huge task, we were committed to bringing countries together to unify the mission.

2017

I often look back through the years at the many hardships and struggles we went through. There were many times I contemplated giving up on the mission and WHAF. Advocacy is not easy, and it comes with thunder and lightning at times—including drama. However, advocacy also comes with more inspiration and hope. The positives ultimately outweigh the negatives. The relationships you build, the people you meet, and the love that fills your heart are worth more than anything else. Our Huntington's and Juvenile Huntington's community has given me my life back.

What about that hammer?

I still have that hammer. I will never get rid of that hammer. I often use it, but when I do, I use it to build and create, not to destroy.

#YouAreLoved

About Dorothy Gerber Pearce

Dorothy Gerber Pearce was born in Kitchener, Ontario, Canada, in November 1946. She grew up in a closely-knit farming community and attended a one-room country school. Following high school and several years of office work, she yearned for adventure and travel. That led to a one-year assignment in a Voluntary Service program under what was then known as the Mennonite Board of Missions and Charities, based in Elkhart, Indiana. That meant living in a group setting and working mainly with local youth in an inner-city setting during a volatile time. The assignment was from October 1968 until October 1969 in St. Petersburg, Florida. It was during the time of the Manson Family murders, the first lunar landing and Woodstock.

After the term was over, Dorothy moved back to Ontario, except this time it was to Ottawa, the capital city of Canada. It was 1971 when she met the man of her dreams. It was gradually revealed that her new husband's mother had HD and that her husband was at risk. Her husband was diagnosed in 1991, and that was two years before the predictive test became available.

Her daughter was diagnosed in 2005, and her son in 2010. By that time, the family had moved back to Kitchener, Ontario. Dorothy eventually learned how to balance caregiving with a full-time career, working for municipal government in the Regional Municipality of Waterloo until her retirement in 2011.

Her husband and daughter have both succumbed to HD, and her son is now in long-term care. Dorothy hopes to settle into a more tranquil existence now that the overlapping caregiving is over, and she can now concentrate on helping her son with his continuing HD battle.

In the meantime, her motto is to be kinder than necessary because every one of us is fighting some kind of battle. Educating others about HD is also a priority.

10

Weathering the Storm

After many decades of upheaval and heartache, my current life seems reasonably calm. I have been a widow since November 2014, and I lost my daughter in December 2017. Only my son remains, and he is now in long-term care. I will turn 72 years old later this year, and it is calming to know that, for the most part, I have weathered the storm. HD has done its worst, and I can now regroup and settle in for the rest of my life.

I have also discovered in the last years that one of the benefits of aging is that we now know for the most part how our lives have turned out. Our bodies are prone to the issues of advancing age, but we can still enjoy the good things in life. I have not always been this philosophical, but somehow, losing two members of my immediate family with the knowledge that I will also lose the third person, unless I succumb first, has put things into sharp perspective.

The horror of HD is not as traumatic as it had been for many decades. I now know that bad things do not always happen to other people. In some ways, I feel that there has been some good in being part of an HD family. My life has been difficult, but I have also learned some valuable lessons. Compassion for others is much easier when we have also suffered. There is so much that I could have taught the younger me throughout the journey. The younger me was far too impetuous and probably would not have listened anyway.

My Early Years

Some background here could shed light on my journey and the forces that shaped me. I was born in 1946, in Kitchener, Ontario, Canada. The unusual part of my story is that I was born into an Amish-Mennonite community. Many of my ancestors came from Germany (Bavaria) as well as Switzerland and Alsace-Lorraine. Some came directly to Ontario (then known as Upper Canada), and many others landed in the United States (Pennsylvania, Ohio, Indiana, etc.) and then moved to Canada as land became available. I spent my early years in a very sheltered environment governed by a deep abiding faith and the importance of church, family, and a rural lifestyle. Education beyond eight grades in a one-room public school was not encouraged, so I had to conform long enough until I could figure a way around these restrictions.

I was a curious child and read voraciously. I remember my parents describing me as being "independent," and I thought that was a negative thing at the time, but eventually, I learned that it was a desirable trait. However, I had no choice initially but to conform and leave school at the end of Grade 8. Following that, I worked as a housekeeper for various relatives and acquaintances. I also spent three miserable years working in a factory. Luckily, my parents realized how unhappy I was through my teen years and backed me when I finally accessed a retraining program with the Ontario government that included academic upgrading as well as commercial office skills. I ended up with a high school equivalency certificate and then was lucky enough to land office jobs where additional training was provided. That part of improving my life had worked well.

My next step was to move out of my community. The easiest route was to join a Voluntary Service Program through the Mennonite Church. I had already evolved from my more Amish background. The Mission Board for this program in Canada and the United States was in Indiana, so I signed up for a one-year mission and ended up being assigned to an inner-city centre in St. Petersburg, Florida. It was 1968, and a time of great civil unrest and race riots in the U.S., not to mention the assassinations of Dr. Martin Luther King, Jr. and Robert Kennedy. Looking back, I realize that it was a very smart way to handle my sheltered existence. My parents were sad to see me leave but happy that I was doing church work.

The Mission Board had some members of their units in both countries working in hospitals, etc. to support the others who were working in the communities. As it turned out, I ended up employed as a nursing assistant in the psychiatric unit of St. Anthony's Hospital in St. Petersburg, and that was very interesting but also quite stressful. It was intensive on-the-job training. I got to be reasonably good at what I was doing by the time that I left, a year later. It was one of those periods of growth in my life that was difficult at the time but useful by way of life experience. The entire experience came full circle for me decades later when my daughter developed HD and experienced many psychiatric disturbances. She spent time in psych units in a local hospital as well as a neuro-behaviour unit and a mental health unit in a specialized hospital over a period of several years.

What my parents did not anticipate in 1969 was my decision at the end of my term in Florida to apply for a nursing program in Ottawa. By that time, I was missing Canada, and what better plan could exist but to move to the capital city? Off I went for my next adventure. I had never been to Ottawa, but that did not stop me. I booked a room at the YWCA and hopped on a bus with two suitcases. Looking back, there was a lot of naivety mixed in with my plans. My guardian angel must have been working overtime.

Great fortune was on my side again. Initially, I was disappointed because the nursing program was full when I arrived, although I had been told otherwise before my move. The job search was on if I wanted to stay in Ottawa. I applied for and got a job in a law firm specializing in intellectual property (patents and trademarks). The fact that I did not have any experience was not a problem. This firm had many older employees, and they were more than willing to train new and inexperienced people. From that time until I moved back to Kitchener in 1997, I worked primarily in law firms. Most of them were in downtown Ottawa and just a short walk from the Parliament Buildings.

I remember occasionally marveling at the fact that a person of my background and lack of formal education had come so far. Keep in mind that I could not even speak English until I started the first grade in a one-room country school two miles from our farmhouse. My parents spoke the colloquial German dialect that everyone spoke in the community. My older brother had no problem with that, but my sisters and I refused to switch from English to German when we came home from school. We came up with a strange compromise that worked very well for many years. We spoke English, and our parents spoke German, and it was perfectly normal to have two languages in the same conversation. That continued for years until I met and married Bob. The only time that German was heard in their home after Bob's entry into the family was when my mother was chatting on the phone with her sisters or when extended family was visiting.

Marriage

After nearly two years in Ottawa and a failed romance, I decided that it was time to move back to Kitchener. Fate intervened when friends of ours introduced Bob to me in the summer of 1971. By that time, my dad and a neighbour had already travelled to Ottawa and moved my possessions back home. I had just resigned from my job when Bob did some fast talking and convinced me to go home for a holiday and then come back to Ottawa. There was just something about him and his honesty and sincerity that convinced me beyond a doubt that it was a great idea. He had asked me in a serious moment what I wanted from life, and I was reluctant to answer (due to that failed romance that I had experienced), so I turned it around and asked him. He immediately responded with marriage and children and a home. He may have included a dog, too, or that possibly came up in a subsequent conversation! Anyhow, I left Ottawa on August 20, 1971, and returned on Labour Day weekend. We were engaged by September 17, and married on April 27, 1972. It made perfect sense. Bob was everything that I wanted in a husband. He was generous and kind and funny and devoted to his family and friends.

Some questions came up in my mind when I met Bob's parents. His mother had very bad balance and looked rather tipsy when she walked. The words "Huntington's disease" came up, but

I had never heard of it. It was referred to specifically when mentioning two of Bob's aunts. One was in a nursing home and the other in a psychiatric hospital. Again, I overlooked the implications. I had met the man of my dreams, and any peculiarities with his family did not concern me.

In January 1974, we were overjoyed to discover that we were having a baby later in the year. Then my mother-in-law started having more uncontrollable movements and, at times, quite slurred speech. We fell into this uneasy pattern. We were not asking, and they were not telling. Tim was born on September 27, 1974. We were thrilled with our perfect little son. A couple of weeks later, Bob's father admitted to us that Bob's mother had Huntington's disease. Our period of denial had come to a crashing halt.

The phone call from my father-in-law came one evening when Tim was 5½ weeks old. Bob's mother had taken a massive overdose and was in the hospital in intensive care. She eventually recovered and was sent home, and that's when she told me that she did not want her husband to be stuck with a sick old woman. She was well aware of the implications of HD since her mother and grandfather had both suffered from it. Bob and I immediately made an appointment with our family doctor to find out more about HD. He gave us as much information as he had (keeping in mind that there just was not a lot of knowledge about HD at the time) and then made an appointment for us to see a geneticist.

Deciding Whether to Add to Our Family

The geneticist had more information, but at that time, the predictive test to find out Bob's status did not exist. We were made aware of the fact that by the time we found out whether Bob had the defective copy of the gene or not, it would be too late for us to have another child. We had been blessed with a beautiful baby boy, and Bob was the picture of good health. On that basis, the geneticist told us that the decision was ours to make. There was a test that could have been done, but it was very rudimentary and would have involved obtaining blood samples from various relatives in different parts of Canada to send to the lab in Vancouver. The accuracy of the test was not guaranteed, and the geneticist did not encourage us to have it done.

Life went on, and Bob's mother continued to have worsening manifestations of HD. We decided to have another child when Tim turned two. We immediately succeeded, but our hopes were dashed when I had a miscarriage on February 9, 1977. We were advised that there would be no harm in trying again right away and succeeded with another pregnancy, which came to an end on July 2, 1977. I was pregnant again by January 1978, and this time, we were rewarded with the arrival of our beautiful baby girl on October 22, 1978. A few months later, Bob's mother went into long-term care.

Reality Sets In

I have a vivid memory of an incident during our Christmas 1978 visit to my family. I remember sitting in an upstairs bedroom, cradling Christina in my arms and chatting with my sisters. I stared at my beautiful baby and realized the full impact of our decision to have another child and the possible implications. I was heartsick.

In the following years, I was starting to get concerned about Bob. He was his usual calm and pleasant self nearly all of the time, except for occasional sudden outbursts of rage. Occasionally, he would break a piece of furniture or punch a hole into the wall. These outbursts came out of nowhere and were totally uncharacteristic. He never hurt us, but I started feeling vulnerable. I had also noticed from the very beginning that he would be a bit twitchy in bed when I had my head on his shoulder, but I did not connect that with his mother's strange movements. Perhaps I deliberately chose not to make that connection.

I eventually encouraged Bob to visit our doctor about the sudden episodes of rage. By that time, we had lost three parents (Bob's father, my father, and then Bob's mother) in a five-month period in 1988. Bob was referred to a neurologist, who sent him for a series of psychiatric tests and then promptly forgot about following up. Eventually, we saw the neurologist at an information session for Huntington's disease at the Royal Ottawa Hospital. He actually remembered Bob and was most apologetic that there had not been a follow up, which was arranged shortly thereafter.

By that time, there were all kinds of additional signs that Bob either did not see or chose to ignore but that I could see quite clearly. I remember our appointment on May 16, 1991, as if it were yesterday. I knew that it would not end well. I watched as the doctor did all the usual neurological testing. I stood there as he watched Bob walk around the hospital grounds. Then they came back inside, and the doctor turned to us and told Bob that he was in the early stages of Huntington's disease.

Then I heard myself saying to the doctor, "Are you sure?"

He told me gently that if he were not sure, he would not have told us. In the absence of the predictive test, he had diagnosed Bob based on clinical signs. Bob turned to me to reassure me that he would handle the diagnosis with as much grace and dignity as possible.

Planning for a Life with Huntington's

Bob and I strategized when we got home. I had a niece who was getting married six weeks after Bob's diagnosis, so we decided that we would not tell anyone, including our children, until after the wedding. I could not stop crying, so it made sense that it would be good if Bob and I could have the additional time to come to grips with the diagnosis first. I remember the first months after the diagnosis as being a time of great passion between us. It was also a time of overwhelming heartbreak and endless crying on my part. Then I would get up every morning and go to work. That's when I developed a strategy that has worked very well for me.

I discovered early on that it was better to separate HD and my job. Luckily, I loved my job. It was interesting and very fast-paced, with many deadlines on a daily basis, so I immersed myself in my work and dwelled on the HD during my commutes to and from the office. My office was downtown, and we lived on the outskirts of the city. Bob's workplace was a short drive from our house. That was also when I began wondering every day if Bob was holding it together with Tim and Christina. He had stabilized somewhat after the diagnosis, and the periods of rage had decreased. However, it was always in the back of my mind.

Eventually, we got a glimmer of hope. We were told later in 1991 that there would be a drug trial for Lamotrigine starting in

1992, and ending in 1995. By that time, we had admitted to Tim and Christina that Bob had HD but were able to add the encouraging news about the drug trial. The trial would take place at the University of British Columbia in Vancouver. Bob's airfare was covered. We made a decision that we would take advantage of the situation and cover the cost of the rest of us flying to BC with Bob. That was a very wise move. All four of us went for the first two trips. After that, Tim was in university, and Christina went with us for the last two trips. When I look back, I barely remember the hours spent in the lab with Bob and the various tests and procedures, including PET scans, which were not commonly done at that time and not available in many hospitals. Our adventures as a family unit stand out in my mind. In addition to exploring Vancouver, we always took the ferry crossing to Vancouver Island and managed to go orca watching on our last trip in 1995. We also travelled to the peak of Whistler Mountain and tossed snowballs at each other on a hot July day. We were very fortunate to be tourists in a world-class city and a very scenic area of Canada.

It was disappointing to us to be told at the end of the study that Bob had been in the placebo group and had never received the drug during his years of taking the required number of pills every day. However, it did not matter because it turned out that the drug had been ineffective for those who had been taking it. We were philosophical about it because we had our memories of the trips to the west coast and a time of great bonding for our family.

Unfortunately, the illness was taking a toll on Bob's ability to do his job. He was an electronics/computer technician with the Department of National Defence and was rapidly losing his ability to do his job. Of course, I was not completely aware of the difficulties because Bob was unaware of the gaps. He started getting bad performance reviews, and I remember feeling quite indignant on his behalf. It was only later when I had a chance to review some of the documents written by his superiors that I had to admit to myself that it was time for Bob to go on medical retirement. That happened in the summer of 1994 (three years after his diagnosis) and became a paperwork nightmare as we had to navigate through a maze of appointments to get everything in order. It turned out that the disability income would come from three different sources. It seemed to take forever for everything to click into place, but eventually it did. I remain grateful to this day because I still receive some benefits as his widow.

It was late in 1996 that Bob came to me with a proposition. He suggested that we should leave Ottawa and move to the Kitchener-Waterloo area. Tim was already studying engineering at the University of Waterloo, and Christina was in her last year of high school. This was a very selfless act on Bob's part because his family was in Ottawa, whereas my family and most of my relatives were in the Kitchener-Waterloo area. Bob told me that he knew that I would need family support as his illness progressed. It made sense to me, and we took nearly a year to carry out our plan. It was not an easy decision because we all loved living in Ottawa, and I regretted leaving my job. Finally, we were able to sell our house in Ottawa and buy one here in Kitchener. I left my job in August 1997, and Christina moved into residence at the University of Waterloo. Tim had returned from an extended work term in the United Kingdom and was resuming his engineering classes. Our family was together again.

I am now overwhelmingly grateful to Bob for coming up with the plan for our future. Since our return, I have received tremendous ongoing support from my immediate family and also from many relatives who live in the area. I am now in touch with cousins and friends from long ago. Sometimes one can go back home again.

Reality sank in shortly after our move that we would not be able to live on Bob's disability income, so eventually, I found a part-time temporary job to tide us over. Bob was progressing steadily with HD, and we were starting to get some assistance with home care. Then it got to the point that we had to set things into motion with long-term care. In spite of the assistance that we were receiving, Bob's needs were greater than my ability to care for him. His involuntary movements were out of control, resulting in many falls and injuries. He was not sleeping well, either, and was getting up numerous times throughout the night. That prevented me from sleeping. It got to the point that we needed to request crisis placement. Bob and I had three years together in our new home before he was placed in a nursing home in October 2000. Again, my tears flowed. Bob was his usual accommodating self and adapted readily. By this time, the rage in him had completely disappeared.

Reinventing Myself Once Again

In the meantime, it became obvious that I would have to reinvent myself again. I tried but did not succeed in getting employed in the intellectual property field. That led to a government-funded program that was geared to helping people become employed again. Eventually, it led to the right contacts with regional government, and I landed a temporary position. Luckily, it was on the same floor as a permanent position that had just been posted. I applied for the permanent position, and that is how I became employed with the Region of Waterloo from December 2001 until my retirement in December 2011. It is also how I started my last full-time permanent position at the age of 55 and managed to hold on until I turned 65, even as the HD in our family now had both of our children firmly in its clutches. My employment improved our financial situation immensely. An added benefit is that it gave me a sanctuary away from the cursed illness.

Backtracking now, it became obvious by the time that Christina was in high school that our lively and spirited daughter was changing. She had always been very talkative and happy. She started becoming morose and withdrawn. I would try to talk to her about it, and she would stare right through me but refuse to engage. Given that she was in her mid-teens at the time, I assumed that she was just having a difficult adjustment to adolescence. I tried not to think that it could be HD and reassured myself that she did not have any involuntary movements. She still had a wide circle of friends and was still doing well in school. I decided that it had to be a phase that she was going through, so we carried on.

She settled into university life after our move from Ottawa, but she hit various speed bumps along the way. There were complications with a period of academic probation and the repetition of most of her second-year courses. She was also into her first serious relationship at this point. There were also time periods when she lived at home with us before Bob went into long-term care, and I was trying to become employed. The big hurdle came at the end when she discovered that she was short one-half credit just before graduation. That meant graduating a full year later. By that time, her boyfriend had moved back to Montreal, and Christina was firmly ensconced with me. Then a nightmarish period of fatigue, frustration, and conflict followed while I was trying to help Bob adjust to long-term care and also help Christina with life decisions while working full-time in my new job.

HD Strikes the Next Generation

Christina eventually received her B.Sc. (Environmental Science) in 2003. She managed to get a few low-paying jobs in retail but seemed unwilling or unable to seek employment in her field. Up until that time, she was not exhibiting any chorea or other obvious signs of HD until I began to realize that she had developed a shuffling gait. That was enough to hear alarm bells, but Christina was not open to discussing issues around HD at the time. Luckily, she had just found a new family doctor. I knew that she was having a complete check-up on an initial visit. I wrote a letter to the doctor, outlining the family history and my suspicions. Much to my relief, he referred her to a local neurologist, and her blood sample was then sent to a Huntington's Clinic in Toronto.

We knew that there would be a long wait to receive the results but were unprepared for additional delays in meeting with our local neurologist. That made it very difficult to deal with the various agencies that could have given us guidance. It also made me less than credible when I told people from these agencies that Christina had HD, but there had not been a definitive diagnosis. We desperately needed the results.

In the meantime, our situation worsened, and it became obvious that Christina and I could no longer live in the same house. Christina refused to engage in any way, other than going to her retail position in a dollar store. Other than that, she sequestered herself in her bedroom. One evening, I got so desperate that I called the police for help. She realized that I had called them and was pretending to be asleep when they arrived. The officers told me that she was fine but that I was distraught.

A short time later, I succeeded in finding a place for her through a social services agency. It was with a woman who took in troubled teenagers. Christina was 27 at the time but presented as much younger. It seemed like a good fit until her increasingly disturbed behaviour became more obvious. The situation came to a head one morning when I started getting calls from Christina and then from her landlady who had come home from work to sort out the situation. By that time, I had called the police and asked them to take Christina to the psych unit at a local hospital and told them that I would meet Christina there. This was not the first time that I'd had to involve police. Her landlady also made it clear that Christina had to leave her house permanently. Christina had gone out of control in her new home. She was very unwilling to share a bathroom and had developed some rather bizarre routines that had started at my house. One was to stand in the bathroom and run the water tap, even though she was not using the water. Even more disturbing was her tendency to stand in front of a mirror for long periods of time without moving and just staring at herself. On that particular morning, the landlady was upset at having to come home to sort things out and told me that Christina had to leave her home permanently.

After I arrived in the hospital and found Christina, my heart sank when a staff member in the psych unit sat with us to discuss Christina's care plan. I knew that he did not understand HD very well at all. We had just mentioned Christina's degree earlier in the conversation. He finished taking her history and then turned to us and said, "Now let's put that degree to good use!"

He did not seem to hear that Christina had been spared being fired from her job in a dollar store when I met with her manager and explained the illness. She was then able to resign from her position rather than being let go. What the staff member did not realize was that Christina had lost the cognitive ability needed in order to use her degree.

The situation at the hospital got worse. A staff psychiatrist phoned me a day or two later to let me know that Christina was being discharged immediately. I was told that she would be sent by cab to a local shelter for homeless women if I failed to pick her up. I dropped everything and involved the agency in charge of long-term care and made a case for having her admitted on an emergency basis. No other agency would take her because HD presents with both physical and psychiatric needs. It had to be one or the other. By the end of the day, Christina was on the list for long-term care, but I had to pay for a bed in a retirement home until they could find a bed in a nursing home.

It was during her stay in the retirement home that we finally got the call from the neurologist's office, letting us know that he had the test results. On the day of our appointment, I can still remember Christina turning to me and saying, "I guess that I will get diagnosed today."

By that time, it was a foregone conclusion for both of us. Her CAG repeat was 55. The neurologist told us that it was not JHD but that it was in the early onset category.

Huntington's Strikes a Third Time

Our luck improved a month later when a place opened for her in the same nursing home where Bob lived. She moved in on November 4, 2005. However, the other shoe dropped when my son, Tim, came back from an employment term in Japan. By that time, he had finished his engineering degree, had lived and worked in India for over a year, and then had moved to the east coast of Canada (Halifax) to start a fine arts degree. I had a bad premonition in the days leading up to his return. I was very happy to see him walk toward me at the airport, but at the same time, all I could see was the involuntary movements. My heart sank. It was January 4, 2006, exactly two months after Christina had been placed in long-term care. I could not deny what I was seeing, but Tim was very happy to see me and to be back home.

Tim's immediate plan was to apply at Ryerson University in Toronto to finish his fine arts degree. I made appointments with both my family doctor and a social worker that I had been seeing through my workplace plan. Both of them advised me not to tell Tim my suspicions and to let him carry through with his plan of completing the degree in Toronto. I was at his convocation in June 2009, when he received his degree. It had been ten years since he had earned his engineering degree, and he was now considerably older than all of the fresh-faced graduates in his class. They were looking forward to endless opportunities ahead. I knew that Tim would barely be employable, even with his newly earned diploma. In the meantime, I was paying his rent and supporting him financially. Tim was able to get an entry-level job in a camera shop that summer but was dismissed a few days later. He was reluctant to talk about it but finally admitted that he was told that he was not catching on to the job quickly enough. I told him that I could no longer afford to support him in Toronto and asked him to move back to Kitchener and live with me. That happened in November 2009.

I was searching for a way to tell Tim about the HD manifesting itself when fate intervened again. My older brother died unexpectedly in January 2010, and I had to tell family members that Tim was in the early stages of HD. He was an obvious candidate to serve as a pallbearer, and I had to alert the others that there could be difficulties so that they could strategize where to place Tim. I had kept it a secret for four years because it would not have been fair to tell others when Tim himself did not know.

After the funeral, I had a chat with Tim and told him my suspicions. He did not have a family doctor, so off we went to an urgent care clinic. The doctor was very low-key and said that there was definitely something wrong and suggested an appointment with a neurologist. That came to pass, and again, a blood specimen was sent to the Huntington Clinic in Toronto. Although he was showing signs of HD in January 2006, Tim was not officially diagnosed until the results came back positive in July 2010. Tim's CAG was 42. He was 31 when I knew that he had HD and 35 when it became official.

In the meantime, Christina was not adapting well at her nursing home. She had given up on life and refused to eat or drink a few months into her stay, and that resulted in hospitalization in January 2006. It got to the point that a feeding tube was the only option, and an appointment was set up. At the last minute, Christina refused the tube and promised to start eating and drinking again. She followed through on her promise, but it was months later before her weight stabilized.

Christina's situation improved in the next few years, and then the bottom fell out again. I received a late evening phone call in April 2009, letting me know that Christina had been assaulted by another resident but that it did not require a trip to the hospital and that there was no need for me to show up. I will always regret that I did not immediately go to the nursing home, but instead, I went first thing in the morning to meet with a police officer. It turned out that the person who had called me the night before had understated the assault.

Christina had gone to a vending machine area in the evening, and the resident had sexually assaulted her. A nurse happened to walk past at the same time and threw the resident off Christina and then called for help. The resident was mobile but had dementia. He was not in a secure unit. It also turned out that he was a repeat offender. The police officer told me that he would not be able to charge the resident because of the dementia. He was unable to answer basic questions, and charging him would have been futile.

I fought this long and hard for many months, in spite of obstacles and impossible circumstances.

Long-term care is handled by provincial governments in Canada rather than by the federal government in Ottawa. I had a hard time dealing with the bureaucracy and an even harder time dealing with a legal organization advocating for seniors in long-term care. It did not help that Christina had HD and that she was not in the usual demographic for long-term care. Again, it seems to be hard to categorize those with HD. Luckily, my Member of Provincial Parliament (MPP) belonged to the party in power at that time, and he was able to direct our case to the cabinet minister in charge of long-term care. I waited for many months for a response. Eventually, we got a letter of apology stating that the incident should never have happened.

I began to realize that I had to forgive the way that it had been handled and move ahead. It was doing too much damage to me. Forgiveness was a good thing because my son is now in the same nursing home and is doing very well. I should add that they now have security guards in the home, starting in the early evening until the following morning. I can only assume that the assault on Christina was the catalyst for change, but by that time, she was no longer living in that home. Changes to security have been made, though, and that is the important thing.

Unfortunately, Christina began another downhill slide after the assault, and there were several incidents involving police and psych units. Christina started acting out violently and sometimes hitting staff and other residents or knocking over clothing racks and laundry containers. She also deliberately destroyed or threw out many of her valued possessions. Months later, after one of her stays in the psych unit, the home refused to have her back, and she ended up in a neuro-behaviour unit in a nearby longer-term care hospital for a year, and that was followed by another trip to a psych unit and then over two years in a mental health unit.

The violent outbursts and Code White situations followed her from one place to another. It was not uncommon for me to visit Christina after work and find her strapped to a gurney. I would sit with her and talk to her until eventually she would be calm enough for the staff to remove her restraints so that I could help her with her meal. It was heartbreaking. I had flashbacks to the psychiatric ward in the hospital in Florida all those years ago. At that time, all nursing homes in our area refused to admit her. It was not until July 2013 that she was deemed to be rehabilitated enough to go back into long-term care.

It then got better. She ended up in a small home with kind and compassionate staff members, and, eventually, she learned to trust again. I knew that we were on the right track when I walked in a couple of months into her stay, and she announced, "Mom ... I'm eating again!!"

From that time until her death, she endeared herself to staff and residents and other family members. Every day when I arrived, I would ask her how she was doing. The answer was always the same: "Much better now that you're here!"

Goodbye to a Beloved Husband and Dad

Our next crisis was in October 2014, when I got the call that Bob's condition had deteriorated after many years of decline but no critical changes. He had been on thickened fluids and pureed food for many years. A decision was made to put him into palliative care, and he passed away peacefully, early in the morning of November 4, 2014, at the age of 67. He had not been very responsive in the preceding years, but in his final hours, he was very aware and kept his eyes on my face as I kept reassuring him that I would look after Tim and Christina. His breathing calmed, and he looked past me as he was taking his final breath, and the look of joy on his face was his last precious gift to me.

Christina's speech was becoming difficult to understand by that time, but just before Bob's funeral service, she turned to me and said clearly, "I want to hold Dad's hand and kiss him goodbye." Tim and I helped her out of her wheelchair and held on to her as she said goodbye on her own terms. Then Tim and I said our goodbyes, and the three of us followed Bob into the chapel. Later, during a visit to her neurologist and the recounting of the loss of her dad and the service and burial, Christina announced, "I was included." She had already decided just after Bob's passing that he was now our guardian angel.

I did not cry at his passing or at the visitations or the funeral. His long journey had been completed. I found after his passing that many memories of our early days and of special times spent with a loving husband and dad came flooding back to me. Now, I think of the times when we were young and happy rather than the long and difficult decline.

In the years following Bob's passing, it was becoming obvious that the caregiving was taking a toll on my health. I had to start negotiating for long-term care for Tim. My initial attempts were an exercise in futility because he presented well and was able to take showers by himself in a specially outfitted shower stall. That all changed a year ago when Tim fell from the top of the stairs down to the lower level and managed to split open the back of his head. That required a trip to the hospital for staples and bandages. I grabbed my phone and took a sequence of photos to show to the placement person. She then decided that he could apply for long-term care. Even better, she told us that he could have the sibling reunification provision since Christina was already in long-term care. That would expedite placement for him in the same nursing home. Our situation had improved.

Confronting the Loss of a Child

Everything changed when my phone rang at 4:45 in the morning on Saturday, December 2, 2017. In my sleepy haze, I realized that it was a staff person from Christina's nursing home. It then registered that she was talking about a fall. That was not uncommon with Christina. She had a lot of falls. I said, "Is

Christina all right?" As soon as the words came out of my mouth, I realized that it was a redundant question, given that the call was coming to me during the night. However, nothing could have prepared me for the response: "Christina isn't anymore."

I do not remember much of the rest of the conversation, except that I told her that I would be right over, and she made me promise not to come by myself. Luckily, my partner, Gary, was visiting for the weekend. Before we left, I woke Tim to give him the news and to promise him that we would be back to pick him up as soon as possible.

When we got to the home, the administrative staff was already there, and the coroner was on his way. We went up to Christina's floor and were asked if we would like to see her. Nothing can ever prepare a parent for the sight of a lifeless child. My first impression was that she was asleep but very white. Then I had to fight the urge to shake her and tell her to wake up. I kissed her and talked to her, and then we went into a room to wait for the coroner. It was a long wait because he had to interview the two staff members who had been there. His opinion from the position of her body was that she had gotten out of bed and then stumbled and fallen backwards, hitting her head on the nightstand. That would have caused her head to fall forward and block her airway. He gave the cause of death as positional asphyxiation, due to a fall in an accidental manner. I pulled out my purse calendar and had him write it down. It was very important for me to know and remember. He also wrote down his name and phone number and asked if I would like an autopsy. I declined because it would not change anything.

Gary and I went home to pick up Tim and then went back to the nursing home. We attended the customary honour guard service held when a resident passes away and is carried out to the funeral home vehicle. It was very moving to have staff and other residents stand as Christina left the home where she had been very happy in her final years. It was particularly emotional for me because I had the staff cover her with the "Grandma quilt" that my mother had made years before and which had been on her bed in her final hours.

After the funeral arrangements had been made, we went to

the nursing home to pick up some framed items from her wall for the visitations. I was not prepared for the outpouring of grief from the staff. It was very affirming and of great comfort to me to know how her death was affecting her caregivers. Again, I did not cry. The pain was too much for the tears to flow. I should add that many staff members came to Christina's visitations and funeral. It was very reassuring to know that she had been loved and cared for with great compassion. She was 39 years old when she left us.

I cope with my loss by having my favourite photo of Christina inside my front entrance. She was probably about ten years old, and she is the picture of good health, and her beautiful blue eyes are sparkling. She will always be my sweet little girl.

There is a footnote to the nursing home situation for my son. The priority placement for siblings was revoked after Christina's death. However, Tim has since been placed in the nursing home where Bob died and where Christina had been placed in 2005.

Tim is very popular with the staff. One told me that Tim is her hero. Another told me that she loves Tim as she does her own sons. He continues to be very low-key and polite and stands out in a crowd of mostly elderly residents. It is heartwarming because everyone knows his name! He quite enjoys the fact that he can stroll down to the tuck shop on the lower level and buy a drink and snack and charge it to his account.

I am saddened by Tim's continual decline but am determined to spend as much time with him as possible. The outings are more difficult but very important. He is my last family member with HD. Every day is a gift. He inspires me with his positive outlook and pleasant demeanor. He is truly his father's son.

Life Outside of Huntington's

I need to add a section for my partner, Gary. Every so often, HD gives back to us, and that happened in our case. Gary lost his wife to HD in 2001. He then wrote and published a book of poetry in her memory. I read the notice in the Huntington Society of Canada newsletter and ordered a copy. Luckily for us, we live in the same part of Ontario, and he is an hour's drive from me. He is my dear friend and companion. We tell each other our stories from our past lives, and we never tire of each other's company. He is a daily reminder that I have been exceptionally blessed in my life, in spite of the difficult times.

This is for you, Gary:

Grow old along with me!
The best is yet to be,
the last of life,
for which the first was made:
Our times are in His hand
Who saith, "A whole I planned,
Youth shows but half; trust God: see all, nor be afraid!"
– **Robert Browning**

About Terry Tempkin

Terry Tempkin, NP-C, MSN, is an Adult Nurse Practitioner who spent 18 years working with Huntington's disease families at the University of California Davis Health System. During her time there, she worked with the HD team to build one of the largest HD programs in the country, noted for their expertise in HD/JHD care. She participated in over 18 clinical trials in Huntington's disease.

Terry currently serves as a Medical Director on the Executive Board of Help 4 HD International Inc. Although she retired from the Health System in 2016, she did not retire from the passion to care for families coping with HD.

Afterword

—— ෂ෧ ——

The Lessons of Huntington's and Juvenile Huntington's Disease

Some of my deepest personal friendships and my most awe-
iring moments have come from almost twenty years of caring
ople with Huntington's and Juvenile Huntington's disease. I
uently humbled by their courage and inspired by their
They are people who fight to live their best lives possible
tremely difficult circumstances. I have considered it a
o share their journeys. They have taught me so much
I have given them.

learned that people matter and can accomplish
ble things when they share a common vision. Committed
of people can change the course of history. It is because of
ared vision of a world without HD/JHD that we have
ific advances and compassionate care for families. It is our
ation to continue to do this work together.

I have learned that it is important to "do something." Not
eryone has the time, energy, or inclination to be a powerhouse
dvocate, but everyone can and should stay informed and be
onnected. Even something as simple as reaching out to another

HD/JHD family helps both of you. Be 'present' for those going through a tough time, as no one knows this journey as well as you.

I have learned that HD/JHD families are required to learn how to make tough choices. It's often an indication there is a need for 'change,' and that can be hard. In preparation, develop a network of trusted confidantes who can help you make those decisions. Understand that when you have tough choices to make, it isn't 'your fault,' nor is it the fault of others.

I want people with HD/JHD to know they are not alone. The journey can be arduous, and the burdens seem endless, but if the journey is shared, connecting with others will help you find the strength you don't think you have. Feelings of isolation lurk constantly. Actively resist it. No one knows the heartache of livi with HD/JHD like those traveling the same road, and whether through print, social media, support groups, phone calls, educational events, or health care visits, each and every famil should reach out and connect with something or someone th meaningful to them.

I want you to know you have many partners worldwid professionals, scientists, HD/JHD organizations, advocat families are working tirelessly to make a difference. You alone, and we care about you.

I want families to know that how you "fight the b something. Until there is a cure, we may not win eacl those of you on the front lines are teaching the ones story may give strength to someone else.

To those in this community that have the strengt out for the benefit of others, you have my heartfelt lov respect. It takes a special strength to put your own grie work for the benefit of others.

Let kindness be the guiding hand on what is undoub toughest journey anyone can face.